Heidegger's *Being and Time*
& Kierkegaard's *The Sickness Unto Death*
as Hermeneutic to Paul's Epistles

Heidegger's *Being and Time*
& Kierkegaard's *The Sickness Unto Death*
as Hermeneutic to Paul's Epistles

BONG-CHOUL HWANG

Foreword by Robert E. Innis

◐PICKWICK *Publications* • Eugene, Oregon

HEIDEGGER'S *BEING AND TIME* AND KIERKEGAARD'S *THE SICKNESS UNTO DEATH* AS HERMENEUTIC TO PAUL'S EPISTLES

Copyright © 2025 Bong-Choul Hwang. All rights reserved. Except for brief quotations in critical publications or reviews, no part of this book may be reproduced in any manner without prior written permission from the publisher. Write: Permissions, Wipf and Stock Publishers, 199 W. 8th Ave., Suite 3, Eugene, OR 97401.

Pickwick Publications
An Imprint of Wipf and Stock Publishers
199 W. 8th Ave., Suite 3
Eugene, OR 97401

www.wipfandstock.com

PAPERBACK ISBN: 979-8-3852-0368-0
HARDCOVER ISBN: 979-8-3852-0369-7
EBOOK ISBN: 979-8-3852-0370-3

Cataloguing-in-Publication data:

Names: Hwang, Bong-Choul, author. | Innis, Robert E., foreword.

Title: Heidegger's *Being and Time* and Kierkegaard's *The Sickness Unto Death* as hermeneutic to Paul's epistle / Bong-Choul Hwang ; foreword by Robert E. Innis.

Description: Eugene, OR : Pickwick Publications, 2025 | Includes bibliographical references.

Identifiers: ISBN 979-8-3852-0368-0 (paperback) | ISBN 979-8-3852-0369-7 (hardcover) | ISBN 979-8-3852-0370-3 (ebook)

Subjects: LCSH: Bible. Epistles of Paul—Criticism, interpretation, etc. | Philosophical theology. | Hermeneutics. | Heidegger, Martin, 1889–1976. Sein und Zeit. English. | Heidegger, Martin, 1889–1976—Criticism and interpretation. | Kierkegaard, Søren, 1813–1855. Sygdommen til døden—Criticism and interpretation.

Classification: BS2650.52 .H85 2024 (paperback) | BS2650.52 .H85 (ebook)

VERSION NUMBER 01/14/25

Contents

Foreword by Robert E. Innis | vii

Acknowledgments | xi

I   Introduction | 1

II   Methodology: Heidegger's Hermeneutic Phenomenology | 30

III   Views of Conscience by Heidegger, Kierkegaard, and Paul | 67

IV   Death and Emptiness by Heidegger and Fa-tsang | 106

V   Death and God by Kierkegaard and Paul | 148

VI   Epilogue | 188

Bibliography | 205

A Framing Foreword

ROBERT E. INNIS

IN A FAMOUS ESSAY from 1896, "The Reflex Arc Concept in Psychology," the American pragmatist philosopher John Dewey criticized the concept of the reflex arc as a unifying principle in psychology's approach to human experience. Dewey asserted that our fundamental experiential relation to the world as conscious beings was not an arc that linked a stimulus of some sorts to an elicited reaction of sensations, thoughts, feelings, and acts. He argued that such a characterization of the components of the putative stimulus and response arc did not capture the most important features of our fundamental relations to the world. The stimulus and response arc, with its differentiation of sensations, thoughts, and acts was, on Dewey's conception, not a "comprehensive, or organic unity, but a patchwork of disjointed parts, a mechanical conjunction of unallied processes."

What it lacked, he thought, was an insight into the implications of how the sensory stimulus with its consequent central connections and motor responses could be viewed not as separate elements or entities but as "divisions of labor, functioning factors, within the single concrete whole, now designated the reflex arc." For Dewey, however, the reflex arc—understood as "sensation-followed-by-idea-followed-by-movement"—does not model the primary relation between ourselves as conscious beings and the multiple environments or life worlds in which we live. The primary relation, the fundamental unit of behavior in the broadest sense, Dewey called "coordination." Indeed, Dewey held that what occurs at the most fundamental level of our experience is not an encounter with sensory stimulus but a self-reconstructing and self-evaluating spiral of responses of different types to qualitatively charged situations or contexts of life.

For Dewey such a self-modifying spiral coordination is a dynamic process of the constitution and reconstitution of the various fields of experience, not all of them perceptual, in which we are located or into which we find ourselves—to echo our author's discussion of Heidegger—"thrown." The fact is, we are already located in a range of fields of experience before we begin to reflect upon them in any critical or systematic manner. A reflective/interpretive locating of ourselves, often provoked by an interruption of some sort, reveals that we have been, as Dewey put it, "funded" by past experience and the meaning systems, codes of conduct, forms of appropriate preferences, and so forth, by which we frame and live out our lies. The earliest phases of this multi-contextual and multileveled process of funding have for the most part taken place without any explicit plan or decision of our own. By being socialized, we have been assimilated into, as well as empowered by and dependent upon, preexisting meaning systems and their supports, in which we now dwell. These meaning systems make up what Heidegger, Kierkegaard, and Gadamer considered to be the operative feeling, interpretive, and agential forestructures that define the unique feeling tones of our unique form of life. Such a unique form of life, our fundamental mode of being-in-the-world with its existential projects, is marked by its ineluctable thrownness into a world one did not create and against which one was not able, in its earliest stages, to defend oneself or to have proper foreknowledge of its existential consequences. Such consequences are not just in our heads as systems of concepts or worldviews handed down to us but in the consequent symbolically charged affective tones of our bodily being as well as in our sedimented patterns of sanctioned or unsanctioned actions or existential projects that make up the sphere of conscience and its demands and its placement in self-interpretation, in the broadest sense, a notion Hwang explores in light of Heidegger, Kierkegaard, and St. Paul.

These systems of concepts, affective structures, and patterns of action make up existential ordering devices, or access structures to the world, that clearly have more than merely instrumental value. As the scientist and philosopher Michael Polanyi put it, we dwell in these systems as if they were parts of our body. They take the form of multi-leveled traditions that are marked by different degrees of stability. In general these traditions are not necessarily internally coherent or closed. They often are amalgams of preexisting traditions, undergoing processes of hybridization for a variety of internal reasons and external (political) causes. The internal reasons are traceable to the need for coherence and involve processes of blending of different conceptual systems and practices. Religious traditions are clear illustrations of these processes. Very few of them, as their histories show, are free of syncretic accumulations of diverse elements from other traditions, often marked by conceptual resistances and physical violence. Religious systems are combinations of unity and difference. They have significant overlappings or family resemblances of their focal concerns as well as different existential realizations and codifications of their contents and demanding claims that make up their forms of life.

Religious systems as complex forms of life, with extensive conceptual articulations and individual and communal ritual practices, ground a defining feeling tone to our existence. Such a feeling tone furnishes an ever-present informing background to our actions and to our conceptual and ethical commitments. These systems arise paradigmatically when we experience ourselves as contingent creatures in a seemingly indifferent universe and strive to establish our locations within it. Such a striving is, as Hwang points, exemplified in the hermeneutic theory and practices of the German theologian Friedrich Schleiermacher, epitomized in his classic *On Religion: Speeches to Its Cultural Despisers* and articulated in his *The Christian Faith*, which offers a rather different approach to the core theological commitments of the author of this book, who, nevertheless, rightly sees the hermeneutical significance of Schleiermacher's work.

Schleiermacher saw and acknowledged the experience of radical contingency or dependency attendant upon the realization of creature consciousness. This experience is an interruption of everydayness and the multiple taken-for-granted frames that define it. It provokes and leads to radical attempts to place ourselves in the cosmos and in the dynamic forces that make up our lives in time. The great religious systems of the world, with their conceptual schemes and ritual practices, embody these attempts at existential placement attendant upon the shock of the realization of our contingency and of our place in nature and its dialectic of creativity and destruction, of emergent novelty and its perpetual perishing, that the process theologians have placed in the center of their developments of the work of Whitehead.

Such a shock of radical contingency, however, is not the core motivating story that lies behind the concerns of this book. The shock that is the focal point of this book is the interruption brought about by the appearance of Jesus of Nazareth and the attempts to formulate its significance and bearing and its present and permanent import. Such attempts make up the core project of the Gospels with their fusion of narrative and interpretive placement of the significance of Jesus and his message. The task of interpretive placement was continued and extended in the missionary work of St. Paul and was codified in different ways in his epistles. Hwang's engagement is not directly with the canonical gospels and their background origins, but with the heuristic fertility of Heidegger and Kierkegaard in supplying hermeneutical keys to access the epistles of Paul and their existential import in a world of radical contingency with its often uncontrollable and deadly disorder and the seemingly inexplicably random deaths of innocents.

Hwang's core motivation of writing this book is not merely scholarly, although it is clearly a work of scholarship, as the references show. It culminates in the later chapters where the moving analyses, reflections, and personal memories confront the permanent shocking enigma of death that interrupts our confidence in existence. It is in these pages that Hwang shows, with focus on Pauline themes, the existential import for him of the hermeneutical intersecting frames of Heidegger and Kierkegaard. Looked at in this way, Hwang's book does not just offer us an analysis of key related hermeneutical theories but also an exemplification of how they can help to supply existential resources for deep personal interpretative engagements with our own life courses and their ineluctable endings in death. In reading this text and engaging its array of analyses and display of commitments, we are caught up in a spiral of reflections and lures to existential commitments that interrupt us and elicit from us serious efforts to locate, or relocate, our lives as finite creatures within its widening gyre of concerns.

Acknowledgments

For my wife, Rev. In-Sook Hwang of the United Methodist Church.

I am deeply grateful for the reviewing and advising made by friends Herbert and Thyra Russell. I could not complete this book without their help. I would like to dedicate this book to God in memory of Professor J. Alton Templin, who taught historical theology and philosophy at Iliff School of Theology, Denver University, and parents Hwak & Jung-Ja Hwang and Hee-Sun & Sun-Mae Park. I am also indebted to Rev. Kil Sang Yoon, who led me to join the ministry of United Methodist Church. I am grateful to those who have prayed for my writing: Karen Downy, a member of Grace United Methodist Church; Rev. Young-Sun Kim, a missionary in Tanzania; Rev. Ha-Jung Min, and Bong-Sun Hwang. I also think of Violet, Preston, Dylan, and Audrey, and many others who have prayed for my writing.

I

Introduction

A. BRIEF DESCRIPTION

The book title *Heidegger's* Being and Time *and Kierkegaard's* The Sickness Unto Death *as Hermeneutic to Paul's Epistles* is a study to understand humanity through examining the being called "*Dasein*"[1] or "*soma*" (σῶμα)[2] that Martin Heidegger, Søren Kierkegaard, and St. Paul discussed in their writings. Heidegger's *Being and Time*, Kierkegaard's *The Sickness Unto Death*, and Paul's epistles[3] explore what the human being is like and how the human being as an individual, ontologically constituted by conscience, guilt or sin, and death, authentically and freely exists, but genuinely and interdependently coexists with others who condition and are conditioned. This is analogous to what Kierkegaard in *The Sickness Unto Death* refers to: he states that his concern is not to seek Christian heroism by the naïve

---

1. Heidegger explains that in both every day and philosophical contexts, "*Dasein*," which refers to the being of human beings, is characterized by their ability to speak (*das Redenkönnen*), suggesting that this capacity fundamentally defines their existence. See Heidegger, *Sein und Zeit*, 25; *Being and Time* [Macquarrie/Robinson], 47; *Being and Time* [Stambaugh], 22. Hereafter, *Sein und Zeit* will be referred to as *SZ*, the translation of John Macquarrie and Edward Robinson as *BTM*, and the translation of Joan Stambaugh as *BTS*.

2. Arndt and Gingrich, *Greek-English Lexicon of the New Testament*, s.v. "σῶμα," hereafter referred to as *GEL*.

3. The Greek word *epistole* (ἐπιστολή) is translated into the letter and the epistle. The letter is a form of written communication for a personal reason, while the epistle is considered doctrinal or instructional in nature. But the letter and epistle are not sharply distinguishable in the style of expressing words. I translate *epistole* into the epistle instead of the letter to stick to the original and Greek term with Paul's literary works. See *GEL* s.v. "ἐπιστολή."

idea of humanity in world-history, but to inquire about relationship to life, relationships with others, and to the reality of personal existence from the Christian point of view.[4]

The issue that Heidegger, Kierkegaard, and Paul forefront in their writings is that *Dasein* or *soma* loses itself because of others who condition *Dasein* and is fated to death due to the temporality of time under which *Dasein* exists; they tell how *Dasein* exists as the constancy of self, brings the lost-self because of conditions by others back to *Dasein*, and projects its future possible being despite unavoidable death. Paul especially seeks to find a way of transcending death in his epistles.

My thesis is that the voice of conscience by philosophers, educators, and preachers besides one's own call of conscience serves *Dasein*, who lost *Dasein*-self in everydayness and publicness, to find its authenticity as "I," and to anticipate the future possibility of existence beyond its death. What they convey encourages *Dasein* to display its distinctiveness in defiance of others' effect; to face one's own death instead of seeing others' death or forcing them in death; to encounter others for the understanding of self as to others; to consider one's existence in ecstatic temporality of time rather than trying to place one's existence in the infiniteness of time; and to project the possibility of future being beyond bounding in temporality and death. This book offers an alternate voice through examining Heidegger, Kierkegaard, and Paul, whose essential views are in conscience, life, guilt or sin, death, time, and projection toward the possibility of future.

Examining those is not to compare what assertions each has, but rather to access and understand Paul's epistles in reference to what Heidegger's *Being and Time* and Kierkegaard's *The Sickness Unto Death* present. What is understood of *Dasein* in *Being and Time* and *The Sickness Unto Death* is called "preunderstanding (*Vorverstehen*)"[5] or "fore-structure (*Vor-Struktur*),"[6] and this preunderstanding is applied to understand Paul's epistles. First, the aim of this study is to understand and experience (*zu erfahren*) (like lived-experience) what Heidegger and Kierkegaard disclose and, secondly, to interpret what Paul reveals from the perspective on what is experienced in *Being and Time* and *The Sickness Unto Death*. Since the issue of "understanding" called hermeneutics is discussed in philosophy and Paul's epistles provide doctrinal ground for Christian theology, *this project offers an access to theology through philosophy*. The book is to be considered the philosophy of Heidegger and Kierkegaard for understanding

---

4. Kierkegaard, *Sickness Unto Death*, 142–43, hereafter referred to as *SD*.
5. SZ 298; BTM 344; BTS 274.
6. SZ 150–51; BTM 190–92; BTS 140–41.

Paul's theology. While the book interprets Paul's epistles on the subject of the human being in light of *Dasein* that Heidegger's *Being and Time* unveils, nuances of Paul's epistles help understand Heidegger's *Being and Time*. It is similar to what Edmund Husserl in *The Crisis of European Sciences and Transcendental Phenomenology* refers to: proportional clarification on one side brings some elucidation beyond confusion on the other, which in turn casts light back on the former under the same subject.[7]

B. ISSUES AND DESCRIPTION IN GENERAL

The issues that Heidegger brings in his *Being and Time* and that this book examines are not concerned with knowing what the human being is, but, rather, understanding the way in which the human being individually exists and interdependently coexists with others in the world. That *Dasein* responsibly exists but genuinely coexists with others implies that it makes its resoluteness (*die Entschlossenheit*) for the care of itself in relation to others in the world. The issue that *Dasein* faces to make its resoluteness as the care for itself with regard to others is what conditions *Dasein* to be pulled to its resoluteness. The conditions, which are considered fundamental and ontological attunements for the being of *Dasein* or *soma*, involve two aspects: (1) *Dasein*'s own conscience along with others called "*das Man*" (anyone or the they), and (2) death as impossibility of existence or no longer existence conditioned by the temporality of time, which compels *Dasein* to see the world including its own existence meaningless, but directs it to project *Dasein*'s future being for the care of its existence.

1. *Dasein's* Own Conscience and Others

a) Heidegger's View of Conscience and Others

As *Dasein* as an individual is thrown into the world, it is surrounded by others, who are different from *Dasein* and thereby to be called strangers. However, *Dasein* individually exists and must coexist with others in the world. The way in which *Dasein* individually exists and interdependently coexists with others is demanded to understand how *Dasein* surrounded by others becomes an individual despite the impact by others on *Dasein* and how others exist and relate to *Dasein*. How does *Dasein* exist authentically and accountably for itself under the influence of others? How is *Dasein*

---

7. Husserl, *Crisis of European Sciences*, 58.

engaged in others who compel it to modify the way of *Dasein*? Conscience is the main constituent that structures *Dasein* and makes *Dasein* to become *Dasein*-self as an individual.

Dasein is determined by anyone called *das Man* in everydayness or publicness; thereby *Dasein* loses itself and becomes everyday-self or *das Man-Selbst* (self). Heidegger claims that with the lostness in *das Man*, *Dasein* enjoys itself as *das Man* takes pleasure; *Dasein* finds beauty and meaning in the arts that are displayed at the gallery as *das Man* finds, praises and judges them.[8] *Das Man*, considered a collection of rules and norms in publicness, decides *Dasein*'s everydayness and makes *Dasein*'s self to fall into anyone-self called "averageness" (*Durchschnittlichkeit*).[9] *Dasein* stands in subjection [*Botmdssigkeit*] to *das Man*, who has taken *Dasein*'s being away from *Dasein*-self.[10] *Dasein* is inauthentically ensnared by *das Man*.

However, *Dasein* is not absolutely enthralled in *das Man*. *Das Man* cannot take the place of *Dasein*. As *Dasein* is thrown into the world, *Dasein* A is *Dasein* A, neither *Dasein* B nor others. If *Dasein* is the same as other *Dasein* and absolutely belongs to others, *Dasein* is not responsible for its existence. If *Dasein* commits a crime, *Dasein* imputes a crime to *das Man*. *Dasein* as a self-responsible being brings itself back (*das Sichzuriickholen*) from *das Man*, reverts to itself, and makes its resoluteness for its own sake. The way that *Dasein* brings itself back to itself from *das Man*'s dominance is called the "*existenzielle Modifikation*"[11] or existentiell modification as ontic adjustment free from the weight of *das Man* to be responsible for *Dasein*'s self.[12]

As the average *Dasein* undergoes its existentiell modification, the modification proceeds along with *Dasein*'s conscience. Conscience is a call. The calling of conscience is a condition that *Dasein* wants to be unbound in *das Man* and, instead, is resolutely responsible for *Dasein*-self. The calling makes *Dasein* bound or indebted to *das Man* be responsible for itself, which is called "wanting to have a conscience (*Gewissen-haben-wollen*)."[13] The calling is carried out by someone who calls as the caller, someone who is called as the hearer, and the calling about something. The caller is *Dasein*; the hearer is *Dasein*; the call from *Dasein* to *Dasein* is about the ensnared *Dasein* under *das Man* and the possible-being of *Dasein* free from *das Man*.

8. *SZ* 126; *BTM* 164; *BTS* 118.
9. *SZ* 43, 129; *BTM* 69, 167; *BTS* 41, 121.
10. *SZ* 126; *BTM* 164; *BTS* 118.
11. *SZ* 268.
12. *SZ* 268; *BTM* 312; *BTS* 248.
13. *SZ* 288; *BTM* 334; *BTS* 265.

INTRODUCTION 5

The voice of calling from *Dasein* to *Dasein* is *Dasein*'s way of being responsible for its existence despite its thrownness into the world.

While *Dasein* turns from *das Man*-self to authentic *Dasein*-self by the call of conscience, *Dasein*-self is not a solitary self away from the world where *das Man* and *Dasein* coexist. As *Dasein* summons *Dasein*'s self, who is shadowed under *das Man* and thereby becomes *das Man*-self, it makes its own resoluteness in reference to *das Man*. *Dasein* that makes its resoluteness in connection with others is called the "genuine (*echte*)" *Dasein* instead of the "authentic (*eigentlich*)" *Dasein*. *Dasein*'s genuineness (*die Echtheit*)[14] makes *Dasein* have its determination or resoluteness in light of *das Man*'s effect, for *Dasein* cannot absolutely exclude its relatedness with *das Man* as long as it exists in the world.

Heidegger's view of *Dasein*'s genuineness is confronted by the question of what *Dasein* is on account of *Dasein*'s determination as to others. Can *Dasein* be considered itself as "I" authentically, if *Dasein* must make its resoluteness in reference to others? How does *Dasein* come out of *das Man*-self, who is used to being embedded and enthralled in *das Man*? If authentic *Dasein* cannot flee from the inducement of *das Man* in publicness, and its authenticity is beset under *das Man*, how does *Dasein* modify it from inauthenticity to authenticity and free it from the weight of *das Man* to *Dasein*'s responsible being of one's self? Is *Dasein*'s own call of conscience powerful enough to bring out *Dasein* whose self is lost in everydayness under the weight of *das Man*? Do some other conditions, that is, the calling of conscience by others beyond *Dasein*'s own voice, let *Dasein*'s inauthentic self, who is shadowed under *das Man*, turn to authentic *Dasein*'s self, who is encouraged by the voice of others to determine itself?[15]

Heidegger's view of *Dasein*'s calling of conscience is confronted by two questions. The first is, "Is *Dasein*'s own call of conscience powerful enough to bring out *Dasein* whose self is already embedded in the weight of *das Man* and thereby loses itself in everydayness?" Do some other conditions, that is, the calling of conscience by others beyond *Dasein*'s own voice, let *Dasein*'s anyone-self turn to authentic *Dasein*'s self? The second question is where the lost-self is gone, after *Dasein* brings itself from *das Man*'s dominance.

The first question brings in Søren Kierkegaard's view of the voice of conscience by others, including the voice of the Infinite, and Paul's view of the Spirit, different from what Heidegger emphasizes of *Dasein*'s own calling of conscience despite referring to the "voice of the friend (*die Stimme*

---

14. SZ 127; BTM 165; BTS 119.

15. The voice of conscience by others is like the piping of the human being, the piping of the nature, and the piping of Heaven beyond one's own voice, which are discussed in *Chuang Tzu*. See Watson, *Chuang Tzu*, 31.

des Freundes)"[16] or "conscience of others (*das Gewissen der Anderen*)."[17] My thesis is that the voice of conscience by others besides one's own call of conscience allows *Dasein* to find its authenticity. The second question—whither the lost self or the old self is gone—brings in the issue of death and time concerned with oblivion or evasion, memories, and repetition (*Wiederholung*), historicality or historicity (*Geschichtlichkeit*),[18] projection toward future possibility of being, and *parousia* (παρουσίᾳ) or the presence of divinity that Paul claims to encounter in the future.[19]

b) Kierkegaard's View of Conscience by Others and the Infinite:

Søren Kierkegaard talks about the voice of others who warn *Dasein*'s *das Man*-self and summons *Dasein* to come out of the lostness of "I" under *das Man*. He in *the Journals* introduces the parable that one gander preaches to geese that their authenticity called "I" is to fly freely in the sky. Since geese are used to being comfortable in everydayness, they do not need to hear their voices called by their conscience. Nevertheless, the gander proclaims, apart from whether geese hear what the gander encourages, that they are distinctive geese, different from other animals, and their distinctiveness is to fly away to distant regions, where properly they were at home, for here they were only strangers.[20]

In *The Present Age*,[21] Kierkegaard points out the lostness of students' uniqueness in the public school. He says the rule of the public weakens students' distinctions and makes everyone fall into a universal, uniformed person.[22] He argues those, who fell into averageness or publicness, are in need of others' voices because of discouragement of self under the uniformed principles, for averaged ones are already bound in *das Man* and keep from hearing their authentic voices of conscience.

Kierkegaard in *Fear and Trembling* also talks about the voice of others from the Infinite or religious God. Abraham, to whom Kierkegaard refers in his work, takes pleasure in the complacent zone where he, his wife Sarah, and his son Isaac, who was born to Abraham's old age, happily live together

---

16. *SZ* 163; *BTM* 205; *BTS* 153.
17. *SZ* 298; *BTM* 344; *BTS* 274.
18. *SZ* 390; *BTM* 442; *BTS* 356–57.
19. Heidegger, *Phenomenology of Religious Life*; Sheehan, "Introduction to Phenomenology of Religion," 40–62.
20. Kierkegaard, "Tame Geese," 433.
21. Kierkegaard, *Present Age*, 258–69.
22. Kierkegaard, *Present Age*, 260.

and in wealthiness. Abraham is so captured by Isaac that he tends to lose his voice of conscience. Abraham hears another voice of conscience from the Infinite, who said to him to take his only son Isaac into the land of Moriah and offer him there for a burnt offering upon the mountain.[23] Abraham builds an altar, lays the wood in order, binds Isaac, and lays him on the altar, upon the wood to slay Isaac. But he did not kill his son, but caught a ram and offered it as a burnt offering. Although he did not kill his son, he attempted to murder his son. God's voice suspends ethics.

Although Abraham fails to slaughter Isaac, what does to prepare to kill his son cannot be ethically accepted. He could be judged as the convicted murderer. On the other hand, he is praised as the father of faith in Judeo-Christianity. For Abraham, the ethical is ignored and is even considered the temptation (*die Anfechtung*) so that he must resist the ethical to join the Infinite. Kierkegaard calls such ignorance of and resistance to the universalistic demands of morality a "teleological suspension of the ethical."[24] The suspension of the ethical is that an individual pursues a higher and ultimate *telos*, and the achievement is not carried out by keeping ethical norms and objective values that people observe. Instead, an individual must bracket ethical norms and aim at following God's voice.

Although Kierkegaard brings in the voice of the Infinite beyond *Dasein*'s own voice of conscience sustained by Heidegger, the voice of God is to be challenged. Kierkegaard's view of conscience by the Infinite could undermine an individual's distinctiveness and worthiness of one's own being. While universalistic principles and ethical norms do not entirely acknowledge an individual's ownness and gifts but regulate them in some respects, the entire suspension of ethics could fall into annihilating human dignity and distinction. Instead of completely removing ethical principles, some different way of being toward individuals is demanded to alternate with Kierkegaard's voice of the Infinite. Paul brings in the voice of the Spirit of the Resurrected Christ.

c) Paul's View of Consciences in Variety:

Kierkegaard's voice of the Infinite that suspends the ethical can be challenged—by which God's voice might allow us to perform unsympathetic deeds, and thereby God's voice is to be seen as the one that annihilates one's existence and distinctiveness. In contrast, Paul in his epistles introduces the voice of the Spirit of the resurrected Christ to those who lost themselves

23. Kierkegaard, *Fear and Trembling*, 27, hereafter referred to as *FT*.
24. *FT* 67.

and encourages them to hear what the Spirit cheers as a personal talent and property. The voice of the Spirit is accessed to those who lost themselves and encourages them to find individual distinctiveness, ownness, and genius. Furthermore, Paul in 1 Corinthians 12:27–31 talks about the voice in variety manifested by apostles, prophets, and teachers. These voices are diverse and distinctive. While each voice is valuable and respected, the voice in variety could fall into chaos and conflicts. Paul presents the unity of various distinctions based on the voice of the Spirit of the resurrected Christ. The unity of various distinctions is carried out in the community of faith, which is considered the origin of the Christian church.

2. Death and Beyond Death

a) Heidegger's View of Death through *Angst*

What Heidegger brings in death as the issue of *Dasein* is not to define what death biologically is, when the extinction of life arrives to *Dasein*, what will happen after death, but, rather, to explore how death or anticipation of death conditions the existence of *Dasein* or how death affects *Dasein* to determine *Dasein*'s way of being. Heidegger calls death (*Todd*) as "dying *(Sterben)*," which does not simply mean the end of life, but an ontological condition like conscience that orients *Dasein*'s existential being.

As soon as *Dasein* or the human being is thrown into the world, it did not already become, but is potential, becomes, and exists.[25] *Dasein*'s becoming of existence is called the being of "being-there," which implies openness and possibility. *Dasein* does not rest but grows, and is followed by one's projection and drives one's future. However, if *Dasein* projected and lasted in an endless way, it would be boundless and unable to be called *Dasein* in totality. Insofar as *Dasein* incessantly lasts and projects one's possibility through and through, there is nothing outstanding to grasp *Dasein* as a whole; *Dasein* is not conceived in totality. Death conditions and bounds *Dasein* in individualistic being, free from the expanse of an interminable and indefinite existence. Heidegger's discussion of death aims at framing *Dasein* within the being bordered by death.

For example, *Dasein* A is *Dasein* A, not *Dasein* B, which is called a theory of identity. The theory of identity does not make *Dasein* confuse it with another *Dasein*. Each *Dasein* is distinct from other *Dasein*s. *Dasein* does not exist boundlessly but is bordered in its totality or wholeness (*die*

---

25. *SZ* 236; *BTM* 279; *BTS* 219–20.

Ganzheit). Death makes *Dasein* in its totality (*die Ganzheit*). One *Dasein* in death can and must exist in distinction from another *Dasein*.²⁶

Death is divided into *Dasein*'s own death and others' death. While others' death is considered indirective, objective death, *Dasein*'s own death is directive, existential death ("*das heißt existenzialer Begriff des Todes*"²⁷). Heidegger avoids examining others' death, but focusing on investigating *Dasein*'s own death as the issue of *Dasein*'s being, for death is experienced like suffering in *Dasein*'s ownness in a genuine sense, not others'.²⁸ When Heidegger focuses on *Dasein*'s death instead of others' death, he also implies that death should not belong to others executed by unjust leaders who murdered innocent people, but be reckoned to one's own death. As death is actualized in *Dasein*'s ownness, *Dasein* can neither share *Dasein*'s own death with others nor describe it for others, for *Dasein* no longer exists in actuality of death. If someone refers to one's own death, the one is not yet dead. While *Dasein*'s own death is neither exposed nor discussible, others' death or the indirective death of others is objectively disclosed and debatable.

While the indirective death is not the same as *Dasein*'s own death, it makes possible an analysis of *Dasein*'s own death. We hear of others' death from the newspaper and TV and discuss them. Everyone learns of death through the death of others on account of incapability of sharing *Dasein*'s own death with others. If death is learned through others, the death is not empirical to *Dasein* but gives information about death or something unalive and objective (*objective*) to *Dasein*. Nevertheless, *Dasein* recognizes one's own possibility of death through others' death.

If death is only learned through others apart from *Dasein*-self, the death is not revealed in "mineness and existence"²⁹ [*Jemeinigkeit und Existenz*] of *Dasein*. *Dasein* cannot access others' death so that it is released to *Dasein* by inference. Since to disclose or disclosedness is to lay open, to obtain death from others by implication is not to be the issue for *Dasein*.³⁰ *Dasein* experiences its own death authentically, but not the death of others. Death that Heidegger explores in *Being and Time* is that death as the fundamental issue of *Dasein* is to be exposed primarily and authentically in *Dasein*'s own death.

Dasein's own death is called *Dasein*'s anticipation of death or being-toward-death. *Dasein*'s anticipation of death includes its death is in ownmost

26. SZ 240; BTM 284; BTS 223.
27. SZ 234.
28. SZ 239; BTM 282; BTS 222.
29. SZ 240; BTM 284; BTS 223.
30. SZ 75; BTM 105; BTS 70.

(*eigenste*), non-relational, unsurpassable (*unuberholbare*), and certain possibility despite indeterminate time when death reaches *Dasein*.[31] *Dasein*'s anticipation of death means *Dasein* is constantly running (*zu vorlaufen*) towards its death without expecting its actualization. If death is actualized in *Dasein*, it exists no more. *Dasein*'s own death does not take the place of another, and no one pays for *Dasein*'s own death to let *Dasein* avoid its death. Heidegger says, "*Keiner kann dem Anderen sein Sterben abnehmen*"[32] [*No one can take the other's dying away from him/her*]. *Das Man* neither substitutes for *Dasein*'s own death or my death nor helps shun my death, but, rather, I certainly die. Thus, the anticipation of death makes *Dasein* something ownmost, and brings *Dasein*, which lost itself in *das Man* and became *das Man*-self or an averaged and public one, back to *Dasein*-self or authentic solitude, which carries a non-relational character. Heidegger states that *Dasein* makes it authentic in the nonrelational character of death, that is, in the anticipation of its own death.[33]

Death that Heidegger discloses is "*die Unmöglichkeit der Existenz*"[34] [no longer existence or impossibility of existence], or "*Nicht-mehr-dasein-könnens Nicht-mehr-dasein-könnens*"[35] [no-longer-being-able-to-be-there]. Anticipation of death is that *Dasein* is anxious about *Dasein*'s impossibility of existence or being unable to be there despite uncertainty of when. Anticipation of death as to the impossibility of existence is called *Angst*, and *Angst* makes *Dasein*'s state-of-mind or attunement (*Befindlichkeit*) to be filled with seeing the world as meaningless due to *Dasein*'s impossibility of existence. Since anticipation of death attunes *Dasein*'s state-of-mind, some secret, sectarian religious groups use the condition of death to threaten some naïve people, saying that if they do neither follow their regulations nor join their groups, they fall into death, which eventually leads to hell. The world collapses in *Angst*, and *Angst* eradicates the significance of the world. *Angst* is a mood of uncanniness and groundlessness of existence in the world on which *Dasein* relies and the world becomes emptiness or nothingness.

As *Dasein* in *Angst* views the impossibility of existence, including *Dasein*'s own existence, and the world as meaningless, *Dasein* faces to view the possibility of *Dasein*'s existence beyond impossibility of existence in response to *Angst*'s nothingness. In *Ecstasy, Catastrophe: Heidegger from Being*

---

31. *SZ* 250–51; *BTM* 284; *BTS* 223.
32. *SZ* 240.
33. *SZ* 263; *BTM* 308; *BTS* 243
34. *SZ* 262; *BTM* 307; *BTS* 242.
35. *SZ* 262; *BTM* 307; *BTS* 242.

INTRODUCTION

and Time to the Black Notebooks David Farrell Krell states that *Angst* affects *Dasein* to fall into its uncanniness but disrupts its dogmatic stubbornness.[36]

While *Angst* makes *Dasein* be under uncanniness as to impossibility of *Dasein*'s existence, *Dasein* projects *Dasein*'s possibility of existence beyond impossibility of its existence. Projection is anticipation toward "one's own potentiality-for-being."[37] Projection (*Der Entwurf*) means "throwing or casting off." The relationship between the impossibility of existence and the possibility of impossibility of existence by *Angst* is like a crisis that carries an opportunity. While in *Angst*, *Dasein* lies in the meaninglessness of the world or the non-existence of *Dasein*-self; this brings it face to face with the possibility to be itself, and to be itself carries an impassioned freedom toward death, a freedom which has been released from the illusions of *das Man* to which *Dasein* clings.[38]

Since everything and the meaning of the world groundlessly collapses in *Angst*, *Dasein* sees a turning point to change for its own sake, and anticipates a new world beyond its collapse. "When the 'ground' is [void], . . . the effect is a radical displacement and departure, a rapture that is more a rupture."[39] For that reason, *Angst* is considered an ontological mood of rupture of *Dasein*'s being-in-the-world for *Dasein*'s new and possible future. The experience of *Angst* viewed as emptiness or nullity of the world makes *Dasein* project its new, significant, possible world. Thus, *Dasein*'s death is not the end of existence but, instead, the possibility of the impossibility of existence of its existence.[40] While *Angst* or anticipation of death brings *Dasein* down to emptiness of the world, it as a condition serves *Dasein* to see its future, that is, to project the new world or the possibility of impossibility of existence, for *Dasein* facing "being-toward-death" cares for itself beyond emptiness or the impossibility of existence ("*Die Sorge ist Sein zum Tode*").[41] *Dasein* in *Angst* projects its possibility of impossibility of existence.

While *Angst* has *Dasein* see the world on which *Dasein* relies insignificant and thereby collapse the world and makes *Dasein* be no longer dependent on the world, *Angst* causes *Dasein* to become itself as being unbound in the world. *Dasein* seeks the possibility of *Dasein*'s existence as counter to *Angst*'s uncanniness, and projects *Dasein*'s future possibility of existence to care for itself. *Dasein* in *Angst* anticipates a new world beyond

36. Krell, *Ecstasy, Catastrophe*, 47.
37. SZ 193, 266; BTM 238, 311; BTS 180, 245.
38. SZ 190–91, 266; BTM 235, 311; BTS 178, 245.
39. Krell, *Ecstasy, Catastrophe*, 49.
40. SZ 250; BTM 294; BTS 232.
41. SZ 330.

its insignificance or meaninglessness of the world; *Dasein* here comes to have a radical displacement and departure. The radical displacement and departure are carried out by seeing the world as insignificance called "nothingness (*die Nichtigkeit*)"[42] or "emptiness."[43] Nothingness that Heidegger refers to releases *Dasein* from the attachment to the world into nothing or liberates itself from the world. Nothingness or emptiness helps *Dasein* openly see the world.[44] *Dasein*'s death is not the end of existence but the possibility of the impossibility of existence.[45] *Angst* is to be considered meritorious and advantageous, for it affects *Dasein* to be free from being bound in the world, and *Dasein* becomes authentic in *Angst* and projects the possibility of *Dasein*'s future being for the sake of its own existence. Emptiness or nothingness that directs *Dasein* to see the world openly and to project its future possible being is not only explored in Heidegger's philosophy, but also in Eastern Buddhist philosophy. The Eastern Buddhist philosophy that emphasizes the significance of emptiness is especially prominent in Fa-tsang's Hua-yen Buddhism that is to be examined in the third chapter of this book.

b) Understanding of Death through Kierkegaard's *The Sickness Unto Death*:

In contrast to Heidegger's view on *Angst* that leads to project the possibility of impossibility of existence beyond remaining at the meaningless world by *Angst*, Kierkegaard in *The Sickness Unto Death* raises a question: "Is despair an advantage or a drawback?"[46] He answers the question that there is no merit in being in despair, while aesthetically it is seen as an advantage.[47] While *Angst* makes *Dasein* see the world in collapse and unbound, and thereby becomes *Dasein* in the authentic *Dasein*-self, Kierkegaard argues that *Dasein*'s self in despair cannot "remain in equilibrium and rest by itself,"[48] but falls into being misfortune and misery,[49] or destructive,[50] which

---

42. Heidegger, "What Is Metaphysics?," 105.
43. See Zimmerman, "Heidegger, Buddhism, and Deep Ecology," 240–69.
44. Heidegger, "What Is Metaphysics?," 112.
45. SZ 250; BTM 294; BTS 232.
46. SD 147.
47. SD 232.
48. SD 147.
49. SD 148.
50. SD 172.

is to be considered "perdition."[51] Despair is even regarded as "sin"[52] in *The Sickness Unto Death*.

Kierkegaard raises a question where despair originates.[53] Kierkegaard as a Christian religionist despite being regarded as the founder of existentialism investigates whence despair leading to death comes and how *Dasein* religiously exceeds despair. Kierkegaard asserts that despair brings about by misrelation or disconnection called "disrelationship" to which he refers in *The Sickness Unto Death*. He argues that human beings are a synthesis of the spiritual and physical, that is, a synthesis of the infinite and the finite, the temporal and the eternal, freedom and necessity, which are called contradictory factors.[54] The solution to anxiety is a condition in which the individual has established a relationship with or a commitment to the Power which constitutes the whole relation[55] and thereby is to establish the relationship between two factors. The Power is God or the Infinite. The self is in sound health and free from despair when it is grounded in God.[56] The possibility of *Dasein*'s existence in anxiety or *Angst* is in order by God's help to be able to deliver itself from certain destruction.[57]

Dasein's commitment to God is performed by the "leap"[58] to something transcendental called God. To leap is not an undifferentiated connection like between the one like "A" and the one like "Á," but to jump or cross over from the one like "A" to the other like "B" or from humanity to deity. To leap from one into the other is "absurd"[59] and unreasonable. To leap "A" into the Infinite is called "faith." Faith is that the self in being itself and in willing to be itself is grounded in God.[60] Faith is a commitment by the person who faces feebleness and weakness to flee to God, who saves them.[61] To flee to God is carried out by *Dasein*'s "self-annihilation before God,"[62] and becomes the unity of *Dasein* with the Infinite. What Kierkegaard argues is that a person who denies oneself and sacrifices oneself for duty gives up the

51. *SD* 148.
52. *SD* 149–50.
53. *SD* 149.
54. *SD* 146.
55. *SD* 147.
56. *SD* 163.
57. *SD* 174.
58. Dreyfus, *Being-in-the-World*, 284.
59. *FT* 10.
60. *SD* 163.
61. *SD* 213.
62. Dreyfus, *Being-in-the-World*, 284.

finite in order to grasp the infinite, and that person is secure enough, for the person is connected to the Infinite.[63] While "Heidegger does not accept Kierkegaard's substitution of the goal of creating one's identity *ex nihilo* through unconditional commitment,"[64] Kierkegaard's ultimate aim or end[65] is to leap into, to grasp, and is united with the Infinite.

Despair, sin, death, and commitment to God through annihilation that Kierkegaard argues in *The Sickness Unto Death* can be the preunderstanding to understand what Paul asserts in his epistles in terms of sin, death through crucifixion, faith, and resurrection. While Kierkegaard's perspective is influenced by Paul's, Paul's view is accessed and disclosed by investigating Kierkegaard's view. Conversely, traces of Paul's epistles help understand Kierkegaard's *The Sickness Unto Death*, as Husserl argues that relative clarification on one side casts light back on the other side.

c) Paul's View of Adam's Death and Jesus' Death:

Paul as a Christian believer discloses whence death comes and how *soma* transcends death. Paul contends that separation or disconnection became the beginning of death. The disconnection evolves three ways: the split between the flesh (σαρξ) or the corporeal and the spirit (πνεῦμα) or the incorporeal, the alienation or isolation into one's ownness excluded from other selves in the community, and the estrangement of *soma* from God. The split between the flesh and the spirit is like the misrelation or disrelationship between the spiritual and physical, the infinite and the finite that Kierkegaard elaborates in *The Sickness Unto Death*. The isolation into one's ownness excluded from other selves is like the disengagement of an organ with other organs in the body that Paul elucidates in 1 Corinthians 12 and Romans 13; each organ represents a distinctive and gifted person in the faith community. The solution to the disconnection is carried out by a fundamental condition in which the individual makes a connection with Jesus Christ, for he is considered repairing the alienation between God and humanity. Paul introduces two kinds of deaths, Adam's death and Jesus' death in order to find the way of surpassing the disconnection leading to death.

Adam's death arose from his initial disconnection with God through transgressing God's Word and has been spread to all people in the world, as Paul states in Romans 5:12. Sin came into the world through Adam and death through sin, and so death is spread to, and reigns over all human

---

63. FD 125–28.
64. Dreyfus, *Being-in-the-World*, 305.
65. FT 64–69.

beings. Adam's disconnection with God leading to death is similar to Rudolf Bultmann's statement in *Theology of the New Testament*[66]: human life is a life with others and it implies mutual trust; if mutual trust happens by such as a single lie, mistrust or sin is established and brings in violence, and then the defensive violence called law is organized to serve the interests of individuals. It is hinted at by 1 Corinthians 5:6, saying "Do you not know that a little leaven leavens the whole lump?"[67]

Paul traces Adam's death as the origin of death for all humans. Adam in the past transgressed against God's Words, made him disconnect with God, and thereby came to his death. However, Adam's death is always opening up—has an effect on all of *soma*'s existence—and the influence of the past is still working and will be in the future. What Adam did in the past does not vanish, but makes others be in no longer beings, as Heidegger says: the past of the self-loss does not vanish,[68] but is rememberable in the future.

Paul introduces Jesus' death and resurrection as therapeutic treatment to humans who are constituted by the past of Adam's sin and death. Paul argues the human being needs to break off the root of humans transferred from Adam's sin and death and then transplant it by Jesus' death and resurrection. Paul discusses the view of the graft in Romans 11:17–24. While Paul discusses in Romans 11 is about the relation between Jewish tradition, including Mosaic Laws, and Gentiles' salvation, the essential point that Paul asserts in the epistle is what is transferred could be grafted by Jesus' death and resurrection. Paul claims the old tradition inherited from Adam's death or no longer possible being should be replaced by the new tradition initiated by Jesus' crucifixion and resurrection or the future being of possibility. Paul in Ephesians 4:22–23 proclaims that Ephesians need to remove the old self (*ton palaion anthropon*, τὸν παλαιὸν ἄνθρωπον) based on Adam or the past self, but, instead, to fill in the new self (*ton kainon anthropon*, τὸν καινὸν ἄνθρωπον) grounded on Jesus.

As Paul brings the tradition or heritage of Jesus, he projects his future as the encounter with the advent of the resurrected Christ called *"parousia"* (παρουσία). *Parousia* is used in the general sense of the "arrival" or "coming" as well as "presence."[69] In *Theology of Hope: On the Ground and the Implications of a Christian Eschatology*, Jürgen Moltmann refers to *parousia* as the expectation of the coming of Christ (*adventus Christi*, not *praesentia*

---

66. Bultmann, *Theology of the New Testament*, 1:253.
67. Meeks, *Harper Collins Study Bible*.
68. *SZ* 424–25; *BTM* 477; *BTS* 389.
69. Buttrick, *Interpreter's Dictionary of the Bible*, s.v. "parousia," hereafter referred to as *IDB*.

Christi).⁷⁰ Jesus' disciples and followers have to experience Jesus' departure despite his resurrection from them and their own unavoidable death. In this anxiety Jesus promised them that they would experience the coming of the Spirit of Comfort called "Paracletes (*Parakletos*, Παράκλητος)," who is also called the Consoler, Comforter, or Intercessor;⁷¹ they would also encounter *parousia* or the presence of divinity beyond their death. *Parousia* brings about two questions: first, what it is like, and when it comes about.

Parousia that Paul argues in epistles involves Jesus Christ's incarnation in the world or Jesus' embodiment in the flesh of the human being despite the sameness with God in quality. *Parousia* to which Paul refers is also the encounter with the resurrected Christ in the future. Human existence is always "*at the point of death*" called "*eskhatos* (ἔσχατος),"⁷² as Sartre in "Merleau-Ponty" states, we are born at the moment of death.⁷³ In response to *eskhatos*, Paul proclaims that people have belief, hope and projection toward *parousia* of Christ, who died but was transformed into the living being as the first fruit of humanity.

When *parousia* takes place is a significant question. Paul's answer to the question is in 1 Thessalonians 5:1–2. He writes that we don't need to write to you about the timing and dates; the day of the LORD is going to come like a thief in the night, which means the sudden time (*kairos*, καιρός) instead of the chronological time (*chronos*, χρόνος). The time of *kairos* (καιρός) is a favorable, proper time or the time determined by God.⁷⁴ Heidegger argues that what Paul emphasizes as *kairos* instead of *chronos* is concerned with how early Christians comport themselves to it in actual life, called "factical life-experience,"⁷⁵ which matters how people in temporality live but project their future being, and enact individually but genuinely interrelate with others and God. Thus, the way I comport myself to *parousia* in actual life is not to sleep like a drunkard, but stay awake and stay sober. First Corinthians 6:9–10 says that the immoral, idolaters, adulterers, sexual perverts, thieves, the greedy, drunkards, revilers, or robbers will not experience the encounter with divinity. The question of the *when* of the *parousia* is replaced with *how* of life with awakening.⁷⁶

70. Moltmann, *Theology of Hope*, 31.
71. *GEL* s.v. "παράκλητος."
72. *GEL* s.v. "ἔσχατος"; "ἐσχάτως."
73. Sartre, "Merleau-Ponty," 304.
74. *GEL* s.v. "χρόνος"; "ὥρα"; "καιρός."
75. Sheehan, "Introduction to Phenomenology of Religion," 57.
76. Sheehan, "Introduction to Phenomenology of Religion," 57.

The shift of the when of *parousia* to the how is established by pursuing Jesus' way of being called emptiness (*kenosis*, κένωσις) and crucifixion. Philippians 2:5–8 says that although Jesus Christ was in the form of God, he emptied himself, taking the form of a servant, being born in the human likeness in the world, and even took death on a cross. Emptiness is Jesus' emptying of the God in the condition of humanity. To seek crucifixion that Jesus Christ endured is to be considered cruciformity, which Michael J. Gorman in his *Cruciformity: Paul's Narrative Spirituality of the Cross* described: "Cruciformity" is Gorman's own term and it means to conform and to make an effort on the crucified Christ in the factical life of humanity.[77]

C. SIGNIFICANCE OF THE EXISTENCE OF HUMANITY AND HERMENEUTICS AS METHODOLOGY

Heidegger raises a question in "What Is Metaphysics?"[78] and *An Introduction to Metaphysics*, saying, "Why are there beings at all, and why not rather nothing?"[79]—the question of being or the being-question (*die Seinsfrage*). The question of being implies that anything extant or entities cannot be without presupposing the being (*das Sein*) of entities instead of the nonbeing of them. The being (*das Sein*) renders beings or entities (*die Seienden*) to be possible. Why things or beings instead of nonbeing or nothing are there depends on the being of beings; being is presupposed in all entities that are to be considered extent.[80] At the same time, non-being or nothing that Heidegger refers to in "What is Metaphysics" is not a negative or empty term, but its meaning is connected to nothingness or emptiness.

The term "being (*Sein*)" is "no more than an empty word."[81] Being is non-conceptual (*unbegrifflich*).[82] Being does not indicate an entity or thing, or the nature of a thing or a thing-itself or thing-ness. According to Heidegger, while the being of entities is neither an entity nor a concept, being (*Sein*) determines entities as entities.[83] Hubert Dreyfus, who examines Heidegger's *Being and Time*, says, "Being is not a substance, a process, an

---

77. Gorman, *Cruciformity*, 4.

78. Heidegger, "What Is Metaphysics?," 112.

79. Heidegger, *Introduction to Metaphysics*, 7. In fact, the question, "Why is there something rather than nothing?" has been raised by Gottfried Wilhelm Leibniz, who holds Monadology. Leibniz had put it this way: "*Pourquoi il y a plutot quelque chose que rien?*" Heidegger rephrases it in a different way. See Steiner, *Martin Heidegger*, 35–36.

80. *SZ* 8; *BTM* 27; *BTS* 6.

81. Heidegger, *Introduction to Metaphysics*, 35.

82. *SZ* 437; *BTM* 488; *BTS* 398.

83. *SZ* 6; *BTM* 25–26; *BTS* 4–5.

event, or anything that we normally come across; rather, it is a fundamental aspect of entities, viz. their intelligibility."[84] The meaning of being is engaged in what it is that makes entities intelligible as entities. Being (*Sein*) enables an entity to be present and lets the occurrence of the entity be illuminated (*zu erhelen*).[85] Thus, being (*Sein*) is to be considered lighting (*Lichtung*) to let the thing unveil, even if being is "non-conceptual (*unbegrifflich*)."[86]

The question, "What is it something to be?" or "Why is there anything rather than nothing," is to be rephrased by the question, "What renders something or entities (*die Seienden*) possible to be?" "What lights entities to be revealed as entities?" The question can be extended to the question, "What is it for *Dasein* not to be non-being or death?" Some people define "death" as the cessation or the end of biological function of *Dasein*. Heidegger describes the end of biological function as "perishing" (*Verenden*). The perishing is not what Heidegger answers to the being-question of death. Instead, *Angst* is the answer to the question of "What is it for *Dasein* to be death or non-being?" or "What does render *Dasein* to be in death?" *Angst*, which Heidegger answers to the question of why death, instead of life, is the response to the being-question of death. *Angst* as *Dasein*'s state-of-mind or attunement renders *Dasein* to be in death or the impossibility of existence viewing the world as meaningless or nothingness; however, *Angst* makes *Dasein* project "its own potentiality-for-being"[87] beyond impossibility of its existence.

Kierkegaard, in *The Sickness Unto Death*, raises a question, "What does render the human being death?" The answer, for Kierkegaard, is *Angest* (anxiety).[88] Anxiety that Kierkegaard brings in his *The Sickness Unto Death* is like *Angst* that Heidegger discusses in his *Being and Time*. While Heidegger is influenced by Kierkegaard, both have their own ideas regarding the being question of death. Since either *Angst* or *Angest* renders *Dasein* the impossibility of its existence or no longer existence, both Heidegger and Kierkegaard are concerned with how to surpass death. Heidegger examines how *Dasein* faces *Angst* and projects *Dasein*'s future being for the care of *Dasein* beyond *Angst*. In contrast, Kierkegaard finds a solution to *Angest* in faith in God.

---

84. Dreyfus, *Being-in-the-World*, xi.
85. Richardson, *Heidegger*, 6.
86. SZ 437; BTM 488; BTS 398.
87. SZ 193, 266; BTM 238, 311; BTS 180, 245.
88. *Angest* in Danish that Kierkegaard refers to is equitable with *Angst* in German that Heidegger explores.

Paul in Corinthians 12 of the New Testament raises the question of being or the being-question of the church. Why is in Corinth the church or the community of faith for Christians rather than nothing? His answer to the question is based on the being of the church instead of the church building or the temple. The being of the church is the recognition of one's distinctiveness, acknowledgement of others and their gifts, communication, and association with others instead of building a high temple.

To distinguish *Angst* and *Angest* as the primordial meaning of death from the ordinary or vulgar (*vulgäre*) notion of death as the end of biological function brings about two questions. The first is who makes and understands two different views of death? The second is how do we make, understand, and interpret it differently? The answer to the first question is *Dasein* as the being of language, who is to be considered lighting (*Lichtung*) to understand and interpret beings, and the second answer is hermeneutics (understanding and interpretation) called "hermeneutic phenomenology,"[89] to which Heidegger refers in *Being and Time*.

1. *Dasein* as the Being of Language

Dasein is the human being[90] and the type of being that humans have.[91] *Dasein* consists of *Dasein* as being (*Sein*) and *Dasein* as an entity, which exists and displays in a region called *da*. *Dasein* "occurs essentially in such a way that the being is the 'there' [*das 'Da'*], that is, the lighting of being. The 'being' of the *Da*, and only it, has the fundamental character of . . . being."[92] *Dasein* as the being of entity exists with the question of its own being: why does *Dasein* exists instead of non-being's existence?[93] *Dasein* asks a fundamental question to itself, "Why is *Dasein* there rather than nothing?" Michael Inwood in *Heidegger: A Very Short Introduction* refers to *Dasein*, which makes an issue of its being, saying "*Dasein* has a preliminary understanding of being [*Sein*],"[94] prior to understanding and interpreting the meaning of being in general, and considers *Dasein*'s own being a means to interpret the being of any entities.

---

89. Dreyfus, *Being-in-the-World*, 2.
90. Inwood, *Heidegger*, 9.
91. *SZ* 25; *BTM* 47; *BTS* 22. See Inwood, *Heidegger*, 22.
92. Heidegger, "Letter on Humanism," 205.
93. *SZ* 191; *BTM* 236; *BTS* 179.
94. Inwood, *Heidegger*, 21.

Dasein's understanding is carried out by "language (*die Sprache*)."[95] Heidegger states that *Dasein* is delineated as the creature whose being is essentially determined by its ability to speak.[96] Entities of the world are lightened insofar as *Dasein* brings language to entities.[97] *Dasein* as "the lighting of being (*Lichtung des Seins*)"[98] illuminates (*zu erhelen*)[99] the occurrence of entities of the world, and its illumination is performed by language.

Heidegger in "Letter on Humanism" states that to be *Dasein* reveals itself in the world. *Dasein* is neither lodged in its environments nor closed to its places like plants and animals, but, rather, it manifests and discloses itself by the being of language.[100] In *The Basic Problems of Phenomenology* Heidegger states that *Dasein* as the being of existence or the being of openness in the world unveils or uncovers its existence through assertion by means of language. Language is not the sum total of all the words printed in a dictionary or book. Instead, language is, as *Dasein* is, and exists in openness or speaking. When *Dasein* unveils itself, *Dasein* speaks itself out and expresses itself.[101] If someone or system blocks or covers over *Dasein* whose ability to speak is denied, it is not *Dasein* and the blocked *Dasein* is a dead one or nothing. So far as it exists, *Dasein* is opened, uncovered, and unveiled through the manifestation of language.[102] The term "existence" of *Dasein* comes from German term "*Existenz.*" Heidegger breaks it up with a hyphen *Ek-sistenz* in order to stress *Dasein*'s standing out.[103] That *Dasein* is considered the being "stands out there" implies *Dasein* ontologically manifests itself. Language serves *Dasein* to be conceived as the being of standing out or the being of disclosedness (*die Erschlossenheit*). Hence, *Dasein* has language as long as it stands out.

2. Hermeneutics as Methodology

Heidegger in *Being and Time* presents a way of access to unfamiliar texts and entities called "hermeneutics"[104] [*die Hermeneutik*]," which is defined as the

---

95. *SZ* 349; *BTM* 400; *BTS* 320.
96. *SZ* 25; *BTM* 47; *BTS* 22.
97. Heidegger, "Letter on Humanism," 193.
98. Heidegger, "Letter on Humanism," 191.
99. Richardson, *Heidegger*, 6.
100. Heidegger, "Letter on Humanism," 206.
101. Heidegger, *Basic Problems of Phenomenology*, 208.
102. Heidegger, *Basic Problems of Phenomenology*, 208.
103. Heidegger, "Letter on Humanism," 191.
104. *SZ* 37; *BTM* 62; *BTS* 33.

methodological principles of understanding and interpretation, "making what was presented in a foreign [unfamiliar] language accessible in our own [familiar] language."[105] Heidegger's view of understanding and interpretation is called "hermeneutic phenomenology."[106] Phenomenology is a search for what the being or existence of entities discloses, while hermeneutics is concerned with understanding and interpreting what is disclosed and illuminated (*erhellen*). Phenomenology is indeterminate and unbounded; hermeneutics is determinative and adequate.

a) Hermeneutics and Epistemology:

The hermeneutic phenomenology is contrasted to epistemology with which traditional, philosophical-religious thinkers approach beings or entities. While the traditional, epistemological access to entities aims at having objective, epistemic knowledge, and knowing the essence or substance of the entity, the hermeneutic phenomenology is concerned with understanding and interpreting through participating in instead of objectively observing beings which are present and illumined instead of nothing.

Epistemology, as the theory of knowledge, is inclined toward gaining the knowledge of beings or entities under these questions: how can we know, what can we know, to what extent can we know, and what essence and substance can we know? The epistemological approach seeks knowledge or grasping objective, impartial essence of entities. The impartial knowledge is oriented toward obtaining something unbiased, indifferent, and detached from the inquirer's interests, beliefs, and perceptions. For gaining something unbiased and indifferent by the inquirer or knower, the knower suspends the knower's conditions on which the knower stands; the knower gazes at things, turns into, and contemplates the entity to have unprejudiced knowledge. How is it possible for the observer to access objectively, contemplate, and gain the knowledge of the entity apart from one's conditions or standpoints? If observers believed to have objective, dispassionate knowledge about what is out there, disconnected, and indifferent from the knower, which might be considered truth, they fall into the subjective (knower)/objective (being known) split, subject/object separation between the knower's mind to put what is perceived and the reality of the fact out there, which leads to the dissociation between theory and reality, and the issue of the truth of correspondence by mind with the external world.

---

105. Martin Heidegger, *Ontology*, 9.
106. Dreyfus, *Being-in-the-World*, 2.

b) Encounter with Others in the World:

Heidegger does not rule out the relation between the subject and the object when something as the object is perceived by the subject. Heidegger states that the perception is an extant relation between two extant entities, that is, the experiencing subject and the experienced object.[107] But this epistemological relation is a derivative discontinuous condition that presupposes a more fundamental way of relation beyond the relation of perception between the subject and object.[108] The fundamental way of relation is grounded on the idea that the subject and object preconceptionally are already ontologically interrelated in the world prior to epistemological perception, which is to be referred to as "the subject-object-in-the-world." Heidegger calls such an ontological relation of the being of entities "the being-in-the-world"[109] [*das in-der-Welt-sein*].

"Being-in-the-world" seems to imply that any independent entity does not exist in the world, but an entity is bound to every other entity. The being-in-the-world looks like a ring or loop that connects and yokes all entities into one circular link, ignoring the significance of a discrete entity. In fact, the term "the being-in-the-world" serves to imagine (*zu einbilden*) the beads of a rosary concerning entities. However, the rosary, which consists of idiosyncratic beads, cannot exist without connection of distinct beads. What Heidegger says of being-in-the-world is that an entity is neither enclosed within itself, nor disclosed only by itself, but is structurally and ontologically interrelated by the joining of many other entities in the world.

Heidegger calls such a participation by many other entities in the world as "to encounter (*zu begegnen*)." Heidegger states that *Dasein* of the factical being or being-with-others exists as an entity within-the-world or being-in-the-world in such a way that it can understand itself as bound up in its destiny with the being of those entities which it encounters within its own world.[110] For that reason, Heidegger divides *Dasein* into two modes of *Dasein*: *Dasein* as an individual and *Dasein* as the being of being with (*das in-der-Welt-sein als Mit- und Selbstsein*) others (the being-with-others) in

---

107. Heidegger, *Basic Problems of Phenomenology*, 59.
108. Dreyfus, *Being-in-the-World*, 5.
109. See *SZ* 52–62; *BTM* 78–90; *BTS* 49–58.
110. *SZ* 56; *BTM* 82; *BTS* 52.

the being-in-the-world.[111] *Dasein* is seen as the "intraworldly [individualistic] existence, and co-existent *Dasein* in its being."[112]

Since the entity is disclosed in the facticity of the-being-in-the-world that the entity of the being is disclosed by encountering or joining other entities, the argument that the entity, apart from other entities in the-being-in-the-world, independently exists, is grasped and is discovered by itself, is not successful. Hence, Heidegger claims that *Dasein* as an entity discloses itself in acquaintance with others in the world.[113] While an entity is independent, and attempts to conceptualize what the entity itself is, the being of entity is not conceptualized (*unbegriffen*) but understood (*verstanden*) and interpreted by *Dasein*'s encountering entities.[114] *Dasein* to which Heidegger refers can be stated as the entity in itself, but "the being of the entity is found only in encounter and can be explained, made understandable, only from interpretation of the structure of encounter.[115] What Heidegger says has two points about *Dasein*: first, a being or entity is in itself as it is, second, "being is there [*es gibt*], [which implies that being is disclosed in contrast to the entity that is in itself]."[116]

As *Dasein* encounters others, *Dasein* is not familiar with others; others possibly confront and challenge *Dasein*. The being of others reveals their modes, languages, and engagements that are divergent from *Dasein*. Others could be children whose languages and expressions are not definite to and familiar with adults. While others whom *Dasein* encounters in the-being-in-the-world are unfamiliar or foreign, *Dasein* neither avoids encountering the foreign nor forces to transform what others manifest, being directed by what *Dasein* favors. The meaning of "*begegnen*" or "encounter"[117] involves "*gegen*" or "counter (against)." To encounter (*zu begegnen*) implies *Dasein*'s being in "counter" or standing over the engaged, like the anti-thesis in contrast to the thesis that Immanuel Kant and Friedrich Hegel discuss in their philosophy. Although *Dasein*'s encounter with something else gives rise to the counterpart, the counterpart becomes a partner, which enriches *Dasein*'s being.

---

111. See *SZ* 113–25; *BTM* 149–63; *BTS* 107–18. See also Heidegger, *Basic Problems of Phenomenology*, 291–302.

112. Heidegger, *Basic Problems of Phenomenology*, 280.

113. *SZ* 183; *BTM* 228; *BTS* 172. See Dreyfus, *Being-in-the-World*, 255.

114. *SZ* 183; *BTM* 228; *BTS* 172.

115. Heidegger, *History of the Concept of Time*, 217.

116. Heidegger, *Metaphysical Foundations of Logic*, 153. See Dreyfus, *Being-in-the-World*, 256.

117. *SZ* 44; *BTM* 70; *BTS* 42. See also Inwood, *Heidegger Dictionary*, 202.

c) Appropriation: Understanding and Interpretation by Preunderstanding:

The manifestation of others, like a strange voice, is alienated from the encountered so that it should be made into significance and familiarity by the engaged. How can *Dasein* encounter strangers? How can *Dasein* make others as partners be in the being-in-the-world? How can *Dasein* transform the unfamiliar one into the familiar as *Dasein*'s own, not an alien? *Dasein*'s transformation of unfamiliarity into familiarity is called as "appropriation (*Zueignung*)." Others are distant from *Dasein* and have nothing to do with *Dasein*. *Dasein* must make others in encountering be in the-being-in-the-world; that is, others as *Dasein*'s own. "Interpretation [appropriation] . . . wants [others] to assimilate in the sense of making similar [to *Dasein*'s]."[118]

The appropriation (*die Zueignung*) is considered "understanding and interpretation." Heidegger claims that understanding is not a mode of cognition but the basic determination of existence that *Dasein* deals with others that are alien and veiled, and understanding is not related to an isolated punctual ego but to relationally existent being with others in the world.[119] And, the appropriation to which Heidegger refers as "interpretation" is to make what is remote or indefinite into the friendly or definite. As *Zueignung* (appropriation) literally is the compound word of *zu* (to) and *die Eignung* (suitability, making its own), it is to make something unfamiliar or unsuitable into something familiar and fitted to a person. Appropriation is "translation [interpretation]: making what was presented in a foreign language accessible in our own language."[120]

As the appropriation is carried out by making what is manifested by the other's foreign language to be accessible and suitable to *Dasein*'s own language, *Dasein* primarily has *Dasein*'s own language or structure. Heidegger states that in the Dasein's existence there is something like "an antecedent understanding of world."[121] As *Dasein* encounters an unfamiliar one, *Dasein* has already understood something in advance called "preunderstanding (*Vorverstehen*)" or "fore-structure (*Vor-Struktur*)," which is divisible into three ways of fore-structure: "fore-having (*Vorhabe*), fore-sight (*Vorsicht*), and fore-conception (*Vorgriff*)."[122] For instance, if I encounter a foreign word, I appropriate or interpret what the foreign word expresses in my local language. Heidegger claims that whenever something is interpreted, the interpretation is based on the interpreter's own fore-structure;

---

118. See Ricoeur, *Interpretation Theory*, 91–92.
119. Heidegger, *Basic Problems of Phenomenology*, 277–78.
120. Heidegger, *Ontology*, 9.
121. Heidegger, *Basic Problems of Phenomenology*, 296.
122. SZ 148–53; BTM 188–95; BTS 139–44.

an interpretation is not a presuppositionless apprehending of something presented to interpreters.[123] All interpretation depends on what has already been characterized and understood.[124]

The operation of interpretation, carried out under what is already understood, is not free from *Dasein*'s own ideas that are already working apart from others. That is, the preunderstanding is seen as prejudice, and prejudice does not enable *Dasein* to understand purely and objectively what the other discloses; the preunderstanding does not provide a new experience and understanding for *Dasein*. If what *Dasein* understands and interprets is based on *Dasein*'s preunderstanding or fore-structure that *Dasein* already owns, it seems to be nothing new or something in a circle. Heidegger calls this circle as "vicious." The circular understanding is tautological.[125]

In response to the criticism that *Dasein*'s preunderstanding prevents from understanding objectively and purely what others disclose, Heidegger argues that if we see this circle as a vicious one and then attempt to avoid it, we cannot get out of it, for understanding is not to get out of the circle but to come into it in the circular way; this circular understanding is the expression of the existential fore-structure of *Dasein* itself.[126] Heidegger argues that the world cannot be understood without *Dasein* constituted by its fore-structure and *Dasein* is not existent without the world, which is considered a hermeneutic circle. In addition, *Dasein* is enriched by encountering the world filled with aliens, and the world is meaningless without being understood by *Dasein* through making something indefinite or unspecified data into definite and specified ones fit to the fore-structure that *Dasein* already owns.[127]

D. OUTLINE

The book will have six chapters: (1) *Introduction*; (2) *Methodology—Heidegger's Hermeneutic Phenomenology*; (3) *Views of Conscience by Heidegger, Kierkegaard, and Paul*; (4) *Death and Emptiness by Heidegger and Fa-tsang*; (5) *Death and God by Kierkegaard and Paul*; (6) *Epilogue*.

1. The introduction addresses these questions: (1) Why is the book planned and what is the main idea? (2) What issues are discussed? (3) What is its methodology? The answers consist of three parts. The first tells what the book will discuss and why, with a brief description of the book. The second part focuses on issues, and discloses the thesis. The third tells

123. *SZ* 150; *BTM* 191–92; *BTS* 141.
124. *SZ* 152; *BTM* 194; *BTS* 142.
125. *SZ* 152; *BTM* 194; *BTS* 142.
126. *SZ* 153; *BTM* 194–95; *BTS* 143.
127. *SZ* 256; *BTM* 300; *BTS* 236.

why Heidegger's *Being and Time* is important, particularly "hermeneutic phenomenology."

2. The second chapter discusses methodology through three approaches: Friedrich Schleiermacher's psychological hermeneutics, Martin Heidegger's hermeneutic phenomenology, and Hans-Georg Gadamer's philosophical hermeneutics. Hermeneutics was first systematically studied by Schleiermacher, the father of modern hermeneutics. His hermeneutics was developed into Heidegger's hermeneutic phenomenology via Edmund Husserl. Heidegger's hermeneutic phenomenology was advanced into Gadamer's philosophical hermeneutics.

Heidegger's hermeneutic phenomenology is thought of as a constructive hermeneutics that the reader activates, and then transforms a text into his or her likeness for one's own sake in reference to conditions—including *Dasein*'s own conscience and death, and the effect by others. A key question is, can the reader make any kinds of manifestations revealed by the text acceptable, agreeable, and unifiable? This chapter will disclose Heidegger's hermeneutic phenomenology in reference to Schleiermacher's psychological hermeneutics, and Gadamer's philosophical hermeneutics.

3. The third chapter will investigate views of conscience. It begins with Heidegger's view of conscience; conscience is *Dasein*'s faculty that directs the way of its existence and a fundamental attunement that encourages *Dasein*, who turns to *Dasein*'s authentic self. Heidegger's investigation of conscience is mostly concerned with the voice of *Dasein*'s own conscience, for "conscience of others" or the "voice of the friend" is considered belonging to others. His view of conscience faces the challenge from Kierkegaard and Paul who argue that *Dasein* is embedded in publicness leveled by *das Man* and thereby is questioned whether it is to be directed only by its own conscience. Doesn't *Dasein* need to hear the voice of conscience by others besides *Dasein*'s own voice? The voice by others includes the voice of God. While Kierkegaard and Paul equally underscore the voice of God, each argues the voice of God in a different way.

Kierkegaard in *Fear and Trembling* writes the voice of the Infinite whose calling is heard by Abraham to kill his son Isaac and to make Isaac a burnt offering to God. The voice of the Infinite to sacrifice Isaac is regarded as a "teleological suspension of the ethical," which resists the ethical or universalistic norm to avoid killing innocents. As the voice of God suspends ethical, universalistic principles, Kierkegaard's voice of God can be confronted, by which God's voice might allow unsympathetic deeds and violence against weak people, and thereby show God an uncaring being. If God's voice ignores how one treats others fairly, God's voice does not serve to direct those who lose themselves to turn back to their authenticity, but, rather, to discourage them to come back to themselves. In contrast, Paul introduces the voice of the Spirit of the resurrected LORD to those who lost themselves and encourages them to hear and conform to what the Spirit allows and cheers a personal talent and property. The voice of the Spirit accesses *Dasein* through acknowledging individuals' distinctiveness, ownness, and geniuses. However, if individuals' distinctiveness and ownness is only emphasized, chaos and conflicts could follow. Paul presents the unity of various distinctions grounded on the voice of the Spirit caused by Jesus' crucifixion and resurrection. Paul highlights the voice of the Spirit that acknowledges individuals' uniqueness and the varieties of individuals.

4. The fourth chapter will discuss death and emptiness that Heidegger and Fa-tsang explored in their writings. Death in the state-of-mind or attunement called *Angst* that Heidegger examines makes *Dasein* regard the world as nothingness (*die Nichtigkeit*). *Die Angst* directs *Dasein* to fall into uncanniness or not-being-at-home. Uncanniness has *Dasein* face its being-in-the-world as the meaninglessness of the world and its impossibility of existence, but it is anxious in the (*die*) *Angst* about its ownmost potentiality-of-being[128] to sustain its existence. While *Dasein* in *Angst* sees the world on which *Dasein* relies as insignificant, *die Angst* causes *Dasein* to become itself as being unbound in the world. *Dasein* thus seeks the possibility of its existence as counter to *Angst*'s uncanniness, and projects *Dasein*'s future possibility of existence to care for itself. Heidegger argues that the anticipation of death called "*Angst*" brings about *Dasein*'s projection toward its future possibility of being for the care of itself. *Dasein* has a radical displacement and departure in nothingness. *Dasein*'s death is not the end of existence, but the possibility of the absolute impossibility of existence.[129]

The examination of Heidegger's view of nothingness is referenced by the emptiness that Fa-tsang's Hua-yen Buddhism discloses, as Michael E. Zimmerman in "Heidegger, Buddhism, and Deep Ecology" discusses. The examination of Fa-tsang's view of emptiness offers a preunderstanding to comprehend the view of nothingness that Heidegger discusses in his writings. Conversely, what Heidegger argues in terms of nothingness is also a preunderstanding to comprehend Fa-tsang's emptiness. Husserl refers to relative clarification on one side bringing some elucidation on the other side under the same subject. While nothingness or emptiness directs *Dasein* to see its new existence beyond its death, emptiness that Fa-sang argues is to be seen a negative approach to attain the new existence of the sentient being (*chung-seng*) like *Dasein*. In the place of emptiness, Fa-tsang introduces

---

128. *SZ* 276; *BTM* 321; *BTS* 255.
129. *SZ* 250; *BTM* 294; *BTS* 232.

chung-seng and its relatedness with and dependence on others called "*li* (principle)-*shih* (phenomenon)-*mu-ai* (non-obstruction)," and "*shih-shih-mu-ai*," as well as *chung-seng*'s emptiness.

5. The fifth chapter will examine views of death and God that Kierkegaard and Paul discuss in their writings. While Heidegger argues that the anticipation of death called "*Angst*" brings about *Dasein*'s projection toward its future possibility of being for the care of itself, Kierkegaard does not consider "*Angest*," or *Angst* meritorious and advantageous. Kierkegaard contends that *Angest* (*Angst*) is sickness or sin that *Dasein* has to "eradicate."[130] He asserts that *Angest* brings about disconnection or disrelationship to which he refers in *The Sickness Unto Death*. Human beings are "a synthesis of the infinite and the finite, of the temporal and the eternal, of freedom and necessity."[131] The solution to free from *Angest* is grounded on God and makes *Dasein* be in a condition in which the individual has established a relationship with or a commitment to "the Power which constituted the whole relation."[132] *Dasein*'s commitment to God is performed by faith in something transcendental called God. Faith is a commitment by the person who faces "frailty and weakness . . . to flee to God, . . . [who] saves from all sin."[133] To flee to God is carried out by *Dasein*'s "self-annihilation before God,"[134] Kierkegaard's ultimate aim is to die oneself and to leap into or flee to God.

Angest, sin, death, and commitment to God through annihilation that Kierkegaard argues in *The Sickness Unto Death* can be a preunderstanding to understand Paul's views of sin, death, faith, and resurrection or transformation. To interpret what Paul's epistles reveal is referenced by the perspective on what *The Sickness Unto Death* discloses. Paul as a religious-theological believer unveils the origin of death and discusses how to transcend death. Paul asserts that death is originated from the destruction of mutual, trustful relationships. The destruction of the mutual, trustful relationship as the nullity or impossibility of *soma*'s being or existence includes the disconnection between the flesh (σαρξ) or the corporal and the spirit (πνεῦμα) or incorporeal, between a person and others, and between God and *soma*. Paul claims that the disconnection between God and *soma* is originated from Adam who transgressed against God's Words, and spread his sin to all human beings. The estrangement of *soma* from God is overcome by a

---

130. *SD* 19.
131. *SD* 17.
132. *SD* 18.
133. *SD* 131.
134. Dreyfus, *Being-in-the-World*, 284.

INTRODUCTION

fundamental condition in which the individual makes a connection with Jesus Christ, who reveals himself through his crucifixion and resurrection. Paul predicts those who connect themselves to Jesus' crucifixion and resurrection would experience "*parousia* (παρουσία), which means the second coming of resurrected Christ.[135] Paul in Thessalonians 4 says that some might experience *parousia* before death. Others might misunderstand the time that *parousia* happens in his/her age for him/her, which brings about the issue of time. The issue of time, which this chapter will discuss, begins with Heidegger's view of time along with ecstasy or "*ekstasis*" (ἔκστασις) as a moment in the twinkling of an eye and then Paul's view of time—*chronos* (χρόνος) or a period of time, *hora* (ὥρα) or a short period of time, and *kairos* (καιρός) or a right, favorable, proper time or the time determined by God.[136]

6. The sixth chapter is the epilogue. The epilogue examines why and how I have written this book. The answers to these questions are elaborated by sharing my previous experiences and issues of conscience, life, death, sin, and salvation. The view of salvation addresses the question whether it is offered to all people or to particular persons who belong to the Christian community. The sixth chapter will bring in the ideas of Karl Rahner, Friedrich Bonhoeffer, Jürgen Moltmann, and John Hick in order to discuss the issue of salvation. The issue will end with Paul's view of *parousia*.

---

135. Heidegger, *Phenomenology of Religious Life*, 71.
136. *GEL* s.v. "χρόνος"; "ὥρα"; "καιρός."

II

Methodology
Heidegger's Hermeneutic Phenomenology

THE WAY OF APPROACHING the text is through hermeneutics, the study of methodological principles of understanding and interpretation. "Methodological principle" does not mean an instrument or technique to comprehend and interpret the text easily and exactly, but, rather, the philosophical theory about how the understanding and interpretation arise when the reader engages the book.

The discussion on hermeneutics in this chapter is divided into three parts: Friedrich Schleiermacher's psychological hermeneutics, Martin Heidegger's hermeneutic phenomenology, and Hans-Georg Gadamer's philosophical hermeneutics. While Heidegger's hermeneutic phenomenology is the essential view that this book follows methodologically, his hermeneutics is to be disclosed in reference to other perspectives.

Hermeneutics was first systematically studied by Schleiermacher, who is considered the father of modern hermeneutics. His hermeneutics developed into Heidegger's hermeneutic phenomenology.[1] Heidegger's hermeneutic phenomenology then advanced into Gadamer's philosophical hermeneutics. No matter how people develop and define hermeneutics, it is concerned with the way of approaching the text. Then, we can ask related questions about the text and the reader. How do people gain access to a text? What is the

---

1. Heidegger, "Letter on Humanism," 213. See also Heidegger, *On the Way to Language*, 10.

METHODOLOGY

understanding of the text? When does the understanding of a text occur? These ways of access and understanding are carried out by the hermeneutic phenomenology to which Heidegger refers in his *Being and Time*.

Heidegger's hermeneutic phenomenology is the confluence of two terms, phenomenology and hermeneutics. Phenomenology is a search for what is revealed in beings or entities and how beings let them manifest, while hermeneutics is concerned with how the revealing of entities is intellectually made known to those who are engaged in the entities that unveil. Phenomenology is in character with the revelation or manifestation of beings; hermeneutics is considered a task to understand and interpret what entities reveal.

Edmund Husserl founded twentieth-century phenomenology.[2] Heidegger took over Husserl's phenomenology; while Heidegger's view is enriched by Husserl's view of phenomenology, Heidegger creates his own view of phenomenology, making phenomenology mean the opposite of Husserl's phenomenology.[3] Husserl's view is to aim at indubitable evidence free from prejudice and background upon which the understanding or interpretation takes place.[4] Heidegger in his *Being and Time* maintains that the understanding or interpretation is conditioned instead of gaining unquestionable evidence by the interpreter. Philosophers such as Jean-Paul Sartre and Maurice Merleau-Ponty[5] began with Husserl's phenomenology, but they are not in accord with Husserl but recreate their own phenomenology. Although phenomenology is not regarded as a unitary study, it is the study of phenomena in general.

A. HEIDEGGER'S VIEW OF PHENOMENOLOGY

Phenomena of phenomenology are in contrast with noumena of metaphysics, which Immanuel Kant in his *Critique of Pure Reason* particularly valued. Metaphysics in Western philosophy has sought the foundational being on which all beings rely beyond what and how we engage in our daily lives. The fundamental being is the noumenon whose feature is considered the true reality or the basis of everything called substance. In contrast, phenomenon, distant from the true reality of noumenon, refers to anything we can encounter in everydayness. Phenomenological research, distinct from traditional metaphysics, shifts from focusing on searching noumenon

---

2. SZ 38; BTM 62; BTS 34.
3. Dreyfus, *Being-in-the-World*, 31.
4. Dreyfus, *Being-in-the-World*, 30, 32.
5. See Macann, *Four Phenomenological Philosophers*.

or substance, by which we can uphold nothing other than the substance itself,[6] to dealing with phenomena involved in everyone's ordinary life.

1. Shift from the Study of Noumenon to Phenomenon

We encounter many beings or entities in our ordinary lives. We go to a grocery store to buy food or to a department store to buy something special for loved ones, looking at things through a show window and raising questions. What are they? Why is the small gold ring more expensive than the bigger one? Perhaps the small one is more authentic or purer than the bigger one. Perhaps we were dazzled by the brightness of an entity. This assumption of unreality opens the possibility that behind what the customer first identified may be the true reality or being which they have yet to discover. The question of the true reality of beings is beyond what the customer first intuited brings about three distinctive views on beings: noumena/phenomena, reality/appearance, and unconditioned substance/conditioned beings.

The divisions between noumena and phenomena, unconditioned substance and conditioned beings, and reality and appearance imply a different value concerning beings. Although conditioned beings are confirmed and advocated in our everyday lives, they are not truly extant but a mere appearance. Phenomena as apparent beings are considered secondary, half-true qualities. In contrast, noumena as unconditioned substance are pure, original, permanent, and genuine beings, independent of phenomena.[7] In a sense, noumena are unbound in conditions and disconnected from phenomena. Are noumena totally separate from phenomena? Are any substantial things pure, free from conditions and locations? For instance, how is pure love possible and separate from actual love enacted by people in the world? If such love exists, what good is it to us? No matter how we interpret what pure love is, love has to begin with actual love and the pure love is not apart from the actual love. For phenomenologists, the pure love should be based on the actual love. The view on noumena excluded from phenomena could be naïve and result in dualistic and unsolvable antinomy, as Kant indicated in his *Critique of Pure Reason*. Antinomy is depicted as a contradiction and duplicity that two opposed principles are equally justified.

The metaphysical and transcendental search for reality beyond what is extant in our ordinary lives, that is, noumena behind phenomena, is challenged by the phenomenological search that phenomena are reality themselves instead of noumena and are true reality, not half-reality.

6. *SZ* 92; *BTM* 125; *BTS* 86.
7. Windelband, *Introduction to Philosophy*, 35.

Phenomenologists do not expect any noumena to be excluded from phenomena. The phenomenological search begins with the argument that there is nothing beyond the phenomenon and the true being is not detached from the phenomenon. Heidegger holds that the question of true being by metaphysical pursuit since Plato and Aristotle has passed oblivion in such a way that the true being disengaged from phenomena is concealed and hidden rather than revealed. Thus, phenomenology must take over to disclose the true being called phenomenon. What Heidegger argues is that the revelation of phenomena, instead of being suppressed by traditional metaphysics, is regarded as the truth that phenomenology seeks. Phenomenology, shifted from the search for noumenon to a search for phenomenon, consists of two components, "phenomenon (φαινούμενον)" and "*logos* (λόγος)" or study, so that it is considered the *logos* of the phenomenon in general.

2. The *Logos* of Phenomenon

The phenomenon, originated from the Greek, is defined as what the entity or the being itself shows (*das, was sich zeigt*), as the self-showing (*das Sichzeigende*) or the manifest (*das Offenbare*)[8] of the entity itself; phenomena (φαινούμενα) of the entities (τά ὄντα) that show themselves for themselves represent the totality of what lies in the light of day that can be brought into the light (*das Sich-an-ihm-selbst-zeigende, das Offenbare*).[9] What the entity itself or the being itself manifests means that neither a transcendental being nor something else apart from the phenomenon itself takes place for the phenomenon to reveal. The entity itself shows that the entity is not isolated and hidden in itself but, rather, disclosed out of itself and related to others in contrast to the metaphysical view of substance by which the substance is in itself, distinct from openness and relatedness of the entity.[10] Thus, the *logos* of phenomenon means that the entity is not concealed within itself but, instead, reveals and opens out of itself to the world. The *logos* lies in letting the entity be exposed in its togetherness with other entities in the world, free from being bound in the entity itself.[11] The *logos* of phenomenon is called *aletheia* (ἀλήθεια) or truth, which is disclosure (*Erschlossenheit*) or un-concealment (*Unverborgenheit*) of how entities in the world appear to and manifest the one called *Dasein* to have a part of *Dasein*'s intelligibility.

8. *SZ* 28; *BTM* 51; *BTS* 25.
9. *SZ* 28; *BTM* 51; *BTS* 25.
10. *SZ* 92; *BTM* 125; *BTS* 86.
11. *SZ* 33; *BTM* 56; *BTS* 29.

Truth has traditionally been understood as a feature of statements or propositions about entities.[12] A statement or proposition objectively expresses something, just as it is. The statement "a hammer is heavy" tells something factual. The statement (*der Satz*) or proposition such as "Two plus two equals four" is considered the locus or place (*der Ort*) in which the truth is placed.[13] While a statement or proposition expresses something truthful and reliable, the statement must be affirmed in accordance with facts in order to be regarded as trustworthy. Otherwise, the statement is false and bogus. Truth asserted by conformity and agreement with facts is called the correspondence theory of truth, which is traditionally advocated in philosophy. In contrast, truth that Heidegger maintains is regarded as something unhidden (ἀληθείς) or uncovered (*entdecken*), revealed by the factical being called *Dasein*; or the being of structured facticity that exists as the-being-with-others-in-the-world.

A fact that makes a proposition to be truthful, not false, is distinct from facticity (*Faktizität*) called the structured fact like a-fact-every-other-fact-structured-in-the-world. A stone and a tree that we see in the world are regarded as the fact or *die Tatsache*. Such facts are called the factuality or *die Tatsächlichkeit* that exists alone in themselves in the world. However, the concept of facticity requires that an entity does not exist separately from other entities, but is bound up with, destined with (called destiny—*Geschick*), and encounters some other entities in the world, and thereby it is understood by the reference with others.[14] Facticity is like a root of a tree, while factuality is the stump of the tree that alone stands in the woods. However, if we unearth the ground in which the tree is rooted, we can find that many branches of the root are spread like a web and structurally connected to roots of other trees in the woods (world). Suppose a difference between humanity and animals such as dogs or cats. If a newborn cat leaves in the wood, the cat might survive. However, if a new born baby lies in the wood, he or she cannot survive, for humanity is a factical being surrounded and nurtured by families and communities.

Heidegger considers truth disclosure or un-concealment by *Dasein* as the being of being-out-there that is factically related with others in the world. To be true is to disclose something lying behind "a reservoir of the not-yet-uncovered,"[15] that is, disclosure (*erschliessen*) or un-hiddenness

---

12. Heidegger, *Logic*, 18.
13. Heidegger, *Logic*, 18.
14. *SZ* 56; *BTM* 82; *BTS* 52.
15. Heidegger, *Poetry, Language, Thought*, 60.

(ἀλήθεια).[16] On the contrary, to be false (*Falschsein*, ψεύδεσθαι) is to deceive in the sense of covering up (*verdecken*), such as by putting something in front of something else to let it appear like the being itself, and thereby passing it off as something which it is not.[17] The *logos* of phenomenon is to let the entity itself be revealed. Furthermore, what Heidegger argues is that truth as uncovering is a kind of being of *Dasein*, which can uncover and free beings in themselves.[18] In other words, as truth signifies the uncoveredness of some entity, the disclosedness is carried out by *Dasein*, which is both disclosed and disclosing. Thus, *Dasein* is considered essentially being in the truth.[19]

The text is considered the entity or phenomenon, and it is understood and interpreted as it is engaged by *Dasein*, which let it be revealed through encountering and reading. When *Dasein* encounters the text, the text, as a phenomenon, reveals and shows itself, which is to be called *aletheia* or disclosure, distinct from one simple proposition or statement.

3. The Phenomenon of the *Logos*

Since the phenomenon or the entity discloses itself, its study is concerned with what the entity itself directly shows and thereby excludes the indirective study such as deduction, dialectic arguments, and transcendental affirmation of metaphysics.[20] The study of the phenomenon attempts to understand the immediate illumination by the entity itself prior to any particular speculative and theoretical knowledge. For that reason, the manifest of the entity itself or phenomenon is to be considered the immediate consciousness of the entity itself like the feeling that Friedrich Schleiermacher brings in *the Christian Faith*. However, even though phenomena that we understand directly manifest themselves, we are not conscious of themselves as they directly show themselves to us. A phenomenon manifests itself in semblance (*das Scheinbare*) or seeming (*der Schein*), which means that when a phenomenon manifests itself, it can show itself as something it is not, or it can merely look like so and so. Rather, "they as self-showing can be brought thematically to us."[21] In other words, although phenomena are what they reveal in unthematical exposure, they reveal themselves in the

16. *BTM* 56–57. See Heidegger, *Poetry, Language, Thought*, 61.
17. *SZ* 33; *BTM* 56–57; *BTS* 29.
18. *SZ* 227; *BTM* 270; *BTS* 208–9.
19. *SZ* 256; *BTM* 300; *BTS* 236.
20. Dreyfus, *Being-in-the-World*, 31.
21. *SZ* 31; *BTM* 54–55; *BTS* 27–28.

appearance,[22] and thereby bring about thematic issues and issuable themes about their revelation.

Suppose a child has a fever. The fever does not show what the disease is, for the disease lies hidden behind the fever, in contrast to that which directly shows the reality of the entity itself. Yet, the symptom of the fever is not totally disconnected from the entity itself or illness, but it comes from the disease itself. The illness refers to itself through its symptoms. Thus, the fever is the symptom of illness (*Krankheitserscheinungen*[23]). Studying the fever, the doctor decides that it can be grasped as illness, allergic reaction, or pretension for some purpose. Likewise, when a person coughs and sniffs, that action can be grasped as illness, allergic reaction, or pretension for some purpose. The phenomenon as that which shows itself is revealed at least into three forms of manifestations, the phenomenon by semblance (*das Scheinbare* or *der Schein*), the phenomenon by appearance (*die Erscheinung*), and the phenomenon by mere appearance (*die bloße Erscheinung*), according to Heidegger. No matter how the manifest of the entity itself is modified into many forms, all forms are primordially rooted in the entity itself and come out of the phenomenon; conversely, even if the phenomenon shows itself directly and primordially, multiplicity of phenomenon are designated as unclarified words such as semblance, appearance, and mere appearance of phenomenon that need to be clarified by interpretation beyond obfuscation.

Husserl brings in a method of suspension to clarify thematic revelation of phenomena. The phenomenological method is "the reduction or epoché,"[24] a suspension of judgment, a holding in abeyance of any theory free from the influence of biases or belief in phenomenological inquiry and clarification. The purpose of the reduction is to focus upon the sheer appearances of phenomena. However, in Heidegger's view, Husserl's phenomenological method can never totally articulate the emanation of phenomena in indubitable evidence,[25] for the manifest of the entity itself can be shown in various ways, depending on the way of access (*nach der Zugangsart*) to the entity itself. No matter how many phenomenological methods that Husserl described, his methods aiming at complete freedom from prejudice[26] can never succeed, for *Dasein* engaged in the phenomenon is constituted by prejudices, and it understands the phenomenon in reference to what it is

---

22. *SZ* 30; *BTM* 54; *BTS* 27.
23. *SZ* 29.
24. Williams, *Schleiermacher the Theologian*, 6–7.
25. Dreyfus, *Being-in-the-World*, 30.
26. Dreyfus, *Being-in-the-World*, 32.

conditioned.²⁷ Heidegger examines how *Dasein* is preconceptionally and ontologically conditioned to understand and interpret the manifestation of phenomena, which is to be called "hermeneutics."

Hermeneutics etymologically comes from *hermeneueia* (ἑρμηνεύεια), which means "translation" or "interpretation";²⁸ *hermeneuo* (ἑρμηνεύω) means to "explain" or "interpret" something to someone.²⁹ *Herm* (Ἑρμ) of *hermeneueia* (ἑρμηνεύεια) "simply means *proclaim*, [say something], *discourse on*, without the idea of interpretation."³⁰ No matter how the phenomenon, as what shows the entity itself is fashioned into several modes such as semblance, appearance and mere appearance, the phenomenon itself manifests and illuminates. In addition, what the phenomenon itself or the entity manifests has the character of saying or expressing (*hermeneuo*, ἑρμηνεύω)³¹ through which the entity itself manifests and is known to those who engage with it. The entity lets others know itself through saying (ἑρμηνεύω); what it says is to be transferred to those who encounter it. What the entity shows itself through *hermeneuo* or expressing is that the entity exists as the being of the entity with others instead of isolating the entity itself from others. The being of the entity reveals itself by such as talking (*lego*, λέγω), saying, declaring, proclaiming, and manifesting to the world.

The saying or expressing of entities is carried out in the medium of language in human beings. However, the saying or *hermeneuo* is not limited to linguistic expression but goes beyond what is expressed linguistically. In *I and Thou* Martin Buber, for instance, discusses the sayings of animals: "An animal's eyes have the power to speak a great language. Independently, without needing co-operation of sounds and gestures, most forcibly when they rely wholly on their glance, the eyes express the mystery in its natural prison, the anxiety of becoming."³² The saying or expressing of entities is extensive but unintelligible and obscure. That the sayings of entities are not intelligible is like babies' murmuring. While what they say is originative and immediate, their sayings are primitive, and indefinite. What they say is even strange, like a foreign language to the engaged such as "speaking in tongues" that Paul indicated in his epistles, or like the voice (*pone*, φωνή) in the wilderness, which is not yet articulated and intellectually interpreted. Their

---

27. Gadamer, *Truth and Method*, 183, 239–40.
28. GEL s.v. "ἑρμηνεύεια."
29. GEL s.v. "ἑρμηνεύω."
30. GEL s.v. "ἑρμηνεύω."
31. SZ 38; BTM 62; BTS 33. See Inwood, *Heidegger Dictionary*, 87; Palmer, *Hermeneutics*, 12–32.
32. Buber, *I and Thou*, 96.

sayings need to be made intelligible and appropriated by the reader, who makes them fit. The manifestation of the entity itself, like a strange voice, should be interpreted and appropriated into familiarity.[33] For instance, Violet and Audrey are babies. They say or express (*hermeneuo*, ἑρμηνεύω), but I do not understand them. However, their moms, who are familiar with their babies, interpret what they say for me and I understand what they express. Then I respond to them or what they expressed.

Pretend that I am now studying in my room. Several texts composed of language, such as Heidegger's book *Sein und Zeit* with two translated books titled *Being and Time*, other reference books of *Being and Time*, Paul's epistles which are in an interlinear Greek-English New Testament, and a Greek-English lexicon of the New Testament are on my desk. The unveiling and radiation are neither the entity nor energy, but, rather, it is the being (*Sein*) of beings or the manifestation of entities themselves. The revelation is already existent prior to speculative and metaphysical ideas or knowledge. The disclosed manifestation or light from those texts is shown forth and renders and illuminates me. The manifestation of the texts that the texts are saying and expressing is staying with me in the room. What they are saying or expressing transfers to me but is indefinitely revealed; it is to be interpreted intelligently further. I interpret what the texts say (*hermeneuo*) on my computer. Particularly, I interpret what Paul's epistles say in reference to what Heidegger's *Being and Time* expresses, which is also commented on by other texts.

Paul says in 1 Corinthians 14 that the original manifestation called "speaking in tongues" is strange, original, spiritual, and primitive unless it is intelligently known and interpreted. Some Corinthian church people in the first century manifested themselves in speaking in tongues. Speaking in a tongue has its own significance. Paul did not reject speaking in tongues. But he warned if those who only emphasized speaking in a tongue do not interpret the primary sayings into intelligent words, that is to say, unless speaking in tongues is intellectually interpreted to people who encounter them, it could be meaningless. Hermeneutics is an approach to making strange and primitive sayings understandable and interpretable to the engaged; hermeneutics is concerned with how indefinite sayings are definite and interpretable. Hermeneutics is to be defined as the study to make abnormal or incommensurate sayings normal or commensurable.[34] Heidegger in his *Being and Time* explores how indefinite and unfamiliar sayings are hermeneutically and understandably transformed into the definite and familiar ones.

33. See Ricoeur, *Interpretation Theory*, 91–92; Taylor, *Deconstructing Theology*, 67.
34. See Rorty, *Philosophy and the Mirror of Nature*, 320–33.

B. HEIDEGGER'S VIEW OF HERMENEUTICS

While Heidegger's view of phenomenology is based on Edmund Husserl's phenomenology, Heidegger's view of hermeneutics is affected by Friedrich Schleiermacher's. As Heidegger's hermeneutic phenomenology is the confluence of phenomenology and hermeneutics, Schleiermacher's view involves two aspects, one the immediate consciousness of dependence that implies Husserl's phenomenology, and the other, the discipline (*Kunstlehre*) of hermeneutics. Schleiermacher, who lived one hundred years before Husserl made phenomenology, "was practicing something very much like it [Husserl's phenomenology]."[35] Since Husserl's phenomenology is recently established, Schleiermacher's immediate consciousness of dependence is not the same as Husserl's phenomenology. Nevertheless, Schleiermacher's immediate consciousness of dependence is understood in reference to Husserl's phenomenology and vice versa.

Just as Heidegger states that there is more than one phenomenology in philosophy,[36] so more than one hermeneutics is to be argued. Hermeneutics was an understanding mostly for the Bible and classical antiquity until Schleiermacher formulated the theory of hermeneutics. He is considered the father of hermeneutics and impacted Heidegger's hermeneutics.[37] Although hermeneutics is viewed in many perspectives, it is concerned with interpreting what the entity itself or the text (that is also called "Thou" to which Gadamer refers in *Truth and Method*) manifests. Schleiermacher has shifted the awareness of the entity from the traditional study of epistemology to the phenomenological, immediate consciousness of dependence, which is considered the pre-conceptional awareness.

Epistemology as the theory of knowledge aims at gaining the true and essential knowledge about the entity, seeking grounds for any knowledge about the entity with the questions: how can we know, what can we know, and to what extent can we know? The questions mean that we doubt if beings really occur to us as they are informed to our perception. A suspicion is behind the assumption that our perceived knowledge may be misinformed and needing replacement by better knowledge beyond simple perceptions.[38] This assumption of misgiving opens the possibility that, behind what we perceived, something as the fundamental being (called the noumenon) or true knowledge beyond the phenomenon may be. Hermeneutics, in contrast

---

35. Williams, *Schleiermacher the Theologian*, 6.
36. Heidegger, *Basic Problems of Phenomenology*, 328.
37. See Heidegger, *On the Way to Language*, 10.
38. Windelband, *Introduction to Philosophy*, 33–34.

to epistemology, seeks to understand and interpret how the reader relates to the entity or the text and how they interpret the relatedness between the reader and the manifest of the entity itself instead of grounding the knowledge about the entity that the traditional epistemology has sought.

1. Turning from Epistemological Knowledge to Immediate Awareness by Schleiermacher

The epistemological knowledge is characterized as objective, impartial of the object. The impartial knowledge is gained by unbiased, indifferent inquiries detached from the knower's interests. The way of access to the entity in epistemology is to disengage the observer's interests and conditions on which the observer is grounded when they gaze at things, turn into, and contemplate the entity to have unbiased knowledge. How is it possible objectively to contemplate the entity without one's interests and conditions? If we, as observers, want to have objective knowledge about what is out there, disconnected and indifferent from the knower, we fall into the subjective (knower)—objective (being known) split, the dualistic separation between what we representationally know in our minds and the reality that objectively is known out there, which leads to discrepancy and disconnection between theory or knowledge and reality.

Hermeneutics avoids the epistemological knowledge of the subject as the knower stands over against what is to be known, the objective world. Instead, hermeneutics upholds immediate awareness prior to splitting the knower and the known, and the immediate awareness is characterized as cooperation and unity between the knower or I and the known or Thou (the text). Gadamer in *Truth and Method* finds the meaning of hermeneutics from a scenario carried by I, the text, audiences, and environments.[39]

Schleiermacher, the phenomenological, hermeneutic theologian-philosopher, responded to epistemological dualism, and sought pre-epistemological awareness called the feeling (*das Gefühl*), which does not cleave but unifies the knower and Thou.[40] Schleiermacher's perspective is viewed in two ways: (1) immediate awareness or immediacy of awareness called an immediate consciousness of dependence or "a modification of feeling or of immediate self-consciousness"[41] and (2) hermeneutics that is a discipline of understanding the text. The consciousness of dependence is divided into the dependence on the world and the dependence on Deity or God or

39. Gadamer, *Truth and Method*, 91–114.
40. Williams, *Schleiermacher the Theologian*, 2.
41. Schleiermacher, *Christian Faith*, 5.

METHODOLOGY

"the immediate feeling of the Infinite and Eternal."[42] The consciousness of dependence is disclosed in *On Religion: Speeches to Its Cultured Despisers* and *The Christian Faith*, which implies Husserl's phenomenological method and attitude. Hermeneutics is discussed in *Hermeneutics: The Handwritten Manuscripts*.[43]

While a life of person as the self-identical person is given in the world, the person does not invariably remain at what is given, but, instead, grows and projects toward their own possible being. As the being grows, the one is conscious of oneself that the one is not originated from oneself, but, rather, is understood as the existence of inexplicable givenness by others in the world. "Self-consciousness [of the person] arises in response to . . . others."[44] The one is conscious of which others, including nature, culture, and tradition, exist already and impact on one's existence. The person, who is consciousness of which they are neither self-original, nor self-sufficient, nor independent of others in the world, is groundless and dependent on others. The consciousness of the non-origination of the existence and dependence on others does not come from epistemological knowledge, but is arisen from pre-reflective, immediate awareness,[45] as the self-consciousness of the person arises in response to others. The pre-reflective and immediate awareness is called the feeling (*das Gefühl*) of dependence, which is "'original expression of an immediate existential relationship' the form of self-consciousness that is anterior to all subject-object relations."[46] William James in *The Varieties of Religious Experience* refers to the feeling as the deeper sense or consciousness of others which are to be called the source of religion.[47] Feeling is a direct apprehension of the thing itself, while knowledge is an abstract notion of the entity.[48]

The feeling of dependence is neither metaphysical knowledge, theoretical formulations nor moral deeds, but immediate awareness or consciousness of reality, which is directive and pretheoretical.[49] Since the feeling is directive and pretheoretical, the person, to gain the immediate consciousness, is to suspend dogmatic disciplines, any ideologies, metaphysical ideas, and anticipatory systems methodologically prior to pre-reflective and

---

42. Schleiermacher, *On Religion*, 16.
43. Kimmerle, "Foreword to the German Edition," 35.
44. Niebuhr, "Friedrich Schleiermacher," 24.
45. Williams, *Schleiermacher the Theologian*, 4.
46. Niebuhr, "Friedrich Schleiermacher," 30.
47. James, *Varieties of Religious Experience*, 337.
48. Williams, *Schleiermacher the Theologian*, 48.
49. Williams, *Schleiermacher the Theologian*, 4.

directive awareness" like Cartesian doubt or Husserl's reduction or epoché that means the suspension of judgement.[50] The feeling is "the immediate presence of the whole, undivided personal existence, . . . the unity of the person."[51]

The feeling of dependence or the immediate self-consciousness is not simply brought in by the subject who impartially observes the entity and who is detached from the entity, but, rather, arises from the cooperation between the engaged and the manifest of the entity itself. "Such feeling arises . . . not in the isolated-man but in the participant of the world of humanity. It is called forth by the gestures and . . . addresses of others, and, more generally, by the whole style of their personal bearing, and it takes on the historical character of the particular community in which the individual is nurtured."[52] Otherwise, the feeling is to be considered a devoid fantasy created by the subject. Instead, the feeling is the awareness of something or entities with which the person has a relationship.

Schleiermacher in general brings in three fundamental entities: the self-conscious, the feeling of dependence on the world, and the feeling of dependence on God, which occurs in the human's immediate self-consciousness. Schleiermacher in *the Christian Faith* says, "*The common element in all howsoever diverse expressions of piety, by which these are conjointly distinguished from all other feelings, or, in other words, the self-identical essence of piety, is this: the consciousness of being absolutely dependent, or, which is the same thing, of being in relation with God.*"[53] In other words, he states that in the feeling of dependence we are self-conscious but it is not simply consciousness of ourselves in unchanging identity separated from others, but are conscious of others and God with whom we are concerned.[54]

The God that Schleiermacher remarks is to be a pantheistic God who pervades the world, saying, "the universe is put for [here] God and the pantheism of the author is undeniable."[55] In addition, the God whom Schleiermacher advocates is the personal God. Schleiermacher states that everyone must recognize God as an almost absolute necessity for the highest stage of piety or feeling in contrast to the transcendental and absolute being beyond human relationship and the universe.[56] Schleiermacher

50. Williams, *Schleiermacher the Theologian*, 7.
51. Niebuhr, "Friedrich Schleiermacher," 31.
52. Niebuhr, "Friedrich Schleiermacher," 31.
53. Schleiermacher, *Christian Faith*, 12.
54. Schleiermacher, *Christian Faith*, 12–17.
55. Schleiermacher, *On Religion*, 24, 97–98, 115.
56. Schleiermacher, *On Religion*, 116.

refers to "the immediate consciousness of the universal existence of all finite things, in and through the Infinite, and of all temporal things in and through the Eternal."[57] Karl Barth in *The Theology of Schleiermacher* states that in Schleiermacher's *The Christian Faith* God based on pantheism is only characterized as "source of my involvement with my fellow humans,"[58] which excludes the view of transcendental God despite acknowledging the significance of immanent God.

What makes the feeling of dependence on the world different from God is that God indicates the Infinite and the Eternal, like something idealistic such as Plato's Idea[59] that serves to determine a person's mind, while the world indicates the universal existence of all finite things on which the human being depends. Schleiermacher argues that while I for myself am supposed to prefer the impersonal form of the highest being, I think that it is truly Christian to seek for piety everywhere, and to acknowledge it under every form.[60] God is known in the sense that there is a certain analogy between knowing and feeling. In knowing, the subject is determined by the object, submits himself to the object, and in feeling, the subject is aware of being determined by God.[61]

The immediate self-consciousness or the feeling of dependence on God bases the meaning of religion. While the immediate self-consciousness or the feeling of dependence is to be considered original and pre-reflective prior to epistemological knowledge, the feeling of dependence is primitive, abnormal, mystical, indefinite, and un-understandable. James says, "Feeling is private and dumb, and unable to give an account of itself. It allows that is results are mysteries and enigmas, declines to justify them rationally, and on occasion is willing that they should even pass for paradoxical and absurd."[62] Thus, Georg Wilhelm Friedrich Hegel comments that if the religion rests on the feeling of dependence, a dog would be the best religious being, for a dog has the feeling of dependence when it is satisfied by a bone. "In 1824, Hegel comments that 'If we say that religion rests on this feeling of dependence, then animals would have to be religious too, for they feel this dependence.' In 1822 he makes a more pointed comment. 'If religion in man is based only on a feeling, then the nature of that feeling can be none other than *the feeling of dependence*, and so a dog would be the best Christian for it possesses this

---

57. Schleiermacher, *On Religion*, 115.
58. Karl Barth, *Theology of Schleiermacher*, 272.
59. Williams, *Schleiermacher the Theologian*, 5.
60. Schleiermacher, *On Religion*, 12.
61. Niebuhr, "Friedrich Schleiermacher," 30–31.
62. James, *Varieties of Religious Experience*, 338.

feeling in the highest degree and lives mainly in this feeling. The dog has feelings of deliverance when its hunger is satisfied by a bone."[63] For Hegel, feeling is an instinctive sense without rational reflections and, thereby, it is meaningless and senseless. However, what Schleiermacher wants to say by the feeling of dependence on God is that as the dog depends on his master and something to eat and to possess, human beings as religious beings not only depend on worldly entities, but also on the Deity, which can neither arise from reflective thoughts nor be demonstrable by rational evidence but by pre-reflective awareness that humanity depends on some infinite and idealistic being beyond finite beings. Nevertheless, Schleiermacher's phenomenological view of immediate self-consciousness and the feeling of dependence is challenged because his views are not understandable and intelligible. As a matter of fact, Schleiermacher surrenders his view of phenomenological, immediate awareness to the view that offers understanding and intelligibility, which is considered hermeneutics. William James (1842–1910), whose approach is psychological-philosophical in contrast to Friedrich Schleiermacher (1768–1834), whose view is psychological-religious, claims that the feeling or the immediate awareness is needed by some disciplinary restrictions to avoid indefinite and unintelligible consciousness of dependence on others.[64]

The immediate awareness is indeterminate like a raw material such as crude oil. Crude oil is an original source but useless unless it is refined. Hermeneutics is like the procedure to turn the crude oil into condensed gas to be useful for motors. Just as the oil company distills the crude oil and makes it high-level gas through the oil refinery process, so Schleiermacher intends to transform the primitive, immediate awareness to the level of intelligent, definite awareness through the art of interpretation or hermeneutics. Although the immediate awareness is continuously effective in the daily understanding and does not cease to function, Schleiermacher aims at having a better awareness and comprehension through hermeneutics.[65]

2. Move from Immediate Awareness to the Art of Hermeneutics by Schleiermacher

The immediate self-consciousness and the feeling of dependence could be individualistic, not universal, and therein incommunicable, as the term feeling (*das Gefühl*) implies personal consciousness. Feeling is a spontaneous

63. de Nys, *Hegel and Theology*, 77.
64. See James, *Varieties of Religious Experience*, 337–56.
65. Kimmerle, "Hermeneutical Theory or Ontological Hermeneutics," 108.

and pre-reflective awareness of the phenomenon that might lead to personal illusion. As a consequence, Schleiermacher endeavors to offer some means or art to let the reader understand and intelligently interpret the text; he departs from the original immediate, phenomenological consciousness and replaces the immediate consciousness with the deliberate understanding of the phenomenon.[66]

To counter unintelligibility and inarticulateness of phenomenon, Schleiermacher shifts from the focus on the immediate awareness to hermeneutics. He introduces the "rigorous (scientific) understanding, with the help of hermeneutic rules."[67] "Interpretation is an art (*Das Auslegen ist Kunst*)."[68] Hermeneutics becomes the doctrine of the art of understanding (*die Kunstlehre des Verstehens*). Schleiermacher differentiates two ways of the art (*die Kunst*) of understanding (*das Verstehen*). The first is the lax practice in the art of understanding, while the second is the rigorous practice in the art of understanding. The lax practice (*Die laxere Praxis in der Kunst*) is that no matter how we practice, understanding occurs in any way.[69] The rigorous practice (*Die strengere Praxis*) is that misunderstanding occurs, and so understanding must be willed and sought at every point to avoid misunderstanding by means of rigorous practice.[70] Schleiermacher argues that misunderstanding is normally present whenever the reader engages in the text, and understanding must be desired and sought at every point through a rigorous hermeneutic procedure. Understanding becomes an art or a rule that is performed by rigorous hermeneutic rules.[71]

The rigorous understanding, along with the coherent relatedness called the hermeneutic circle between the part and whole, the author and the audience, individuality and totality, contains two fundamental rules or methods: (1) grammatical interpretation and (2) psychological or technical interpretation. The grammatical interpretation is achieved by studying philology, grammar, and history, while the psychological interpretation is concerned with seeking the author's creative act or gifted intention through which the text was produced to say or to express. Schleiermacher emphasizes that these two hermeneutical tasks are completely equal, and there is no higher or lower task to interpret the text.[72] Instead, the two forms of interpreta-

---

66. Kimmerle, "Hermeneutical Theory or Ontological Hermeneutics," 108.
67. Kimmerle, "Hermeneutical Theory or Ontological Hermeneutics," 107.
68. Schleiermacher, *Hermeneutik*, 82; *Hermeneutics*, 100.
69. Schleiermacher, *Hermeneutics*, 109.
70. Schleiermacher, *Hermeneutics*, 110.
71. Kimmerle, "Hermeneutical Theory or Ontological Hermeneutics," 111.
72. Schleiermacher, *Hermeneutik*, 81; *Hermeneutics*, 99.

tion supplement one another; the two interpretations are considered the hermeneutic circle of part and whole[73] and the parts cannot be interpreted without an understanding of the whole, and the whole cannot be grasped without an understanding of the parts.

Hermeneutics is not only the art of understanding, but also is the art of avoiding misunderstanding. Causes of misunderstanding include indefiniteness or ambiguity of words, contradiction, or inconsistency in word usage. The grammatical interpretation requires that the interpreter analyze the language, sentence structure, and literary forms that the author has expressed in the text or spoken to the audience. The grammatical interpretation is based on two principles. The first is that the text is composed of individual words so that understanding is one of individuality (conversely, individual words are extant to build the sentence, phrase, and the whole work).[74] The second is every word of the text is meant by the relatedness with other surrounding words. Hence, Schleiermacher claims that a word is never isolated, occurs with other words in its context.[75] The grammatical interpretation determines the meanings of particular words in terms of sentences, the sentences in terms of paragraphs, the paragraphs in terms of the whole work, the whole work in terms of genre to which it belongs—which are considered the contextual coherence of parts in the whole work.[76]

In psychological interpretation, the reader is to identify with the author of a given text and to empathize with the lived experience of the author, for Schleiermacher regards each work as a part of the author's life.[77] The linguistic utterance or sentence is not only composed of words, but also relates to the life of the author who produced the text. While the grammatical interpretation is a method of understanding how meaning is determined by the way in which language is used, psychological interpretation is a method of understanding the author's intentions through which the text emerges. The psychological interpretation as pre-reflective experience is to find the mental context in which the motivation of the author is understood. The psychological interpretation is based on the facts in an author's individual life and the language that the author makes and uses.[78] Specifically, the interpreter is concerned with recreating the author's brilliant ideas or spirit

---

73. Warnke, *Gadamer*, 13.

74. Kimmerle, "Hermeneutical Theory or Ontological Hermeneutics," 109.

75. Schleiermacher, *Hermeneutik*, 92; *Hermeneutics*, 121.

76. Schleiermacher, *Hermeneutik*, 34, 59, 69, 85.

77. Schleiermacher, *Hermeneutik*, 113, 202. See also Kimmerle, "Foreword to the German Edition," 39.

78. Barth, *Theology of Schleiermacher*, 179–80.

through which the text is created so that understanding is "the reproduction of an original production."[79] By the psychological interpretation, the interpreter attempts to enter into the spirit of the speaker or writer, and thereby the interpreter achieves a divinatory identification with the author through placing themselves within the author's world and life history,[80] for the author's creativity is illuminated by finding the attached relationship between the author and the world.

While the interpreter using Schleiermacher's hermeneutics is to avoid miscommunication and misunderstanding through the grammatical interpretation and to relive and recover the author's disposition by dwelling on the creative intent of the author, his grammatical and psychological interpretation might miss the focus on the manifest of the text. His subject matter is not to understand what the text phenomenologically reveals, but, rather, to enter the mind and world of the author as well as the structure of language that the author uses in the text. Focusing on finding the divinatory identification with the author's intention might sidestep proper understanding of the text itself. As a consequence, the text could be considered the secondary value in Schleiermacher's hermeneutics; Schleiermacher's view is to be driven to eliminate the manifest of the text.[81] The question is raised whether the text is understood or not when the reader simply searches for the intention of the author. Schleiermacher confronts the criticism that his rigorous hermeneutics does not contribute to understanding and interpreting the text or the phenomenon, but to center on recovering the intention of the author, which is to be considered subjective. In *Truth and Method* Gadamer maintains that the text is not of a kind that we presuppose that the meaning that the reader discovers in the text agrees with what its author intended. Just as the events of history do not agree with the subjective ideas of the person who stands and acts within history, so the sense of a text in general reaches far beyond what its author originally intended. The task of understanding is primarily concerned with the meaning of the text itself.[82]

Roland Barthes in his *Image, Music, Text* argues that the author is dead but the text is alive, so that the reader or interpreter must focus on the text, not the author.[83] Barthes maintains that readers need neither to find who the author is nor connect the text to its creator or author, for the text is drawn from innumerable ways of culture rather than from one or individual

---

79. Gadamer, *Truth and Method*, 263.
80. Schleiermacher, *Hermeneutics*, 44.
81. Kimmerle, "Hermeneutical Theory or Ontological Hermeneutics," 108, 112.
82. Gadamer, *Truth and Method*, 335.
83. Barthes, *Image, Music, Text*, 142–48.

experience. The text itself is primarily significant in hermeneutics, and the essential meaning of hermeneutics depends on the reader instead of the author.

Heidegger explores *Dasein*, which engages in and interprets the text, in contrast to Schleiermacher's psychological hermeneutics that search for the divinatory identification with the author's spirit or intention. *Dasein* is primarily the subject of hermeneutics, and hermeneutics is even to be considered the manifest of *Dasein* ("*Das Dasein ist seine Erschlossenheit*")[84] in advance of disclosing the text. In the relationship between *Dasein* as the reader and the text, Heidegger argues that the text manifests insofar as the reader understands and interprets it. Texts do not have meaning in themselves; their meaning arises only in the reader's understanding and interpreting. However, Heidegger also maintains that while the reader, who understands and interprets the text, lets the disclosure of the text be meaningful, the reader is not understandable unless the text phenomenologically reveals and throws light to the reader. The word of the text speaks, and the reader determines what the word unveils (*Das Wort unverbergt*). In a sense, the revelation and interpretation of the text are mutually cooperative and complementary.

3. *Dasein* by Its Thrownness and Projection

Heidegger's view of hermeneutics takes precedence to examine *Dasein*, as the text itself phenomenologically says (*hermeneuo*, ἑρμηνεύω). Heidegger's *Being and Time* "works back from a phenomenon to [*Dasein* as the reader]. 'We do not ask what must be actual for something else to be actualized, but about what must be possible for something else to be possible.'"[85] Heidegger's hermeneutics is focused on exploring *Dasein*, which make the text intelligible prior to disclosing the text.[86]

Examining *Dasein*, one is concerned with what constitutes *Dasein*, and what constitutes *Dasein* is how to condition the being of *Dasein*. Heidegger explores the possibility of *Dasein*'s ontological constituents and conditions to make the text understandable and intelligent. Two fundamental and ontological constituents or conditions that serve *Dasein* to interpret the text are conscience and death, the latter of which will be discussed in the next chapters. He elaborates on how the interpreter has already realized

---

84. *SZ* 133.
85. Inwood, *Heidegger Dictionary*, 171.
86. Hoy, "Heidegger and the Hermeneutic Turn," 182, 193.

METHODOLOGY

ontologically conscience and death regarded as *Dasein*'s state of mind (*die Befindlichkeit*) that conditions to interpret the text.

Dasein is primordially disclosed in two ways: thrownness and projection. Both lead to understanding and interpretation. As *Dasein* is thrown into the world, *Dasein* is not thrown into the worldless (*weltlose*) regions, but, rather, is cast into the factical world where many different beings already exist and are intertwined, which is called *Dasein*-with-other-beings-in-the-world. What is factical means that *Dasein* is structurally bound up with other beings in the world. *Dasein*-with-other-beings-in-the-world exist ahead of the thrownness of *Dasein* so that *Dasein* must exist together with other beings as the being of being-with (*Mitsein*) and is affected by *Dasein*-with-other-beings-in-the-world presently and futuristically. It is like the birth of the child who is conditioned by its families, friends, and culture. Since *Dasein* is thrown into the world where family, language, history, and tradition already dwell, *Dasein* lies in a past which inevitably conditions *Dasein*'s existence in the effective history.[87] Heidegger states that *Dasein* exists as it has already been characterized ontologically by being-ahead-of-itself as factical conditions and being together with other beings. *Dasein* in being-ahead-of-itself lies in the existential and ontological condition of the possibility of being for its care of future being.[88] What *Dasein* is or exists implies in some sense that *Dasein* is not in *Dasein*'s own control.

Since *Dasein* is thrown into the being-together-with the world and does not exist in its own control, the existence of *Dasein* seems to be determined and finalized. However, as *Dasein* is thrown into the world, it is neither finalized nor remains at what is already given. Instead, *Dasein* projects or anticipates *Dasein*'s own possible being. Thrownness leads to projection or anticipation. *Dasein* is the possibility of being for its ownmost potentiality of being.[89] Projection (*der Entwurf*)[90] to which Heidegger refers is to see the possibility (*die* Möglichkeit) of *Dasein* and to encounter the future that the thrown *Dasein* would become the new, possible being. *Dasein*'s projection is like *Dasein*, which forgets its givenness of the past but strains or runs toward (*zu laufen*) what is ahead. To anticipate and encounter the possible being of *Dasein* passing the thrown *Dasein* is to penetrate the possibility of *Dasein* in reference to every dimension of what is thrown and disclosed to *Dasein*.

---

87. Tracy, *Analogical Imagination*, 103. The term "the effective history" comes from Gadamer's *Truth and Method*.
88. *SZ* 193; *BTM* 237; *BTS* 180.
89. *SZ* 144; *BTM* 183; *BTS* 135.
90. *SZ* 145; *BTM* 184–85; *BTS* 136.

Projection does not consist of making deliberate plans. Projecting is not a plan or strategy with which *Dasein* arranges its being, but, rather, is carried out as a provisional, preliminary drafting awareness by *Dasein* prior to reckoned schemes or theory. To the extent *Dasein* exists, *Dasein* projects and always anticipates its future in terms of possibilities of *Dasein* for *Dasein*'s sake. The word "projection" etymologically comes from the Latin *proicere*, "to throw forward." The meaning of the terms "projection (*der Entwurf*)" and its verb "to project (*zu entwerfen*)" in German is originally that of throwing off (*ent*) or away from one. To throw off means a sketch, outline, and draft.[91] Just as Schleiermacher's immediate consciousness is indefinite and indeterminate, so Heidegger's projection seems to be undecided like a sketch.

While *Dasein* projects its possibility, *Dasein* as an existential being does not project a free-floating possibility of being.[92] Rather, *Dasein* projects not only its possibility in reference to what is already thrown, which is also called the past, but also projects its possibility in the concrete situation in which other entities are embedded together in the world. *Dasein* projects or anticipates itself into definite possibilities under some conditions of the past. Projection is alive and meaningful insofar as it is carried out in the definite situation and determined in reference to where *Dasein* already lies. When *Dasein* projects its possibility in reference to what *Dasein* is thrown into *Dasein*-with-other-beings-in-the-world and its projection is carried out in the definite situation, the projection is to be called interpretation (*die Auslegung*). While projection breaks out in indefinite and unbound awareness, the projection is developed into the concrete and lineate one. The development of the projection from indefinite to definite one is equivalent to *Dasein*'s development from understanding to interpretation.

Dasein's projection of possibility is also called the understanding (*das Verstehen*). The understanding is *Dasein*'s mode of being through projection ("*Das Verstehen ist, als Entwerfen, die Seinsart des Daseins.*")[93] Understanding is a hunch and basic ability to be aware of something others or something new beyond what *Dasein* is already given, which *Dasein* holds in itself. Understanding is an ability to know or handle something in everydayness.[94] Heidegger states that in ordinary language, we use the term "understanding" when we say how to handle people and how to talk with

---

91. See the footnote of *BTM* 185; Inwood, *Heidegger Dictionary*, 176–77.
92. *SZ* 144; *BTM* 183; *BTS* 135.
93. *SZ* 145.
94. *SZ* 143; *BTM* 183; *BTS* 134.

them. So understanding means knowing how and being capable of. And being capable of means having the possibility for something in oneself.[95]

I sit on my chair in my room to study and write this book. An electric lamplight stand that I understand is on my table. Before I click the switch of the light, the room is so dark that I could not read the Greek-English dictionary, which is full of small print. I have the knowledge of the lamp made of some metals, plastic materials, glass, and wood. I project the light, and it becomes something else when I turn it on. When I click it on, the light shines, and heat emanates from the light. Then the light becomes something else that is transformed from the stand of the lamplight made of metal and wood to the radiating light. When the light is on, I clearly see and read books on my bookshelf and continue studying. I understand the lamp by projecting it onto something else.

Understanding something is in the sense of "being able to manage something," "being a match for it," "being competent in something," ["*etwas verstehen*" in der Bedeutung von "*einer Sache vorstehen können*," "*ihr gewachsen sein*," "*etwas können*"],[96] with which *Dasein* deals in ordinary and everyday being. In *The Basic Problems of Phenomenology* Heidegger refers to understanding in reference to German. He states that a German term "*zu verstehen*" or to understand something literally means to stand in front of or ahead of it, that is, stand at its head, administer, manage, preside over it. This is equivalent to saying that he or she understands the know-how in the sense of being skilled or expert.[97]

Understanding is prior to conceptual comprehension. One can understand a being without comprehending it, for understanding is an initiative and prereflective awareness[98] like Schleiermacher's feeling in everydayness. Heidegger states that understanding is neither a definite kind of cognition, nor specialized scientific ideas or skills, nor a cognition in general in the sense of grasping something thematically,[99] but the mode of being of *Dasein* that it handles everything in the ordinary life in the world. Our competencies in everydayness are existential, not epistemological, so that the thing with which we are able to handle is not the issue of what the thing is analytically, but how to exist and relate to that.[100] Existence is more than mere cognition

95. Heidegger, *History of the Concept of Time*, 298. See Dreyfus, *Being-in-the-World*, 184.

96. SZ 143; BTM 183; BTS 134.

97. Heidegger, *Basic Problems of Phenomenology*, 276.

98. Heidegger, *Basic Problems of Phenomenology*, 18, 117.

99. SZ 336; BTM 385; BTS 309. See also Heidegger, *Basic Problems of Phenomenology*, 276.

100. SZ 143; BTM 183; BTS 134.

in the sense of knowledge by the spectator and such knowledge presupposes "the original existential concept of understanding"[101] that *Dasein* is able to do or handle something basically in its own ability.

Understanding is already prereflectively given to *Dasein*. *Dasein*'s understanding as "knowing-how" that is given to *Dasein* is like *Dasein*'s thrownness into the world. As *Dasein*'s being is thrown into the world, it projects or anticipates or throws itself toward what can be in the future for its own sake. As *Dasein* has an initiative awareness called understanding, *Dasein* does not remain at what it basically understands. While understanding is fundamental and able to be aware of others in everydayness, understanding is neither ended in something definite nor owned by *Dasein*. Understanding is not fixed and perpetual in *Dasein*; understanding is to be developed into the specific and owned ability to *Dasein* called interpretation. While understanding is considered a basic determination of existence as *Dasein*'s possible manner of comportment, interpretation is *Dasein*'s development or the working-out of possibilities in understanding under some conditions. However, understanding and interpretation are not separate from each other. Understanding is operative as interpretation and is realized in interpretation. Heidegger refers to the relationship between understanding and interpretation that interpretation is existentially based in understanding, and not the other way around; interpretation is not the acknowledgment of what has been understood, but rather the development of possibilities projected in understanding.[102]

4. Understanding as Projection and Preunderstanding that Lead to Interpretation

As *Dasein* is thrown into the world, *Dasein* is cast into the world where others or anyone called *das Man* already exist. *Dasein* is thrown into the midst (*in das Inmitten*) of *das Man*, including environments, tradition, technology, and culture. *Dasein* cannot avoid what is already in the world, but, rather, must encounter and deal with them.

Dasein's thrownness is beforehand given to *Dasein* as the past called givenness, but projection is hereafter opened to *Dasein* for its own future. *Dasein* understands or projects its future in reference to givenness of the past. What is thrown and given to *Dasein*'s being is to be called "preunderstanding (*Vorverstehen*)"[103] or "fore-structure (*Vor-Struktur*)"

---

101. Heidegger, *Basic Problems of Phenomenology*, 276.
102. *SZ* 148; *BTM* 188; *BTS* 139.
103. *SZ* 298; *BTM* 344; *BTS* 274.

that is already operative in *Dasein* in advance of later understanding or projection. Then, *Dasein* projects or understands its possible being in reference to the preunderstanding (*die Vorverständigung*),[104] which is called interpretation. Interpretation even executes *Dasein*'s understanding fit to its preunderstanding.

As *Dasein* is thrown into the midst of *das Man* embedded by tradition and culture, *Dasein* must encounter and be in reference to them, even if what *Dasein* encounters and relates is uncomfortable and foreign (*fremd*). What is foreign possibly confronts and challenges *Dasein*. Encounter is not idiomatic but unpleasant, unsympathetic, and harsh.[105] The meaning of "*begegnen*" or "encounter" presupposes "*gegen*" or "counter" against what *Dasein* is. To encounter (*zu begegnen*) implies *Dasein* stands over others. Since *Dasein* thrown into the midst of anyone cannot exclude anyone who is unfamiliar with *Dasein*, *Dasein* must appropriate unfamiliar ones into familiar ones. Such an enactment or operation is called interpretation or translation. While others whom *Dasein* encounters can give rise to the counterpart, the counterpart is constructive,[106] which enriches *Dasein*'s being.

Interpretation involves at least two commitments, (1) appropriation, which is to make the foreign and unfamiliar into the local and familiar (like translating a foreign language into one's own indigenous language[107]) and (2) adjusting understanding to preunderstanding, which is called *Dasein*'s fore-structure. The fore-structure is what is familiar to the interpreter who has already had as some preunderstanding prior to interpreting the foreign; thereby the interpreter fits what is foreign to the interpreter.

a) Heidegger refers to interpretation as the appropriation (*die Zueignung*) that makes what the interpreter indefinitely understood into taking one's definite own. Appropriation, as the term indicates—to make something one's own (own property)—is to make something suitable to a person. As *Zueignung* (appropriation) literally is the compound word of *zu* (to) and *die Eignung* (suitability, making its own), it is to make something alien or unsuitable into something local and fitted to a person. Appropriation is "translation [interpretation]: making what was presented in a foreign language accessible in our own language."[108]

Although *Dasein* understands or projects its possibility of being, what is primarily understood is neither yet clear nor fully unhidden. It is like an

104. *SZ* 11; *BTM* 31; *BTS* 9.
105. See *BTM* 70n2.
106. See *BTM* 70n2.
107. Heidegger, *Ontology*, 9.
108. Heidegger, *Ontology*, 9.

infant whose indefinite anticipation or projection can be modified into a definite one under the one's contemporary circumstances on which the one lies. For that reason, *Dasein* does not remain in understanding but makes what is vaguely understood into being definite to *Dasein*. Heidegger refers to interpretation as making a relevance or appropriation after understanding something that the interpretation operates in being toward a totality of relevance which has already been understood but still veiled, and it becomes unveiled by an act of appropriation.[109] In short, "Interpretation in its last stage wants to equalize, to render contemporaneous, to assimilate in the sense of making similar."[110]

Appropriation is to make what is foreign and does not belong to the interpreter to be local and proper to the interpreter. What is local and proper to the interpreter is not novel but is already used and familiar with the interpreter prior to interpreting. Appropriation is to bring what is presented in a foreign language to the interpreter's own familiar or native language, including culture and tradition. For instance, the text inherited from the ancients such as Greek texts is not familiar to post-modern people who speak in different languages, including English and German. The ancient text is filled with not only the ancient words, but also ancient culture and tradition. The interpreter interprets the ancient text under the condition of post-modern and familiar context that post-modern people are used to being, and post-modern people grasp the issue of text in reference to the post-modern agenda.

Appropriation is to make what is indefinite and global into what is definite or local as something definite such as such-and-such or a so-and-so. The term "as" constitutes the structure of the clarity of what is understood; it contains the clarity of referential relations in terms of what is encountered and understood.[111] However, to appropriate something into "as" of something else does not involve "as" of an apophantical (relating to ablaut—the change of a vowel into another vowel in the root of a word) proposition or "as" of a logical assertion, but, rather, "as" of an existential-hermeneutical interpretation or appropriation. While the logical assertion or judgment is related to factual knowledge, the existential-hermeneutical interpretation is concerned with the factical being[112] which is embedded in a local

---

109. SZ 150; BTM 191; BTS 140–41.

110. See Ricoeur, *Interpretation Theory*, 91–92.

111. SZ 149; BTM 189; BTS 140.

112. *Dasein* known as the factical being is distinct from animals such as cats and dogs, plants, including trees and flowers, and minerals such as gold and silver, which are considered factual things. *Dasein*'s mode of being is called facticity (*Facticity*), while the way of factual things factuality (*Tatsächlichkeit*). Factuality is about discrete things

situation. Thus Heidegger says: "The existential-hermeneutical 'as' [is] in distinction from the apophantical 'as' of the assertion [*Das ursprüngliche 'Als' der umsichtig verstehenden Auslegung (ἑρμηνεύεια) nennen wir das existenzial-hermeneutische 'Als' im Unterschied vom apophantischen 'Als' der Aussage*]."[113]

b) Whenever something is interpreted as something, the interpretation will be carried out on the basis of preunderstanding or fore-structure.[114] All interpretation operates in the fore-structure on which the interpreter has already been conditioned. For that reason, the entity has no objective and neutral interpretation. For instance, when someone encounters a particular text and tries to interpret it with the conviction, "what is there exactly?" which implies self-evident and undisputed prejudice, the question has *a priori* presupposition or fore-structure of the interpreter, who is already conditioned by his tradition, culture, and language, and tries to interpret it based on the condition of the fore-structure.[115] The reader does not choose all the books beyond his or her interests and concerns so much as choosing a book to read on the condition of what they are already pre-structured and interested.

The fore-structure, for Heidegger, is composed of at least three elements: fore-having, fore-sight, and fore-conception. According to him, every interpretation has its fore-having, its fore-sight, and its fore-conception.[116] Fore-having (*Vorhaben*) is the general grasp of the entity to be interpreted and the totality of involvement in which it lies. But to have a general grasp of the entity is not yet to make any particular feature explicit, so fore-sight (*Vorsicht*) is required before anything can become explicit. Fore-sight is a previous sight, which I see in advance. I have a sight on what I want to interpret in fore-sight. Fore-conception (*Vorgriff*) is considered previous grip or grasp, as the term fore-conception implies. Fore-conception that

---

which could be listed in a category. Facticity is about *Dasein* which cannot be categorized, for *Dasein* is constituted in a complicated structure and is related to every other *Dasein*. Facticity implies that an entity within-the world has being-in-the world so that it can understand itself within the world connected with other beings. While factual things like stones spatially exist as a fact (*die Tatsäche*) in the world, they are worldless (*weltlos*), for they do not exist with other beings in the world. In contrast, *Dasein* is factically worldly, for *Dasein* exists as being-together-with or being-in or being-with the world. Of course, to be for *Dasein* tells us *Dasein* is a fact. However, *Dasein* is a being-with-others-in-the-world (*Mitsein und Mitdasein*) as a structured being that dwells and is connected with other-beings-in-the-world which is unable to be categorized.

113. SZ 158; BTM 201; BTS 148.
114. SZ 151; BTM 192; BTS 141.
115. SZ 150; BTM 192; BTS 141.
116. SZ 232; BTM 275; BTS 214.

takes place before an explicit interpretation can occur is fore-conception, in which we grasp conceptually in advance the appropriate way to interpret something. If I encounter a foreign word, I appropriate or interpret it to the extent that the foreign word expresses my local language. Heidegger claims that whenever something is interpreted as something, the interpretation will be based on one's own fore-structure or preunderstanding. An interpretation is never a presuppositionless apprehending of something presented to us.[117] All interpretation depends on what has already been characterized and understood.[118]

If so, isn't the seeing of this sight already understanding and interpreting?[119] Is there any pure and new interpretation about the thing itself, apart from fore-structure or prejudice? If the entity is already pre-understood by the interpreter prior to understanding the entity itself, is understanding/interpretation necessary? The operation of interpretation carried out under fore-structure is not free from *Dasein*'s subjective ideas or prejudices. Heidegger's fore-structure and as-structure are challenged. Any interpretation that is to contribute understanding must already have understood what is to be interpreted.[120] Then, all understanding is circular. Does not the lack of this "as" constitute the simplicity of a pure perception of something? Any new understanding of the things themselves may not exist outside the circle. Heidegger responds to the doubt. He argues that the circular understanding is necessary for *Dasein*, which cannot be avoided in the process of understanding, for *Dasein* as "I" is ontologically constituted by its own fore-structure or preunderstanding. The fore-structure is a condition that *Dasein* holds in its own being. *Dasein* interprets something unfamiliar through something familiar, that is, the fore-structure, and it enlarges its understanding through what it has already owned, namely, the fore-structure.[121] Heidegger argues that no one in the world can stand in presuppositionless apprehending of something that conditions the interpreter (*ein voraussetzungsloses Erfassen eines Vorgegebenen*). Presuppositionless apprehension assumes that the interpreter cannot be free from the subjective prejudice[122] that the interpreter has already determined by his or her disposition to engage with the text. However, fore-structure, on which the interpreter is conditioned, is the interpreter's prior hermeneutic situatedness

---

117. *SZ* 150; *BTM* 191–92; *BTS* 141.
118. *SZ* 152; *BTM* 194; *BTS* 142.
119. *SZ* 149; *BTM* 189; *BTS* 140.
120. *SZ* 152; *BTM* 194; *BTS* 142.
121. *SZ* 153; *BTM* 194–95; *BTS* 143.
122. See Gadamer, *Truth and Method*, 235–74.

("*die hermeneutische Situation*"[123]) that allows what is to be interpreted to be grasped in a preliminary mode. Heidegger affirms that the hermeneutics is ontological, not epistemological, and that *Dasein* factically imbedded in the world cannot be understood without the world, and the world cannot be understood without reference to *Dasein*'s interpretation, which is considered a hermeneutic circle.

In response to the challenge that *Dasein*'s fore-structure prevents from understanding impartially what the text manifests, Heidegger emphasizes that the understanding is carried out by *Dasein*.[124] The text manifests open-endedly object and provides something indefinite or unspecified for *Dasein*. Then, *Dasein* makes something indefinite and indeterminate accessible and suitable under its fore-structure and turns it into detailed explications.[125] Heidegger argues that the text cannot be understood without *Dasein* constituted by its fore-structure, while *Dasein* is not existent without the text. *Dasein* is enriched by encountering the text filled with aliens, and the text is meaningless without being encountered and understood by *Dasein*.

While Heidegger does not ignore the significance of the text and emphasizes mutuality and circularity between the text and *Dasein*, he first explores *Dasein*, for *Dasein* understands the text despite the significance of the text's manifestation.[126] Heidegger's hermeneutics is to uncover *Dasein* that makes the text intelligible rather than the text that reveals to *Dasein*. In response, Hans-Georg Gadamer, who studied hermeneutics with the direction of Heidegger, in his *Truth and Method*, points to the significance of text and emphasizes the dialogue between *Dasein* and the text. As Heidegger's hermeneutic phenomenology is developed from Schleiermacher's phenomenological hermeneutics consisted of both the immediate consciousness and grammatical-psychological hermeneutics, so Gadamer develops his philosophical hermeneutics from Heidegger's hermeneutic phenomenology.

5. Development of Heidegger's Hermeneutics by Hans-Georg Gadamer

When the reader encounters the manifest of the text or Thou and interprets the text intelligently to be understandable, the reader-the-text-relationship or I-Thou relationship[127] is operated. In Schleiermacher's rigorous herme-

123. *SZ* 232.
124. *SZ* 256; *BTM* 300; *BTS* 236.
125. Hoy, *Critical Circle*, 3.
126. *SZ* 256; *BTM* 300; *BTS* 236.
127. Hans-Georg Gadamer discusses I-Thou relationships in his *Truth and Method*.

neutics, the reader has an interest in analyzing the structure of the text, which is composed of language and is created by the spirit of the author to avoid the misunderstanding (*das Mißverstehen*) or misconnection between the author and the reader, between what is linguistically created and the language with which the reader is familiar. The subject matter for Schleiermacher is neither what the text (Thou) manifests nor how the reader understands, but, rather, is concerned with discovering the author. Gadamer shifts hermeneutic focus from the author to the text and the dialogue between the text and the reader.

Gadamer's dialogue between the text and the reader is specifically called "Fusion of Horizons (*die Horizontverschmeizung*)," which Gadamer investigates in his work *Truth and Method* (*Wahrheit und Methode*). A fusion of horizons occurs when the text and the reader encounter. As the reader approaches to understand and interpret what the text says, the text is called "Thou," for the text manifests itself and, thereby, can be treated as Thou.[128] On the other hand, the reader, who reads and understands what Thou expresses, is regarded as the "I." Both the "I" and "Thou" are ontologically different and stand face to face so that each ontological being is called "the horizon" (*der Horizont*) to which Gadamer refers in *Truth and Method*. "The horizon is the range of vision that includes everything that can be seen from a particular vantage point."[129] The fusion of two horizons is an "agreement"[130] between the "I" and the "Thou." The fusion of horizons is the relationship between the "I" and the "Thou" or I-Thou relationship in Gadamer's philosophical hermeneutics.[131]

As the "I" encounters the "Thou," the "I" comports (*verhält*) itself toward Thou. Three modes of I-Thou relationships that the "I" behaves toward the "Thou" are delineated in *Truth and Method*[132]: (1) disjunction, (2) engagement, and (3) dialectic relatedness or interplay.

See Gadamer, *Truth and Method*, 278–333. Martin Buber also discusses I-Thou relationships and I-It relationships in his work *I and Thou*.

128. Gadamer, *Truth and Method*, 159, 298, 321.

129. Gadamer, *Truth and Method*, 269.

130. Gadamer, *Truth and Method*, 158. "To understand means primarily for two people to understand one another. Understanding is primarily agreement or harmony with another person."

131. Martin Buber in his work *I and Thou* makes the distinction between the "I-Thou" and "I-It" relationship. Buber's I-Thou relationship seems to be an ontological relationship, apart from a hermeneutic and linguistic relationship. But some scholars in recent years argue that Buber's I-Thou relationship is not only ontological, but also hermeneutic and linguistic. See Kepnes, *Text as Thou*, 20–32.

132. Gadamer, *Truth and Method*, 310–32.

METHODOLOGY

a) In disjunction, the "I" treats the "Thou" as an objective entity; therefore, the "I" neither engages in any way with the "Thou" nor is affected by the "Thou," just as a professor, who teaches morality or ethical rules, behaves differently from theories or knowledge that they teach in the classroom. In this mode, the "I" treats the "Thou" as objective, and the "I" is value-free and neutral.

b) In engagement, the "I" is concerned with the spirit of the liveliness driven from the author who created the text; the "I" is engaged in the "Thou," not as the text which is strange and alien to the "I," but as the enlivened spirit of the author. The "I" has the same spirit or empathic mind with the author. In this mode, the "I" seeks the same psychological feeling of the writer who constructed the text, as Friedrich Schleiermacher argues in his *Hermeneutics*. The "I" is to identify with the author of a given text and to have an empathy with the lived experience of the author, for Schleiermacher regards each work as a part of the author's life.[133] The linguistic utterance or sentence is not only composed of words, but also is related to the life of the author who produced the text. This mode conceives "understanding as the reproduction [by the 'I'] of an original production [effected by the author]."[134] In contrast, the text for Gadamer is the truth (*aletheia*, ἀλήθεια) about being that the text exists and manifests. Truth is "not an achievement of empathy, which involves guessing the inner life of the [author]. . . . [Truth] is not something that pertains to the [author], but to what is spoken [by the text]."[135] Truth is the opposition of disclosure (*erschliessen*) or unhiddenness[136] and lies behind a source of the concealed[137] of being (*Sein*). Being is what the text phenomenologically radiates and unveils through hermeneutically interpreting the text through language by the interpreter who serves what truth reveals.

c) In the dialectic relatedness or interplay that Gadamer regards as the highest type of mode,[138] the I-Thou relationship begins with disjunction and "temporal distance"[139] between the "I" and the "Thou"; the "I" acknowledges the "Thou" as otherness or strangeness but "in such a way that it [the

---

133. Schleiermacher, *Hermeneutik*, 113, 202. See Kimmerle, "Foreword to the German Edition," 39; "Hermeneutical Theory or Ontological Hermeneutics."
134. Gadamer, *Truth and Method*, 263.
135. Gadamer, *Truth and Method*, 445.
136. BTM 56–57. See Heidegger, *Poetry, Language, Thought*, 61.
137. Heidegger, *Poetry, Language, Thought*, 60.
138. Gadamer, *Truth and Method*, 324.
139. Gadamer, *Truth and Method*, 258–67.

'Thou'] has something to say to me [the 'I']."[140] In this mode, the "I" does not "overlook the claim of the 'Thou' [but] listens to what the ['Thou'] has to say to the 'I.'"[141] As the "I" approaches the text, the "I" responds to what the text speaks by absorbing the back-and-forth movement of the subject matter of the text in "an equilibrium between pro and contra."[142] The "I" responds to the text in dialogue by "having a conversation with the text."[143]

As the "I" has a conversation with the "Thou," both are alien and separated from one another; the "Thou" is truth, and truth is illuminated through the "I." Gadamer argues that truth reveals itself in its being in the form of work or from the work of text or art,[144] even if its disclosure is not an absolute transparency but entails indefiniteness of being (*Sein*).[145] The indefiniteness of being becomes definite by the medium of a language; the strange encounter between the "I" and the "Thou" becomes relational and familiar through the language. Gadamer states that the world is disclosed in linguistic communication, and the linguistic world in which *Dasein* exists is not a barrier that prevents knowing and relating others, but fundamentally embraces everything in which *Dasein*'s insight can be enlarged and deepened by virtue of language.[146] Heidegger refers to language as "the house of being."[147]

As the "I" has a conversation with the "Thou" by the medium of language, the fusion of horizons is not yet accomplished between the "I" and the "Thou." Instead, the revelation of the text, which is indeterminate, is transformed into the certain content under some conditions or standpoints in which the "I" as the interpreter is already imbedded historically and existential-ontologically. The "Thou" first open-endedly exists in no-where (no perspective) and is unbound, but the unbound "Thou" is appropriated as the definite one by the interpreter, who particularly stands in the historical and existential-ontological point. Of course, a standpoint "limits the possibility [openness] of vision."[148]

However, Gadamer states that the historical and existential point where the interpreter stands does not limit the freedom of knowledge, but, rather,

---

140. Gadamer, *Truth and Method*, 324.
141. Gadamer, *Truth and Method*, 324.
142. Gadamer, *Truth and Method*, 326–27.
143. Gadamer, *Truth and Method*, 331.
144. Gadamer, *Truth and Method*, 443.
145. Gadamer, *Philosophical Hermeneutics*, 205. See SZ 308; BTM 356; BTS 284–85.
146. Gadamer, *Truth and Method*, 404.
147. Heidegger, *On the Way to Language*, 63.
148. Gadamer, *Truth and Method*, 269.

METHODOLOGY

makes knowledge certain and definite.[149] Understanding is not indefinitely unrestricted (*freischwebend*) but is certainly and emphatically conditioned and appropriated.[150] Heidegger in *Being and Time* maintains that the text is understood and interpreted under the interpreter's conditions called "preunderstanding"; the preunderstanding is also considered "prejudice."[151] The preunderstanding or prejudice that the "I" has already held as the condition prior to understanding might be an effective direction for understanding the text. Gadamer calls the effective direction for the understanding the text "the principle of effective-history" (*Wirkungsgeschite*),[152] which means the effect upon human beings of a past. When "I," encounters the strange "Thou" or the text, "I" does not agree automatically with and understand the manifestation of the text. Rather, "I" puts the alien text under what "I" have already been used to be; what is used to be might not be directly pointed to something definite, but, instead, be aware of it like tradition. The principle of effective-history leads the gap between "I" and "Thou" to being connected and makes two into one. The term "fusion of horizons" connotes appropriation, reconciliation, synthetic unity, and coherence between the "I" and the text through dialogical conversation.

However, Gadamer's view "fusion of horizons" is challenged by Jacques Derrida, who is skeptical that we can have the fusion of horizons or agreement between the "I" and the text. Derrida refers to the horizon, saying, "As its Greek name suggests, a horizon is both the opening and limit that defines an infinite progress or a period of waiting."[153] Thus, he sees that the text and "I" are continually breaking apart. Derrida questions, "To what extent does this interpretation . . . in its totality and as a whole contain an interpretive decision about the unity or singularity of thinking?"[154] In contrast to Gadamer's "fusion of horizons," the term "deconstruction" that Derrida uses is associated with binary oppositions instead of unity, breakage instead of synthesis, and heterogeneity instead of homogeneity. "There [in Derrida] is a shift of focus from identities to differences, unities to fragmentations . . . presence to absence."[155] Derrida indicates "sorts of crevices, abysses, and undecidable aporias [impasse or irresolvable contradiction]" beyond

---

149. Gadamer, *Truth and Method*, 269, 324.
150. SZ 339; BTM 389; BTS 312.
151. Gadamer, *Truth and Method*, 245–74.
152. Gadamer, *Truth and Method*, 267–74.
153. Derrida, "Force of Law," 26.
154. Derrida, "Interpreting Signatures (Nietzsche/Heidegger)," 59.
155. Sarup, *Introductory Guide*, 53–54.

"showing how underlying its surface unity and coherence"[156] of the text and the relationship between the reader and the text. Nevertheless, I rely on Gadamer's view of the fusion of horizons instead of Derrida's deconstruction. Then, why?

6. The Way of Access to Unfamiliar Texts

When some themes of texts are researched, some significant questions arise, for each philosophical-theological or religious work and its intended audience is embedded in different contexts. St. Paul lived in the first century and Fa-tsang lived in the seventh century, and their works were carried out in the context of Judeo-Christian and Greek-Roman cultures, and Chinese culture. Hence Paul's theology and Fa-tsang's Buddhist religious philosophy are not easily accessible to the contemporary researcher who lives outside of the ancient culture.

How can the researcher who is so differently situated approach Paul's epistles and Fa-tsang's works? How can the modern researcher overcome the distance between his/her contemporary cultural context and a text that is part of a tradition handed down from the remote past? How can the tension between the two sets of horizons in the words of Hans-Georg Gadamer be resolved?[157] My approach to Paul and Fa-tsang will rely on Gadamer's philosophical hermeneutics based on Heidegger's hermeneutic phenomenology. There are several ways in which one can read Paul and Fa-tsang following Gadamer's philosophical hermeneutics.

First, the meaning of a text handed down from the past or transferred from another cultural tradition may be thought to depend on the reader. The reader is already conditioned, subjected as he or she is to particular social conditions. Since the meaning of the text is mainly constructed by the reader or interpreter who is conditioned by his/her own historical existence, and hence not free from impartiality,[158] the tension might be resolved by the reader who appropriates the past, brings it into his/her own stance or situation. Then the content of the text might be recaptured and reproduced by the exegete. This approach is similar to Schleiermacher's psychological hermeneutics. This approach focuses not so much on the reality of the

---

156. Bernstein, "Constellation of Hermeneutics," 277.

157. The term "horizon" is used by Hans-Georg Gadamer to refer to "the range of vision that includes everything that can be seen from a particular vantage point" (*Truth and Method*, 269). For a brief survey of Gadamer's term *horizon*, see Hoy, *Critical Circle*, 95–100.

158. Gadamer, *Truth and Method*, 190.

METHODOLOGY

text as on the subjectivity of the interpreter. The reader in this approach might have some questions about the objectivity of the text's meaning. How can the reader distinguish his/her own ideas from the reality of the text or compare his/her understanding with others? The reality of the text, however, is not simply out there to be recollected by a reader; it is much more. Gadamer sees the process of understanding a written text in terms of art: "The 'subject' of the experience of art, that which remains and endures, is not the subjectivity of the person who experiences it, but the work itself."[159] Subjective reconstruction of the meaning of the text by the reader is an art which is only part of the process of understanding.

It is possible, however, to approach the text differently by focusing primarily on the text itself, prior to the situatedness of the reader. In this approach the reader does not consider his/her conditions, but attempts to find the ideal of the text in itself. The reader tries to bracket the factors that condition him/her, and to discover an unconditioned ideal of the text free from the conditioned reader. This approach is similar to the reduction or epoché of Husserl's phenomenological method. The purpose of overcoming the tension between text and reader is to get into the object, namely, the text, detached from the view of the reader. In this way, an ideal of the text itself through detachment and neutralization from the reader's situatedness is independent of the conditioned reader.[160] However, this approach must still answer the question: Is it possible for a conditioned reader to enjoy impartially the text while the text is independent of the situatedness of the reader? If the ideal object of this approach lies in the text itself, it is separated from its conditioned reader, thus producing a dualistic relation between the text and the reader. Such an approach results in naive objectivism. Gadamer again points out the misunderstanding of such an approach by using art as an analogy. "Art is a particular organ of the understanding of life because . . . life reveals itself at a depth that is inaccessible to observation, reflection and theory."[161] In the same way, Gadamer argues that to interpret means precisely to use one's own preunderstanding or fore-structure so that the meaning of the text can really be made to speak for us.[162]

Another possible approach to the interpreting of a text seeks to make transparent the walls that separate "then" and "now," "there" and "here," until the conversation between the document and the reader is

---

159. Gadamer, *Truth and Method*, 92.
160. Taylor, "Comparison, History, Myth," 39.
161. Gadamer, *Truth and Method*, 208.
162. Gadamer, *Truth and Method*, 358.

totally concentrated on the subjectmatter.¹⁶³ In *The Epistle to the Romans* Karl Barth says that "The conversation between the original record and the reader moves round the subjectmatter, until a distinction between yesterday and today becomes impossible."¹⁶⁴ The concentration on the subject matter bridges the gap and transforms the tension between what the text meant in its past and what it means now into one.¹⁶⁵

Krister Stendahl, however, points out that Barth's argument is distorted because Barth's attempt ignores the tension and transforms the dynamic interactive process of understanding into a different theoretical category of "otherness."¹⁶⁶ Barth's approach is "incapable of enough patience and enthusiasm for keeping alive the tension between what the text meant and what it means. There are no criteria by which they can be kept apart."¹⁶⁷ Instead, Stendahl allows for a tension between the horizons of the text and the conditioned reader and, further, asserts that a proper tension is valid.¹⁶⁸

Likewise, Gadamer stresses the significance of the tension in a hermeneutic task that the task consists in not covering up this tension by attempting a naive assimilation but consciously bringing it out.¹⁶⁹ Why is Gadamer willing to preserve the tension between the past and the present? Does he absolutely reject a fusion of horizons? No. Instead, Gadamer warns against any naive fusion of horizons which neglects critical tension and distance. At the same time he believes that understanding a text entails a fusion of horizons. Naive fusion comes from refusal to recognize that a fusion is the process of fusion and that the process of fusion is continually going on.¹⁷⁰

Gadamer argues that a horizon is not closed, but moves as the interpreter moves. He states that just as the individual is never simply an individual, he/she always involves others, so the closed horizon to enclose a culture is an abstraction. The historical movement of human life consists in the fact that it is not bound to any one standpoint or within a closed horizon. The horizon is something into which we move and that moves with us. Horizons change for a person who is moving. Thus the horizon is

---

163. Barth, *Epistle to the Romans*, 1, 7; *IDB* s.v. "Biblical Theology, Contemporary."

164. Barth, *Epistle to the Romans*, 7.

165. *IDB* s.v. "Biblical Theology."

166. *IDB* s.v. "Biblical Theology." For a brief understanding of the controversial issue between Karl Barth and Krister Stendahl, see Thiselton, *Two Horizons*, 314–19.

167. *IDB* s.v. "Biblical Theology."

168. Thiselton, *Two Horizons*, 318.

169. Gadamer, *Truth and Method*, 273. For a brief understanding of the issue, see *IDB* s.v. "Biblical Theology"; Thiselton, *Two Horizons*, 314–19.

170. Gadamer, *Truth and Method*, 273.

METHODOLOGY

always in motion.[171] Gadamer's meaning of the term reinforces the fusion which acknowledges the character of various horizons as elements, thus emphasizing tension. Further, the fusion is not enclosed in one perspective or one horizon but open toward greater horizons. Consequently, the fusion of horizons, for Gadamer, does not imply that one must appropriate the past into the present, or the present into the past, or strive for naive assimilation through concentrating on subjectmatter. Instead, the fusion is a great broadening of one's horizon, which moves from within and beyond the present horizon through the encounter which "involves the experience of tension between the text and the present."[172] Therefore, a fusion of horizons is "the kind of openness that wills to hear rather than to master, is willing to be modified by the other."[173] A particular horizon, according to Gadamer, can be enriched and broadened through the encounter or the fusion of horizons. "Only through others do we gain true knowledge of ourselves."[174] Practically, how does this broader understanding arise? It comes through the encounter, including comparison, contrasts and critique which let the other be.[175]

So far, we have discussed what and how the text as phenomena reveals directly to those who are engaged in based on Schleiermacher's psychological hermeneutics and Heidegger's view of phenomenological hermeneutics in reference to Husserl's phenomenology and Gadamer's philosophical hermeneutics. Since what the phenomenon shows itself is brought thematically to show itself as semblance, appearance, or mere appearance, distant from the revelation of the phenomenon itself, it imparts some issues to the reader or encounter who has an interest in being conscious of the text to clarify and articulate what the text reveals. While Husserl suggests methods to be unthematized such as "the reduction or epoché" or a suspension of judgment to free from the influence of prejudices and to arrive at indubitable evidence, his methodological undertakings are challenged by Heidegger and Gadamer whose essential ideas are *Dasein* engaged in the phenomenon is constituted by prejudices, and *Dasein* understands the phenomenon in reference to what it is conditioned. Heidegger and Gadamer examine how *Dasein* is ontologically already conditioned to understand and interpret the manifestation of phenomena, which is to be called hermeneutics. That *Dasein* is already conditioned prior to understanding the text is called

---

171. Gadamer, *Truth and Method*, 271.
172. Gadamer, *Truth and Method*, 273.
173. Palmer, *Hermeneutics*, 193.
174. Gadamer quoted in Bernstein, *Beyond Objectivism and Relativism*, 144.
175. Taylor, "Comparison, History, Truth," 42.

"preunderstanding" to which Heidegger refers; Gadamer calls the preunderstanding "tradition." As Heidegger and Gadamer claim that *Dasein* is conditioned, this book also follows what Heidegger and Gadamer claim in the way of hermeneutics.

Prior to examining and understanding the text of Paul's epistles, Heidegger's *Being and Time* and Kierkegaard's *The Sickness Unto Death* are explored. What is understood of *Being and Time* and *The Sickness Unto Death* is called "preunderstanding (*Vorverstehen*)," and this preunderstanding is necessary to understand Paul's epistles. *The aim of this study thus is to experience what Heidegger and Kierkegaard disclose, and then is to interpret what Paul reveals from the perspective on what is experienced in Being and Time and The Sickness Unto Death*. Since the issue of "understanding" called hermeneutics is discussed in philosophy and Paul's epistles ground for Christian theology, Paul's theological and religious doctrine is accessed and understood by virtue of philosophical hermeneutics. The reason of access to Paul's epistles through Heidegger's and Kierkegaard's philosophical works is not to confine Paul's views in his Christian soil but to enrich and broaden Paul's views such as conscience, death, the moment of insight (*Augenblick, ecstasis*), transformation, and *parousia* on philosophical soil. Conversely, Heidegger's and Kierkegaard's philosophical views are also enriched by encountering Paul's theological views.

III

Views of Conscience by Heidegger, Kierkegaard, and Paul

AS A HUMAN BEING called "*Dasein*" is born in the world, *Dasein* is surrounded by many other beings but must relate them to one another. While *Dasein* as an individual being exists responsibly and authentically, other beings condition and affect *Dasein*'s individuality. How does *Dasein* as itself exist in the world? How does *Dasein* engage in and respond to others? How does Martin Heidegger in *Being and Time* show that *Dasein* can exist in its ownness called authenticity (*die Eigentlichkeit*) and that *Dasein* genuinely (*echte*) understands and relates to others in the world? This chapter will first discuss how the call of conscience can shape *Dasein*'s authenticity and responsibility, and how others serve *Dasein* to be in its genuine being despite others' conditions to be under their forces and to fall into inauthentic being.

Heidegger's view on *Dasein* constituted by conscience is challenged by what Søren Kierkegaard takes into consideration of the human being, whose issue is serious with conscience. While Heidegger employs the view of Kierkegaard (of the nineteenth century) to formulate his view of conscience, Heidegger (in the twentieth century) does not symmetrically adopt what Kierkegaard views but instead builds his own view with reference to Kierkegaard.[1] Heidegger finds the significance of *Dasein*'s own conscience in contrast to Kierkegaard, who evaluates the voice of conscience by others. Although Kierkegaard acknowledges the voice of one's own conscience, he seeks the voice of conscience by others, especially the Infinite or deity besides one's own conscience. In this chapter, Kierkegaard's view of conscience by

---

1. See *BTM* 494.

others will be investigated after first examining Heidegger's view of *Dasein's* own conscience.

While Kierkegaard's view of conscience by others is revealed by the voice of teachers or pedagogical philosophers, whom he discusses in *The Present Age*,[2] the voice of conscience by others is attested to in the voice of the Infinite or God, whom he refers to in *Fear and Trembling* and *The Sickness Unto Death*. Kierkegaard's view of conscience by the Infinite suspends the voice of the ethical or the universalistic principle, such as prohibition of murdering an innocent son. The voice of the ethical principle is considered the temptation to undermine *Dasein's* conformity to the voice of the Infinite. Resistance to the ethical or universalistic norm is called a "teleological suspension of the ethical."[3] Although Kierkegaard does not ignore the voice of the ethical in the "stage"[4] of human existence, the most respectable commitment to achieve *Dasein's* authenticity and distinctiveness is carried out by hearing and conforming to the voice of the Infinite, which is to be called the religious stage beyond the ethical and aesthetic stages of *Dasein's* being. The voice of conscience by the Infinite, aiming at relating with or promoting oneself to deity, is engaged in something transcendental beyond and exclusive to the world in which ethical and universalistic directions are involved.[5]

As Kierkegaard's view of conforming to the voice of the Infinite suspends ethical, universalistic principles, his view can be challenged—by which the voice of the Infinite or God's voice might be forced to perform merciless deeds and violence against innocent people. Ethics is to be defined as the discipline dealing with how one person copes with and treats others fairly or unfairly, justifiably or unjustly, suitably or unsuitably in reference to socially accepted culture and universalistic principles. If the voice of Infinite disregards the way or principle of how one relates to others fairly, the voice of God does not serve to direct those who lose themselves and fall into inauthenticity to turn back to their authenticity, but rather to discourage them to come out of the loss of themselves. Nevertheless, the significance of the voice of conscience by the Infinite engaged in something transcendental beyond one's own conscience due to fatigue should not be overlooked. Rather, in response to Kierkegaard's voice of the Infinite, which suspends the ethical commitment, Paul introduces the voice of the Spirit of the resurrected Christ to those who lost themselves, and encourages them

---

2. See Kierkegaard, *Present Age*.
3. *FT* 64.
4. Dreyfus, *Being-in-the-World*, 338.
5. *FT* 70.

to hear and conform to what the Spirit manifests. The Spirit of the resurrected Christ accesses the human being through acknowledging individuals' talents, ownness, and geniuses.

As Kierkegaard suspends the voice of the ethical but jumps to the voice of the Infinite, so the priority between God's voice and *Dasein*'s voice, or the uneasiness between *Dasein*'s voice of conscience and the voice by others, is to be resolute and bring about the issue of how to deal with variety in conscience. Different consciences, including *Dasein*'s own voice of conscience that Heidegger argues, the voice of conscience by others and the voice of the Infinite that Kierkegaard underscores raise a question of how to operate variety in conscience for one's own decisions and resoluteness. Paul brings in the community of faith underlying the Spirit where diverse voices of people are to be acknowledged, tension and strife are to be transformed into enhancement and conciliation, and cooperation and diversity are to be encouraged. Paul discusses the community of faith in which one's own distinctive voice, the voice of conscience by others, and the voice of deity called "the Spirit of the resurrected Christ" coexist, cooperate, and help differences unite into one.

A. HEIDEGGER'S VIEW OF *DASEIN'S* OWN CONSCIENCE

Before examining what, how, and why conscience is, the question of what the human being called *"Dasein"* is will be raised, for conscience is ontologically constituted in *Dasein*. *Dasein* is distinct from other entities such as cats and stones because of conscience, which constitutes it, even if *Dasein*'s excellence from other entities is in language.

The question of what *Dasein* is generally is answered by two terms, *being and time* (*Sein und Zeit*). As his title *"Being and Time"* indicates, it elaborates both views, "being (*Sein*)"[6] or "to be," which implies the existence and presence of an entity (*ein Seinendes*) or entities or beings (*die Seienden*), and time (*die Zeit*), which entails temporality, restriction, and finitude. *Sein* (being) is no class or genus of entities, but it lies in every entity. Every entity or thing presupposes it is (being or Sein), not non-being.[7] That being lies in entities that exist everywhere implies being is indefinite, indeterminate, and unbound. Being (*Sein*) is conceived as the ontological ground or reason for

---

6. I translate *Sein* as "being" and *das Seiende* as "entity," different from John Macquarrie and Edward Robinson, who use an upper case "B" to signify *Sein* ("Being") and lower case "b" ("being") for *das Seiende* in *Being and Time*.

7. *SZ* 38; *BTM* 62; *BTS* 33.

the existence of entities; being is responsible for how entities are intelligibly understood as entities instead of non-being or nothingness.[8]

While being pertains to every entity and indefinitely lies in entities, time converts indefinite being into definite being. Time is identified as a standpoint on which the presence of an entity stands, lies, and conditions the indefinite being, for the existence of entities is not no-time. Heidegger refers to time as the horizon of every understanding of being.[9] Since being (*Sein*) is unbound and indeterminate, being is said to be obscure and concealed. In contrast, time makes the indeterminate being the decisive, restricted, and perspectival one and, therefore, makes the concealed being disclosive, specific, and explicit.

Both terms, "being" and "time," are to be simplified into *Dasein*. *Dasein* consists of two terms, *da* (there or an existential, disclosive region) and indefinite *Sein* (being); indefinite *Sein* becomes definite by *da*. That is to say, *Sein* or being, is conditioned by *da*, and *Sein* (being) is existentially and explicitly unveiled by *da*. Since indefinite *Sein* becomes definite by *da*, *da* serves *Sein* to be in shining and clearing phenomenon. Heidegger discloses the significance of da of *Dasein* by saying that being (*Sein*) is possibly known as being lies in here (*hier*) or there (*da*) or over there (*dort*), this is, when there is a being which has disclosed spatiality as the being of the there. The expression 'there' pertaining to *da* of *Dasein* implies the disclosedness or non-concealment.[10]

In the relation between *da* and *Sein*, *da* becomes nothing significant unless being (*Sein*) validates *da*; being or *Sein*, which is indefinite, is claimed by *da* to be definite. While *da* is to be called a perspective, being (*Sein*) provides something substantial for *da* to let *da* be a perspective. The human being called *Dasein*[11] consists of *Dasein* as being (*Sein*) and *Dasein* as an entity, which exists and displays in a particular region called *da*. The human being (*Dasein*) is the disclosive entity or being, who thinks of its own existence, not non-being, and *Dasein*'s disclosedness or manifestation is especially carried out by *da* through "language (*die Sprache*)."[12]

Heidegger states that *Dasein* is ontically distinguished by the fact that in its being this being is concerned about its very being. It always understands itself in terms of its existence, in terms of its possibility to be itself or not to

---

8. SZ 154–60; BTM 195–203; BTS 144–50. See Heidegger, *Kant and the Problem of Metaphysics*, 8–9. See also Dreyfus, who introduces the character of being in his *Being-in-the-World*, 16–22.

9. SZ 17; BTM 39; BTS 15.

10. SZ 132; BTM 171; BTS 125.

11. Inwood, *Heidegger*, 9.

12. SZ 349; BTM 400; BTS 320.

be itself, which is in a word concerned with life and death.[13] In *Heidegger and Being and Time* Stephen Mulhall refers to *Dasein*'s distinctiveness based on what Heidegger means: *Dasein* is distinctive among entities in that it does not simply exist, but rather it has an issue for itself and about itself in the sense that its continued living of its life and its non-being is the significant issue that it concerns.[14] As *Dasein* is concerned about its being, it is the being of care (*die Sorge*) of itself and it sustains itself by its care.

1. The Priority of *Dasein*'s Existence to Others

Dasein is disclosed in two modes of dimensions in being: (1) *Dasein*, as a proper and authentic being or "I," individually exists and determines itself by and for *Dasein* as the caring being, and (2) *Dasein*, which exists with others in publicness, is conditioned by others and becomes an average and ordinary entity in reference to others of the world. On the one hand, *Dasein* is a private individual, and on the other, a pubic being related to society.[15] Heidegger, in the first part of *Being and Time*, examines *Dasein*'s averageness and everydayness relying on *das Man* (the they, the one or the anyone) in publicness;[16] *Dasein-Selbst* (self) falls into *das Man-Selbst* (the anyone-self) in everydayness as an inauthentic being of *Dasein*.

The second part of *Being and Time* focuses on *Dasein* as a unique, valuable being despite its fallenness into inauthenticity and conformity to *das Man*; the second part highlights how the inauthentic *Dasein* turns back into the authentic *Dasein*; and how *Dasein* treats the lostness of *Dasein* or *das Man-Selbst* (self) for its new being after returning to the authentic from inauthentic being by way of "historicality or historicity" (*Geschichtlichkeit*).[17] In the contrast between *Dasein*'s everyday averageness forced by *das Man* and *Dasein*'s own authenticity, the essential theme of the second part of *Being and Time* is to respond to the question of how *Dasein* authentically determines itself in reference to *das Man*'s force, how *Dasein* copes with *das Man*'s condition without avoiding and excluding the existence and

---

13. SZ 12; BTM 32–33; BTS 10.
14. Mulhall, *Heidegger and Being and Time*, 128.
15. Löwith, *From Hegel to Nietzsche*, 235.
16. The German term *das Man* refers to an unspecified one and is translated into several terms such as the they, the one, the anyone. As there is no perfect English translation, I shall leave *das Man* untranslated.
17. SZ 390; BTM 442; BTS 356–57.

significance of *das Man*, and finally, how *Dasein* makes its resoluteness for its future.[18]

As *Dasein* is cast into the world, *Dasein* as the being of the entity exists in two different modes of being as "I," not others, but must relate to others as "being-with others" beyond "I-in-self" in the world. *Dasein*'s two modes of being as "I" as well as "dealing with others," which are to be called the dualistic, juxtaposing features in *Dasein*'s being, are disclosed as being-in (*In-Sein*) of *Dasein* or *Dasein*-self, and being-with (*Mitsein*) of *Dasein* or social *Dasein*.[19] Being-in of *Dasein* indicates *Dasein*'s unique, self-relating-character, and being-with as *Dasein*'s social, relating-to-others-character of being. *Dasein*'s being-in is its ownness within itself, which is inaccessible by others. Being-with is manifested in *Dasein*'s "care" (*die Sorge*) or "concern (*besorgen*)." Being-in is *Dasein*'s concern toward *Dasein*-self, while being-with is *Dasein*'s matter toward others.

That *Dasein* as the being of care of itself is concerned about its being means that *Dasein* says and emphasizes "I am." "I" is unique and has its authentic property. The authentic *Dasein* or "I" does not belong to others, but is *Dasein*-self like. "I am mine." *Dasein* is basically summed up in the phrase "I am." This "I am" statement is a genuine expression of our existence, something each of us personally owns.[20] In simpler terms, "I am" is what makes us who we are. Just as much as we exist in the world, this "I am" is our own unique existence. Each *Dasein*'s existence is special and unique. All fundamental sorts of types for *Dasein* must converge in such a character in each case mine.[21]

However, *Dasein* as "I" neither exists in an isolated nowhere nor belongs to others, but coexists with others in the world. *Dasein* of *Dasein*'s being-with must relate to others in the world, while *Dasein* of *Dasein*'s being-in as an individual exists and relates to *Dasein*-self. As one coin has at least two sides, front and back, *Dasein* has two sides, *Dasein*-in or *Dasein*-self and *Dasein*-with or *Dasein*-relational-social being. Because we exist together with others, it's not just about us individually. Most of the time, it's about us with others; we live our lives among others and they live theirs among us. In everyday life, no one is truly themselves alone.[22]

---

18. See Mulhall, *Heidegger and Being and Time*.

19. SZ 118; BTM 155; BTS 112.

20. Heidegger, *Begriff der Zeit/Concept of Time*, 6E. I changed several terms of McNeill's interpretation based on German text.

21. Heidegger, *Begriff der Zeit/Concept of Time*, 8E.

22. Heidegger, *Begriff der Zeit/Concept of Time*, 8E.

What Heidegger refers to "I" of *Dasein* or *Dasein*'s self is not the detached self from the world and self-contained self but the self-in-the-world that others exist and a world-immersed self. An isolated and worldless self is not thought of in *Dasein*. Thus, we can neither understand a pure and detached self nor an abstract epistemological subject, while the self is traditionally viewed as the substance of the unchanging identity of the person, or something independent of or separate from others in the world.

As *Dasein* is not the self-substantial being (*Selbständigkeit*)[23] that philosophy and religion have traditionally maintained,[24] *Dasein*, as the existential being, has stood out or stepped out (*ek-sistence* or *Ex-sistenz*) from itself for unveiling itself and dealing with others. Heidegger especially argues that *Dasein* stands out or manifests itself by the way of language in the world. Heidegger calls "*Ex-sistenz*, 'that which steps out of itself,' *das aus sich Heraustretende*."[25] *Dasein* is always connected with others and disclosed in the world so that a self-experience is a worldly experience. Conversely, disclosing the world is concerned with self-disclosure and self-finding. Heidegger states that when you see a window, you're creating a connection between you (the viewer) and the window (the object). The relation of the perception of the window expresses the relation in which the window stands to me as I stand to the window. By this presently existent perception of the window there is an extant relation between two beings, the extant object and the extant subject. If I remove one of the members of this relation, the extant object and extant subject, then the relation itself is also no longer extant. If either the viewer or the window disappears, so does this connection. If I let the other member of the relation, the object, the extant window, vanish, then the relation between me and the extant object, and the possibility of relation, vanishes with it.[26]

2. *Das Man* and Distantiality (*Abständigkeit*)

Since *Dasein* does not exist as only one being in an isolated place but coexists with others and stands out in the world, *Dasein* is related to and conditioned by others called *das Man*. *Das Man* affects *Dasein* to determine *Dasein*'s way of being with reference to *das Man*. While *Dasein* is thrown into the world as *Dasein*-self or authentic *Dasein*, not something else, *Dasein* undergoes its transformation of authentic and inauthentic modes of being through

23. *SZ* 332; *BTM* 381; *BTS* 305.
24. *SZ* 113–80, 316–23; *BTM* 149–224, 364–70; *BTS* 107–68, 292–97.
25. Krell, *Ecstasy, Catastrophe*, 15.
26. Heidegger, *Basic Problems of Phenomenology*, 59.

engagement in the world of *das Man*; thereby *das Man* has a position to have an aspect of *Dasein*'s being. The issue, "Who is *Dasein*?" is answered by *das Man*'s involvement in *Dasein*. Heidegger states that *Dasein* is the one to be in terms of *das Man*.[27] Everyday *Dasein*'s existence is characterized as a feature of *das Man*—the phenomenon that allows *Dasein* to live in a shared world interacting with *das Man*. Since *das Man* has various possibilities of becoming, its involvement in *Dasein* constitutes *Dasein* as something characteristics of *das Man*.[28]

Das Man is translated as "the 'They'" by John Macquarrie and Edward Robinson and by Joan Stambaugh. Hubert Dreyfus and Taylor Carman render *das Man* as "the one." Others refer to *das Man* as "the anyone" or "we" or "the crowd." No satisfactory translation on *das Man* is reached. Just as *Dasein* is untranslated in this research, so *das Man* is mentioned as *das Man* in this study.

Heidegger elaborates on what *das Man* is and how *das Man* conditions the way of *Dasein* especially in §27 of *Being and Time*. His words are debatable to those who study the essence of *das Man*. While Frederick Olafson considers *das Man* a distorted mode of being of *Mitsein* or being-with, Dreyfus and Carman treat *das Man* as social norms that provide for everyday *Dasein* intelligibility. "For Olafson . . . *das Man* is a privative [inauthentic] mode of *Dasein*, while for Carman [and Dreyfus] it makes up an important aspect of *Dasein*'s positive constitution."[29] In this contrasting view, I do not cling to one or the other. Rather, I examine *das Man* based on what Heidegger expounds in *Being and Time* where he calls *das Man* a neutral being, apart from whether it is positive or negative. *Das Man* is like being sexless to prevent an affinity for one side or the other.[30] The issue of whether *das Man* is positive or negative depends on *Dasein*'s resoluteness, for *das Man* entails both positions. No matter how *das Man* is examined, *das Man* as social norms conditions to change the constancy of *Dasein*.

As *Dasein* is thrown into the world, *Dasein* abides in the surroundings where *Dasein* itself and various others or anyone called *das Man* dwell together. While *Dasein* is taken into account of the particular entity called "I," *das Man* is not regarded as a specific entity. *Das Man* has a unique way of existing, always present but elusive when *Dasein* faces decisions. It appropriates all judgments and decisions as its own, alleviating *Dasein*'s burden by

---

27. SZ 126; BTM 164; BTS 118–19.
28. SZ 129; BTM 167; BTS 121.
29. Dreyfus, "Interpreting Heidegger on *Das Man*," 423.
30. SZ 126; BTM 164; BTS 118–19.

providing its judgments and decisions.[31] *Das Man* is to be considered the general crowd or society, not specific individuals. It is not definite others, but represents the anonymous "they" in everyday life, shaping our actions and decisions without us realizing it. We often rely on "*das Man*" to make choices for us, which can lead to a lack of authenticity in our actions.[32]

The others called *das Man* in contrast to "I" exist in the world, as they are and as they do, and are encountered by *Dasein*, which has its own character and concern to itself (being-in) and others (being-with) in the world. As *Dasein* engages *das Man*, *Dasein*, constituted by dual, contrasted features—being-in (*In-Sein*) and being-with (*Mitsein*)—accesses *das Man* by the way of being-with (*Mitsein*). As being-with relates with others and being-in concerns (*besorgen*) *Dasein*'s comportment to itself, *Dasein*'s being-with is care for others that is different and distant from *Dasein* itself. *Dasein*'s care for others distant and different from *Dasein*-self has the character of distantiality (*die Abständigkeit*).

The distantiality belongs to being-with or taking care of others.[33] The distantiality as the character of *Dasein*'s care for and attentiveness to distant beings makes *Dasein* not to be simply in *Dasein*-self but makes it relate with being aloof and different from *Dasein*.[34] *Dasein*'s care for or concern with distant and different beings or any beings like *das Man* called the distantiality makes *Dasein*-self or *Dasein*'s property fall into averageness, and levelling down, as ways of being of *das Man*, which is known as "publicness (*die Öffentlichkeit*)."[35] *Dasein*'s way of being through distantiality is insensitive to every difference of level of beings that the being itself properly holds, and loses to get to "the heart of the matter (*auf die Sachen*)" based on every individual's uniqueness and distinctiveness.[36] Thus, publicness might make what inimitably and uniquely belongs to individuals obscure and lose something individualistic and unique, and then claim that what has been covered over is familiar, commonable, and accessible to everybody.[37]

What *Dasein* loses to get to the heart of the matter characteristically and distinctively given to every individual on account of *Dasein*'s distantiality (being-with) means that *Dasein*'s being-with lessens care for *Dasein* itself but, instead, adheres to care for others in everydayness and publicness.

31. *SZ* 127–28; *BTM* 164–66; *BTS* 119–20.
32. *SZ* 126; *BTM* 164; *BTS* 118–19.
33. *SZ* 126; *BTM* 164; *BTS* 118.
34. *SZ* 126; *BTM* 164; *BTS* 118.
35. *SZ* 127; *BTM* 165; *BTS* 119.
36. *SZ* 127; *BTM* 165; *BTS* 119.
37. *SZ* 127; *BTM* 165; *BTS* 119.

Dasein has an eye on what interests many others and what they are doing about their interests. What and how *Dasein* does, as *das Man* does, mean that *Dasein* is ignorant of itself and is mostly determined by indefinite, nameless others. *Dasein* enjoys itself as *das Man* takes pleasure; *Dasein* reads, sees, and judges art and literature as *das Man* expresses, sees, and judges them.[38] The concept of distantiality related to being-with implies that in everyday interactions, *Dasein* is subjected to others, leading to a state where its own being is overshadowed by the presence of others.[39]

Das Man, as a collection of roles, norms, practices, and behaviors that perform and expose in publicness, determines *Dasein*'s everyday way of being, constituting the everyday self of each particular *Dasein* called as an anyone-self;[40] thereby, *Dasein*-self becomes *das Man-Selbst* (self). *Dasein* is enthralled by *das Man*. Heidegger states that in everyday life, *Dasein* relies on *Das Man* for tasks, rules, standards, and understanding its role in the world. *Das Man* makes these choices without considering *Dasein*. It even hides how it takes these choices from *Dasein*, leaving it unclear who is really making decisions. As a result, *Dasein* becomes inauthentic, influenced by *das Man* without making its own choices.[41]

As *Dasein* makes no choices, gets carried along by unspecified ones or *das Man*, *Dasein* itself is ensnared under the rules of *das Man* and falls into inauthenticity.[42] But *Dasein* is not absolutely captivated in *das Man*. Despite *Dasein*'s coexistence with and conditions by *das Man*, which force *Dasein* to follow rules and social norms provided by *das Man*, *Dasein* is not entirely subject to *das Man*. *Dasein* is the entity itself and has the issue of its own being.[43] *Das Man* cannot take the place of *Dasein*. Otherwise, *Dasein* is not called as *Dasein*, and *Dasein* is not responsible for *Dasein*'s comports but throws the blame on *das Man*. If *Dasein* commits a crime, *Dasein* imputes a crime to *das Man*. *Dasein*, as a self-responsible being, brings itself back (*das Sichzuriickholen*) from *das Man*, and reverts to itself for its own decision and sake. The way that *Dasein* brings itself back to itself from its dominance of *das Man* is called the "existentiell modification (*die existenzielle Modifikation*) [ontic adjustment]"[44] of individualistic *Dasein*

---

38. *SZ* 126; *BTM* 164; *BTS* 118.
39. *SZ* 126; *BTM* 164; *BTS* 118.
40. *SZ* 129; *BTM* 167;*BTS* 121.
41. *SZ* 268; *BTM* 312; *BTS* 247–48.
42. *SZ* 268; *BTM* 312; *BTS* 248.
43. *SZ* 12; *BTM* 32–33; *BTS* 10.
44. *SZ* 268.

oppressed under the force of *das Man* into *Dasein*'s authentic, responsible being-one's self (*zum eigentlichen Selbstsein*).⁴⁵

The way that *das Man* forces the distinctive *Dasein* to fall into an average being and to lose its proper ownness is largely carried out as *das Man* offers it the groundlessness of idle talk (*die Bodenlosigkeit des Geredes*) of publicness. The unnamed and indefinite anyone or *das Man* in the form of the groundlessness of idle talk bestows *Dasein* something unsubstantial along with nonprimordial words that lead *Dasein* to discard its distinctiveness and authenticity. Heidegger refers to idle talk as groundless words. Idle talk, or gossip, spreads easily because it doesn't require deep understanding and passes information along without such solid grounding, becoming more groundless over time. This includes both spoken gossip and written idle talk. It thrives on superficial reading and hearing from others without being aware of the root of gossip. Idle talk distinguishes between well-researched information and gossip. The lack of depth in idle talk makes it easily accessible and widespread, leading to shallow understandings. It thus thrives on superficial knowledge and can be picked up by anyone, making genuine understanding rare. When we lose ourselves in the chatter of society (*Das Man*), we fail to listen to our true selves. To find our true selves again, we need to stop listening to the noise and hear the silent call of our conscience.⁴⁶

What *Dasein* is under the pressure of *das Man*, loses *Dasein*-self, and follows what *das Man* offers in the form of idle talk, is that *Dasein* leans toward and listen to what *das Man* calls. On the contrary, what *Dasein* turns back from being dominated under *das Man*'s idle talk to *Dasein*-self is to be sensitive or to listen to *Dasein*'s own voice called the "voice of conscience (*Stimme des Gewissens*)."⁴⁷ While idle talk is based on what anyone says—like things are so and so because someone says so⁴⁸—the voice of conscience arises from *Dasein*-self. Heidegger states that *Dasein*, when understanding being-with others, can listen, but by getting lost in the publicness and idle talk of *Das Man*, fails to hear itself. To bring itself back from this lost state, *Dasein* must first recognize its own failure to listen to itself. It needs to stop listening to *Das Man* and start a different kind of hearing, one that interrupts the influence of idle talk. This new kind of hearing is a silent and clear call from conscience.⁴⁹

45. *SZ* 268; *BTM* 312; *BTS* 248.
46. *SZ* 169; *BTM* 212–13; *BTS* 158.
47. *SZ* 268; *BTM* 313; *BTS* 248.
48. *SZ* 169; *BTM* 212; *BTS* 158.
49. *SZ* 271; *BTM* 316; *BTS* 250–51.

Dasein's turning back from the inauthentic being or *das Man*-self to the authentic being or *Dasein*-self does not take the place of itself. *Dasein*'s turning back is to choose *Dasein*'s voice of calling instead of *das Man*'s voice in the form of idle talk, which is called "wanting to have a conscience (*Gewissen-haben-wollen*)."[50] This can be accomplished by making up for not choosing (*Nachholen einer Wahl*) between the voice of the idle talk and the voice of conscience; making up for not choosing means choosing to make this choice for *Dasein*'s potentiality-of-being, and making this decision from one's own self based on *Dasein*'s voice of conscience. In choosing to make this choice, *Dasein* makes its authentic potentiality of being possible.[51] That is to say, the process of reversal, by which *Dasein* returns to itself from its lostness due to *das Man*, involves halting the act of failing to hear itself and continuing to listen to *das Man*. *Dasein* must create the possibility of another kind of hearing that interrupts this listening. This breach occurs when *Dasein* is immediately summoned by itself. When *Dasein* fails to hear itself and instead listens to *das Man*, it encounters the 'noise' of the manifold ambiguity of everyday idle talk. However, this listening is broken by the call of conscience.[52]

Dasein's turning back from the lostness of *Dasein*'s self on account of *das Man* to *Dasein*'s self is processed by *Dasein*'s commitment to hear its own voice. To hear *Dasein*'s own voice is to choose and to prefer the call of conscience out of *Dasein* to *das Man*'s voice. *Dasein* chooses the voice of its own conscience instead of *das Man*'s idle talk. The voice of conscience tells *Dasein* to look forward to seeing its possibility called "projection" without remaining at its thrownness and the temptation by *das Man*'s idle talk. *Dasein*'s projection through the voice of call of conscience is *Dasein*'s care for its possible future being. The voice of conscience brings the present *Dasein* to the possible and future *Dasein*.

3. Thrownness and Groundlessness that Lead to *Dasein*'s Guilt

As *Dasein* is thrown into the world, *Dasein*'s existence is brought into its being neither by itself nor of its own accord. *Dasein*'s thrownness is not something that lies behind it as a past event but is a continuous part of its existence. It is not something that happened to *Dasein* and was then separated from it. Instead, *Dasein* is always released to itself, meaning that

50. SZ 288; BTM 334; BTS 265.
51. SZ 268; BTM 312; BTS 248.
52. SZ 271; BTM 316; BTS 250–51.

Dasein is not the ground of its being but is always thrown.[53] Since *Dasein*'s being is granted to itself, *Dasein* primordially and ontologically is owed. Because *Dasein*'s origin does not come from itself, *Dasein* itself is ontologically indebted and groundless. Thus, *Dasein*'s unfoundedness tempts *Dasein* to find its ground from something such as *das Man* or a powerful and mysterious being beyond *Dasein*-self. While a powerful and mysterious being is found in Kierkegaard, who is considered a philosophical-theological thinker, Heidegger does not search for such a being.

Despite *Dasein*'s attempt to find something basic belonging to *das Man*, *Dasein* conscientiously has its own sense that *das Man* cannot be the ground for *Dasein*-self. While *Dasein* loses itself by attaching the idle talk that *das Man* offers, *Dasein*, which is not absolutely enthralled to *das Man*, hears *Dasein*'s own voice called "conscience." *Dasein*, instead of choosing others' voice or *das Man*'s voice, hears the voice of conscience, which observes *Dasein*'s guilt or indebtedness along with *Dasein*'s ineffectively looking for its ground on *das Man*. The voice of conscience speaks *Dasein* of guilt.[54] Being-guilty, which means owing or indebtedness, belongs to the being of *Dasein* itself.[55] What the voice of conscience speaks of guilt is that *Dasein* is in groundlessness (*die Bodenlosigkeit*) or nullity (*die Nichtigkeit*) or indebtedness, no matter how *Dasein* morally and religiously practices doing something. Heidegger refers to the guilty as *Dasein*'s groundlessness that *Dasein*'s being is *not* self-standing, but is empty or null—that is, "*being-the-ground of a nullity*."[56]

As *Dasein* is thrown, *Dasein* is not originated from itself, but owed, indebted, and thereby ontologically groundless. Insofar as it is thrown, *Dasein* is guilty in everydayness. *Dasein*'s nullity indicates what *Dasein* primordially is. *Dasein*'s being guilty as to nullity is *a priori* to *Dasein*'s immoral actions or guilty deeds. Heidegger argues that being guilty does not stem from an indebtedness due to moral deeds or actions; rather, the possibility of indebtedness arises from a primordial state of being guilty. Guilt is not a result of moral or religious actions but comes from the ontological constitution of being. *Dasein* is inherently guilty because it is not ontologically self-originated but is given and thus owed. *Dasein* particularly owes itself because it loses itself in everydayness due to the influence of *das Man*, realizing its voice of conscience. In this sense, *Dasein* is primordially guilty as long as it exists because of its indebtedness to its thrownness and its

---

53. *SZ* 284–85; *BTM* 329–30; *BTS* 262.
54. *SZ* 280; *BTM* 325; *BTS* 258.
55. *SZ* 305; *BTM* 353; *BTS* 283.
56. *SZ* 283; *BTM* 329; *BTS* 261.

lostness to *das Man*.⁵⁷ Guilt does not result from moral or religious deeds but rather from the ontological constitution of being as the primordial character. Heidegger argues that *Dasein* already is guilty, for it is not ontologically originated from itself, but is given and thus owed. At the same time, *Dasein* particularly owes to *Dasein*-self, for *Dasein* lost itself in everydayness by the force of *das Man* with realizing itself by virtue of its voice of conscience. In a sense, *Dasein* is primordially guilty as long as it exists, because of its indebtedness of thrownness and because of its lostness to *das Man*.

Guilt is divisible into non-primordial being-guilty and the primordial being-guilty. Non-primordial being-guilty is to be called as the being-guilty of common sense or vulgar interpretation (*die vulgäre Interpretation des Schuldigseins*); the primordial being-guilty is the being-guilty of the existential-ontological sense (*die existenziale-ontologische Interpretation des Schuldigseins*). The common or vulgar sense's guilt is based on *Dasein*'s liable deeds and actions failing to follow ethical and moral codes. However, *Dasein*'s primordial and ontological guilt is a preconceived condition of existence like *Dasein*'s state of mind preceding moral actions and ethical codes and ontologically renders *Dasein* deficient deeds, for *Dasein* is already existentially indebted, guilty, and groundless as it is thrown into the world. The primordial and ontological guilt is earlier than any indebtedness or guilty, liable deed and not the other way around.⁵⁸

Being guilty in everyday common sense is "owing something," or "having something on account." Indebtedness or "having debts" (*Schulden haben*) that shapes guilt arises from being reprehensible and chargeable in consequence of depriving, borrowing, withholding, and stealing. Imagine that one is supposed to return something to the other as the latter claims. If the former does not give back to the latter something that is due on account, the former is guilty. If someone hurts another person and does not help the injured person to recover, the injurer is indebted to the injured, which is to be guilty. Being guilty is deficiency or failing to do liable or blameless action like the absence of good, which is called "*bonum* [good] and the *privation* [lack]."⁵⁹

However, being guilty does not happen simply because of law-breaking, but rather through having the responsibility for the other's becoming endangered in one's existence, led astray, or even ruined.⁶⁰ For instance, a young boy saw that a neighbor girl was about to be kidnapped

---

57. *SZ* 284; *BTM* 329; *BTS* 262.
58. See *SZ* 291; *BTM* 337; *BTS* 268.
59. *SZ* 286; *BTM* 332; *BTS* 263.
60. *SZ* 282; *BTM* 327; *BTS* 260.

by tall and strong men by taking her into their car. He was too shocked and overwhelmed by fear to come near the girl. He could do nothing for her, and she was eventually kidnapped. He was morally guilty, for he did nothing to rescue her from the predators. His guilt arose from his lack of power or strength, instead of from depriving or stealing something from the girl and failing to pay her back. Becoming responsible to others, Heidegger explains, does not necessitate breaking public laws. Guilt, in this context, is being the reason for a lack in another's *Dasein*, defined by the demand placed on one's being-with others.[61]

Likewise, we can feel guilty if we hear that some radical terrorists devastated a town and took women, elderly people, and feeble men as hostages, for we could do nothing for justice to the city and the abducted. This kind of guilt is based on our powerlessness for the victimized to prevent injustice enacted by dehumanized people.

Since being-guilty in the ordinary sense arises from one's deficiency for the other called the creditor to whom the debtor is obligated, being guilty in everydayness is based on one's insufficiency or obligation to others. This guilt occurs by *Dasein*'s powerlessness or groundlessness to care for others. In contrast, the primordial view of being-guilty is concerned with the groundlessness like powerlessness of *Dasein* to itself rather than others. What *Dasein* is thrown into the world without any consent from *Dasein*-self is considered ontological-guilty beyond *Dasein*'s own power or ground. The ontological sense of being-guilty is based on the idea that *Dasein* is powerless within itself but, instead, it wants to be responsible for itself, and cares for it, apart from answering metaphysical questions such as from whence it comes and why it comes to the world. *Dasein* hears the voice of conscience from the inside, speaking of care for the powerless, groundless *Dasein*.

Dasein's powerlessness or groundlessness begins with *Dasein*'s thrownness. As *Dasein* is thrown into the world, *Dasein* does not determine itself to be born as a woman or a man, European or African, a baby girl as the prisoner of war, or a prince of the king. *Dasein*'s being is given to *Dasein* as it is so that *Dasein*'s powerlessness or groundlessness primordially goes along with its thrownness. Heidegger refers to *Dasein*'s thrownness concerning its groundlessness that as *Dasein* is thrown there or here, it has been brought into there or here without its own consent or not of its own accord.[62]

However, as *Dasein* is thrown into the world, *Dasein* neither remains the same as its being is thrown nor is bound up with what is thrown. *Dasein* projects its possibility of being instead of regretting and blaming what it is

61. *SZ* 282; *BTM* 327–28; *BTS* 260.
62. *SZ* 284; *BTM* 329; *BTS* 262.

given, thrown, and indebted, for its being is not originated from itself but is given and endowed. *Dasein* thrown into the world must exist as the ground for its own sake, and it must project its future to exist. Heidegger explains that being a self, or *Dasein*, means being a thrown being. The thrown being does not come from itself, but released to itself from the ground in order to be as this ground. Existing *Dasein* is this ground and sees itself in terms of possibilities.[63] That existing *Dasein* is this ground is like a person, who is born in the world without their accord and thereby is groundless and not responsible for their existence, but must be responsible for the continuation of their existence and be the ground for their existence. Human existence, as a possibility-being, on basis of this ground, is oriented toward its future (*Zu-Kunft*). Consequently, this ground is always something "still outstanding" about *Dasein*—some possibility not yet actualized, some debt not yet acquitted, some deed not yet done.[64]

Dasein's futuristic attempt begins with hearing its own voice of conscience. *Dasein*'s conscience calls *Dasein*, who is indebted to *das Man* and lost its responsibility and itself in *das Man* back to itself—who is *potential* as it is potentially thrown into the world.[65] *Dasein* projects its possibility of being in response to *Dasein*'s indebtedness to *das Man* by means of the voice of conscience. Heidegger states that *Dasein*'s projection followed by the call of conscience discloses its possibilities ("*Das Entwerfen erschließt Möglichkeiten, das heißt solches, das ermöglicht*").[66] While *Dasein* begins with groundlessness, as it is cast into the world and exists as the thrown being without its own accord,[67] it as a responsible being sees its projection and its possibility, conditioned by the call of conscience. While *Dasein*'s thrownness is groundless, *Dasein*'s own voice of conscience makes its existence be its ground toward its future possible being.

The call of conscience speaks to *Dasein* that *Dasein* is guilty as long as it exists in the world, for it was thrown and not responsible under the pressure of *das Man*; but the call lets *Dasein* awaken to what *Dasein* ontologically is. The awakened state of *Dasein*'s groundlessness or nullity by summoning the voice of conscience serves *Dasein* to have its projection for its possibility of being passing over the nullity or impossibility of being. If the call of conscience summons *Dasein*'s guilt or groundlessness, that is, if *Dasein* is reminded by the call of *Dasein*'s nullity or emptiness, it projects its

63. SZ 284; BTM 329; BTS 262.
64. Krell, *Ecstasy, Catastrophe*, 19.
65. SZ 277; BTM 371; BTS 298.
66. SZ 324.
67. SZ 285; BTM 330; BTS 262.

potentiality of being. *Dasein*'s nullity is like emptiness, openness, or disclosure (*Erschlossenheit*) that leads *Dasein* to a new possible being. Nullity or emptiness by the call of conscience directs *Dasein* to project its possibility. Thus, projection begins with *Dasein*'s nullity or openness—*Dasein*'s being guilty or *Dasein*'s wanting to have a conscience (*Gewissen-haben-wollen*) of being guilty or wanting to be guilty. Wanting to have a conscience of being guilty becomes readiness for possibility,[68] which is followed by projection. Projection (*Entwurf*), which literally means "throwing off," in contrast with "thrownness (*Geworfenheit*)," which indicates *Dasein*'s awakening by the call of non-responsibility, groundlessness, and nullity, turns it to *Dasein*'s openness, responsibility, anchor, and possibility; the call of conscience is the call of care for *Dasein*'s future potentiality.[69]

4. The Call of Conscience

Heidegger refers to conscience as a call. The calling of conscience is vital to drive *das Man*-self to the authentic *Dasein*-self, to make *Dasein* become responsible for itself, and to shift from *Dasein*'s indebtedness to *das Man* to its own responsibility of its future possibility. When *Dasein* is responsible for itself, *Dasein* moves forward for its ownness beyond what is already thrown and given. Conscience calls to *Dasein*'s hidden authentic self under the pressure of das Man to be responsible for itself.[70] When summoned, Heidegger notes that one is called to their own self, not to their everyday roles. This call disregards the worldly aspects of *Dasein* and focuses on the self, causing *das Man* to collapse. If conscience emerges after a misdeed, it highlights the incurred guilt and calls *Dasein* back to its own thrownness and being-guilty, emphasizing care. The call aims to guide *Dasein* toward an authentic self-understanding.[71]

The calling is carried out by someone who calls as the *caller*, someone who is called as the *hearer*, and the calling about something. The caller is *Dasein*; the hearer is *Dasein*; the call from *Dasein* to *Dasein* is about the thrown *Dasein* and the possible-being *Dasein*. If the call begins with *Dasein*, hears by *Dasein*, and calls about *Dasein*, the call of conscience seems to be tautology like the principle of identity in logic (A is A). Heidegger suggests that being (*Dasein*) takes the form of a potentiality-for-being that has listened to itself and dedicated itself to its own potential, though not in an

68. *SZ* 296; Krell, *Ecstasy, Catastrophe*, 51.
69. *SZ* 289; *BTM* 335; *BTS* 266.
70. Dreyfus, *Being-in-the-World*, 241.
71. *SZ* 273; *BTM* 317; *BTS* 252.

inherent manner.⁷² The call of conscience summons *Dasein* ensnared by *das Man* to go back to *Dasein*-self, which was not fallen into *das Man*.

Conscience calls *Dasein* to come out of *das Man*-self or the averaged self in publicness and to turn back to *Dasein*-self or the authentic, distinctive self. However, this does not mean that conscience points to and reprimands what *Dasein* has already done. Rather, conscience summons *Dasein's* ownmost potentiality-of-being that *Dasein* authentically holds instead of reproving what *Dasein* has immorally done against moral codes and religious discipline.

Heidegger discusses conscience, stating that if it arises after an action has been completed or omitted, and if it follows up on the transgression, reminding *Dasein* of the guilt incurred, then conscience indicates a being guilty. This indication, however, occurs not as a summons but as a reminder of the guilt. He explains that the call of conscience is a form of care. In this call, *Dasein* projects itself forward while simultaneously reflecting on its thrownness. This backward call transcends past deeds, referring to a more fundamental state of being guilty that precedes any specific indebtedness. Furthermore, Heidegger notes that this call forward also brings forth a state of being guilty that one must actively acknowledge in their existence—suggesting that authentic being-guilty emerges after the call, not prior to it. He also mentions that the experience of a warning conscience perceives the call as aiming at its future being. This warning function serves to keep one free from indebtedness, seeing its future possibility.⁷³

Heidegger asserts that the properly understood call provides the most positive existential possibility, allowing *Dasein* to call itself back to its potentiality-of-being-a-self. Authentic hearing of this call involves taking factical action. Heidegger emphasizes that a complete interpretation of the call requires an understanding of the existential structure inherent in our response to the summons.⁷⁴ Conscience calls, not to point at what fails to keep ethical and religious instructions, but to orient *Dasein* to its authenticity called the potentiality-of-being of *Dasein* (*das Seinkönnen des Daseins*), whose existence lies in factical beings.

A young woman, whose father is a pastor, is undisciplined. She is resistant to religious norms, rules, and disciplines. The pastor calls his daughter, exhorts Christian disciplines, and even warns her not to be disgraceful. But she does not follow what she is supposed to do based on socioreligious directives. The pastor prays to God, saying, "Why is she, such a delinquent

---

72. *SZ* 284; *BTM* 329–30; *BTS* 262.
73. *SZ* 290–92; *BTM* 336–39; *BTS* 267–69.
74. *SZ* 294; *BTM* 341; *BTS* 271.

daughter, born into my family? Is she worthy to society, family, God, and my ministry?" He prays to God every morning. One day, he seems to hear some voice of conscience. "What about you? Were you disciplined when you were young? Look back on your past. She cannot be measured by what religious regulations stipulate and what you religiously expect. Your daughter is potential, and neither comparable with others nor to be judged by religious standard and norms." He awakens from his prayer and starts to treat her differently. He approaches her to reveal what she properly carries and to help her display her uniqueness instead of stereotyping her on the basis of religious norms. He tries to help her reveal her unique talents instead of judging her by discipline and warning her and pressing her to keep rules and regulations. He communicates her to reveal what she has uniquely, capably, and factually. Heidegger calls *Dasein*'s disclosing (*Erschlossenheit*) or un-concealment (*Unverborgenheit*) as "truth (*aletheia*, ἀλήθεια)."

The call of conscience has the character of an appeal to *Dasein* as the being of mineness to let it be in its ownmost potentiality-for-being-a-self.[75] The call of conscience is to access *Dasein* to find its authenticity. Authenticity is based on what *Dasein* holistically and properly holds, which cannot compare and universally generalize. Authenticity is being owned, peculiar and separate from others. It signifies *Dasein*'s proper potentiality, ability to be *Dasein* itself and something of its own (*zueigen*).[76] Auto of authenticity (*die Eigentlichkeit*), arisen from Greek term *autos* (αὐτός),[77] is self or subject, done by one's own hand, "setting the individual off from everything else."[78] "Authenticity consists in somehow being true to oneself."[79] Authenticity is based on the referring to *Dasein*, which is in general determined by being-mine.[80] "Authenticity is, precisely, owning up to what *Dasein* essentially is."[81] The opposition of authenticity, as being owned called mineness (*Jemeinigkeit*), distinctive, and separate from anyone (*das Man*), is not impurity but everydayness and selflessness forced by *das Man*. Inauthenticity distinct from impurity serves to avoid practicing *Dasein*'s ownmost potentiality and to flee into anonymous, generic forms of *das*

---

75. SZ 269; BTM 314; BTS 249.
76. SZ 42; BTM 68; BTS 40.
77. Inwood, *Heidegger Dictionary*, 22–23.
78. GEL s.v. "αὐτός."
79. Carman, "Concept of Authenticity," 229.
80. SZ 43; BTM 68; BTS 40.
81. Dreyfus, *Being-in-the-World*, 194.

Man. Conscience attests *Dasein*'s authenticity as "an authentic *potentiality of-being-one's-self*"[82] [*ein eigentliches Selbstseinkönnen*]."

When the call is understood with *Dasein*'s individualistic kind of hearing, such understanding is authentic and *Dasein* understands its own being in a nonrelational way, and the call directs *Dasein* forward its potentiality of being. The call does not give us to understand an ideal, universal potentiality-of-being, but it discloses it as what is actually individualized in that particular *Dasein*.[83]

That *Dasein*'s self is lost but brings itself back from *das Man* by the calling of conscience does not mean that *Dasein*'s authenticity totally is exclusively and totally detached from *das Man* of the world. Thus, understanding, Heidegger suggests, is to turn towards the disclosedness of the world for *Dasein*'s own being. It can be authentic, arising from oneself, or inauthentic, influenced by the world. But authentic self-knowledge involves grasping the full being-in-the-world. Resoluteness, as an authentic self, integrates *Dasein* into the world, allowing it to take care of things and lets others be in their potential. Authentic being one's self is not based on an exceptional state of the subject, a state detached from *das Man*, but *Dasein*'s personal modification of *das Man* as factically related beings in the world, not factual, existentiell individual.[84]

Heidegger states that authenticity means neither solitude separated from the world nor stubbornness through blocking hearing from others in the world. While *Dasein* turns from the inauthentic being to the authentic being unbound in *das Man* of the world, *Dasein* as the being of being-with (*Mitsein*) others does not exist in a solitary self away from the world; *Dasein* is not meaningful without the world. *Dasein*'s authenticity is neither impartiality from nor elimination of the world. If *Dasein* attempts to exist as an isolated entity devoid of the world, such *Dasein*'s mode of being is called the "ungenuine authenticity" or "non-genuine authenticity" (*die unechte Eigentlichkeit*); in contrast, the "genuine authenticity (*die echte Eigentlichkeit*)" is openness to the world.[85]

Heidegger discusses the concept of *Dasein*'s self-understanding, noting that its average, everyday self-perception is often seen as inauthentic. However, he clarifies that this inauthentic self-understanding does not imply that it is ungenuine (*unrechte*). On the contrary, he argues that the everyday,

---

82. *SZ* 267; *BTM* 312; *BTS* 247.

83. *SZ* 280; *BTM* 325–26; *BTS* 258–59.

84. *SZ* 130; *BTM* 168; *BTS* 122.

85. *SZ* 146, 178; *BTM* 186, 222; *BTS* 137, 166. See Dreyfus, *Being-in-the-World*, 192–94.

practical engagement with things can indeed be genuine. Heidegger contrasts this with the notion that excessive introspection excluded from many things of the world might be artificial or even pathological. The *Dasein*'s inauthentic understanding of itself via things of the world is neither ungenuine nor illusory, as if what is understood by it is not the self but something else, and instead the self only is emphasized. He emphasizes that inauthentic self-understanding involves a genuine experience of the self as it actually is, in its daily existence, and that this self-reflection emerges from one's engagement with the world.[86]

The relationship between genuine and ungenuine authenticity is disclosed in three ways: ontological, hermeneutical, and dialogical relationship between *Dasein* and others. The ontological relationship is like the relationship between a single tree and the wood that consists of many single trees, a part and the whole of parts. The hermeneutic relationship pertains to understanding of *Dasein* in reference to others. The dialogical relationship refers to *Dasein*'s resoluteness as to *Dasein*-self and others.

a) The ontological relationship is based on the mode of *Dasein*'s being-with others beyond *Dasein* itself. The ungenuine authenticity is like emphasizing a tree of the forest, while the genuine authenticity considers the significance of the woods where a tree lives with other trees. The ungenuine authenticity is like saying that we can ignore the woods for a tree.

b) The hermeneutic relationship between genuine (*echt*) and ungenuine (*unecht*) authenticity is the way of understanding *Dasein*. Genuine authenticity considers *Dasein* a whole of the world, not a self-possessed entity, and thereby understands *Dasein* as being-in-the-world where *Dasein* and others dwell and are factically structured together. Genuine, authentic understanding puts stress on *Dasein* in terms of the whole-being-in-the-world, whereas ungenuine understanding focuses on *Dasein* itself. Heidegger suggests that understanding can primarily turn towards the disclosedness of the world, for *Dasein* can understand itself for the most part in terms of the world. It can be authentic, arising from oneself, or inauthentic, influenced by the world. Authentic self-knowledge involves grasping the full being-in-the-world. In understanding the world, *Dasein*'s being-in is understood. Resoluteness, as an authentic self, integrates *Dasein* into the world, allowing it to take care of things and let others be in their potential. Authentic being-with-one-another stems from resoluteness, not ambiguous societal norms.[87]

c) As *Dasein* brings back *Dasein*-self from *das Man*-self by the call of conscience, *Dasein* determines for itself. When *Dasein* determines itself,

---

86. Heidegger, *Basic Problems of Phenomenology*, 160–61.
87. *SZ* 146; *BTM* 186–87; *BTS* 137.

Dasein does not make its decision in an exclusive way but has its resolution in reference to others-in-the-world. *Dasein*'s decision in reference to others is called resoluteness (*die Entschlossenheit*), which entails openness (*die Erschließung*) to the world as well as decisiveness (*die Entschiedenheit*) by and for *Dasein*. While a resolution such as a New Year's resolution is focused on one's own decision, resoluteness depends on *Dasein*'s decision in reference to others of the world. "To be resolute is to remain sensitive to . . . 'situation' (*Situation*). . . . Resolute agents, that is, maintain a subtle feel for the situations they confront and so are able to deal with them intelligently, skillfully, with finesse."[88]

According to Heidegger, resoluteness does not detach or isolate *Dasein* from its world. Rather, it allows *Dasein* to be with others and to reveal their potentiality through concerned and freeing interactions. The resoluteness toward itself first brings *Dasein* to the possibility of letting the others who are with it in their ownmost potentiality-of-being, and also discloses that potentiality in concern which frees. This authentic mode of being-with-others arises from resoluteness rather than from superficial social conventions or idle talk. Resoluteness always belongs to a factical interconnection with others in *Dasein*.[89] Heidegger also mentions that when *Dasein* becomes resolute, it withdraws from the inauthentic influence of *das Man*. This withdrawal enables *Dasein* to be more authentically present in the "moment of vision (*Augenblick*)," gaining a clearer understanding of its situation.[90] The moment of vision or insight will be discussed in the fourth and fifth chapters of the book.

So far, we have discussed that *Dasein*, as an authentic, individualistic being, as it is thrown into the world, is surrounded, and affected by other beings called *das Man*, and thereby *Dasein* loses itself, and *Dasein*-self becomes *das Man*-self. Despite *Dasein*'s lostness of self under the influence of *das Man*, *Dasein* ontologically constituted by conscience is not entirely subject to *das Man*. The voice of conscience calls *das Man*-self to come out of *das Man* and return to the authentic *Dasein*-self. While *Dasein* returns from *das Man*-self or the inauthentic being to the authentic being or *Dasein*-self unbound in *das Man*, *Dasein* neither exists as a solitary self apart from the world nor impartially excludes others of the world. *Dasein*'s existence, even in its authenticity devoid of the world, is in ungenuine authenticity or blocked authenticity. Genuine *Dasein*, consisting of authenticity and openness, makes its resoluteness involved in *Dasein*'s authentic decision

---

88. Carman, "Concept of Authenticity," 234.
89. SZ 298; BTM 344–45; BTS 274.
90. SZ 328; BTM 376; BTS 301–2.

VIEWS OF CONSCIENCE BY HEIDEGGER, KIERKEGAARD, AND PAUL 89

and openness to the world. Resoluteness is understood as decisiveness for *Dasein*-self in reference to others based on what *Dasein* is authentically and distinctively thrown. Hence, "The structure of *Dasein* must now be displayed in terms of how such a being-with-one-another determined by the world and the common understanding given with it are constituted in *Dasein*."[91]

Then, Heidegger's view of *Dasein*'s genuineness confronts some questions, for example, "Who is it really that understands oneself in such a being-with-one-another?"[92] Can *Dasein*, who is already factically webbed with others-in-the-world, be considered itself and understand others authentically? How does *Dasein* come out of inauthentic *Dasein*, who is already used to being amid *das Man* and who might be even enthralled by *das Man*? If authentic *Dasein* cannot escape the inducement of *das Man* in publicness, and its authenticity is oppressed under *das Man*, how is the inauthentic *Dasein* exhorted to change it from inauthenticity to authenticity? Do some other conditions let inauthentic *Dasein*, who is already shadowed under *das Man*, turn to authentic *Dasein*? Doesn't *Dasein* need another voice or the voice of conscience by others beyond *Dasein*'s own voice, who are not captivated by *das Man*? This need is like a person who wears the same shirt for a while and does not smell of sweat until someone else mentions it. Kierkegaard brings in the voice of conscience by others such as educators, especially the voice of the Infinite, which will be discussed in the next section, for Heidegger avoids arguing the significance of the call of conscience by others but emphasizes finding its authenticity from within its own voice.

B. KIERKEGAARD'S VIEW OF THE VOICE OF CONSCIENCE BY OTHERS AND THE INFINITE

This discussion of Kierkegaard's view of voice of conscience in response to the issue disclosed in Heidegger's *Being and Time* does not mean that Heidegger first brought out the voice of *Dasein*'s conscience and that Kierkegaard then challenged what Heidegger viewed; rather, it is the other way around. While Kierkegaard introduced his philosophical-religious view of conscience in the early nineteenth century, Heidegger, influenced by Kierkegaard, published his *Being and Time* almost one hundred years later in 1927. As Heidegger has some references from Kierkegaard in his work,

---

91. Heidegger, *History of the Concept of Time*, 243. See Dreyfus, *Being-in-the-World*, 144.

92. Heidegger, *History of the Concept of Time*, 243–44.

he did not follow utterly what Kierkegaard maintained but challenged what Kierkegaard asserted of the view of conscience.

We now have both references of what Kierkegaard and Heidegger built philosophically and religiously. Apart from sequential, chronological order, the present research is primarily based on Heidegger's *Being and Time*. Since some scholars dispute Heidegger's view of *Dasein*'s call of conscience, my reply to them is examined on the basis of Kierkegaard's works. Kierkegaard's view of the voice of conscience by others is divisible into two groups. One is the call of conscience by others, such as teachers and philosophers who declare *Dasein*'s inauthenticity and encourage the inauthentic *Dasein* to come out of its inauthenticity; the other is the call of conscience by the Infinite or God.

1. The Voice of Conscience by Others

The conscience of others to which Kierkegaard refers is similar to that of a philosopher or religious-moral pedagogue who speaks of *Dasein*'s potentiality and distinctiveness that it holds in itself.[93] Kierkegaard's *The Present Age* presents the lostness of students' individualistic uniqueness, and argues that the principle or rule of the public weakens people's distinctions and makes every individual to be average and to fall into a regular, universal, uniform person.[94] He argues that the present tends towards equality and tries to put everything at the same level. The principle or rule of public is based on rational reflection and computation. Kierkegaard does not specifically indicate who warns of *Dasein*'s inauthenticity. But that person is a philosophical pedagogue like Kierkegaard, who talks about the voice of conscience as another beyond *Dasein* itself.

Kierkegaard's *Journals* reference the call of conscience by others in a geese story. It involves the lostness of *Dasein*'s authenticity or the lostness of *Dasein*-self in everydayness, the encouragement to rediscover *Dasein*-ownness or property, and the returning to *Dasein*-self filled with potentiality and distinctiveness through summoning the geese's conscience by others. Kierkegaard says:

> Every Sunday, the geese gathered and listened to one of the ganders preach. The sermons were always about their grand destiny and the high goals their Creator had set for them. Every time "Creator" was mentioned, the geese would curtsy and the ganders would bow their heads. The preacher

---

93. Mulhall, *Heidegger and Being and Time*, 143–51.
94. Kierkegaard, *Present Age*, 260.

VIEWS OF CONSCIENCE BY HEIDEGGER, KIERKEGAARD, AND PAUL

would remind them that with their wings, they could fly to distant, blessed lands where they truly belong, as they were just strangers here.

After each Sunday service, they would return to their daily lives, only to come back the next Sunday for more divine worship. This cycle continued, and they thrived, becoming plump and well-fed, until they were eventually eaten on Martinmas Eve. Despite the lofty Sunday sermons, the geese knew that on Monday, they could discuss what happened to a goose that tried to use its wings seriously—it usually ended in a terrible death. Such topics were not suitable for Sunday discussion as it would reveal that their worship was just a farce.

Some geese, who took the idea of flying seriously, became thin and weak. Other geese would say, "See what happens when you take flying too seriously? They don't thrive like we do because their hearts are focused on flying instead of living comfortably and enjoying God's grace."

So, every Sunday, they returned to hear the old gander preach about the high goals set by the Creator, always curtsying and bowing at the mention of the divine. This was how they practiced their worship.[95]

The above story tells us that geese wallow in and enjoy everydayness so that they lose their authenticity-flight. One gander preaches to geese that their authenticity constituted by their ownmost potentiality is to fly freely through the sky, saying: "You are distinctive geese different from other animals and your distinctiveness is to fly away to distant regions, blessed climes, where properly they were at home, for here they were only strangers." Of course, some geese fly faster through the sky than others, depending on their abilities. Nevertheless, their properties are flight through the sky. Since geese do not feel uncanniness and challenge but comfortableness and complacency in everydayness and publicness, they do not need to hear their urgent voice summoned by their conscience toward authenticity.

Kierkegaard, in *The Sickness Unto Death*, describes how a person might lose themselves by becoming overly engaged in worldly affairs. He suggests that such a person might forget their true self and divine purpose, finding it easier and safer to conform to societal norms rather than daring to be their authentic self.[96] Doesn't *Dasein* need another voice of conscience like the gander beyond *Dasein*'s own calling of conscience on which Heidegger emphasizes in his *Being and Time*?

However, Kierkegaard in the story does not indicate whether geese heard the voice of the gander and flew over the sky. The story does not disclose that the gander's speech is eloquent enough to convince geese to

---

95. Kierkegaard, "Tame Geese," 433.
96. *SD* 167.

fly away to distant regions. Kierkegaard warns people through the story of geese that average geese are accustomed to being in everydayness and lost themselves in publicness; they need to get out of averageness to display their own possibilities. But, do geese remain in everydayness and publicness as they enjoy their lives in a comfortable zone? While geese's averageness manifested in their lostness of their property or themselves is informed by the mature goose, we do not know whether geese follow by the gander's proclamation that encourages them to fly through the sky. The geese embedded in the comfortable zone seem to need a stronger or imperative voice than the voice of teachers and philosophers who declare *Dasein*'s inauthenticity and encourage the inauthentic *Dasein* to come out of its inauthenticity. In a sense, average geese need a directive voice from God. Kiekegaard introduces another voice or directive and imperative voice called the voice of the Infinite or God whose voice ignores worldly norms and matters, which is to be called "the religious voice." The religious voice demands its commitment, practice, and participation by its hearers. The religious voice is directive, powerful, and imperative. Kierkegaard in *Fear and Trembling* discusses the call of voice or the directive voice by the Infinite. He introduces the voice of God besides the voice of humanity including teachers and philosophers.

2. The Voice of Conscience by the Infinite

As *Dasein*—proper, authentic, and ownmost potential being, but as the being of being-with in the being-in-the-world and thereby is the conditioned being—is thrown, *Dasein*'s thrownness does not presuppose that something else exists to bring about *Dasein*'s thrownness beforehand. *Dasein*'s thrownness does not allow something else behind *Dasein* to give rise to thrownness of *Dasein*, separated from *Dasein*.[97] Just as a die is cast by chance, *Dasein* is groundlessly thrown into the world. Heidegger as a phenomenologist refuses to talk about something transcendental, something trans-phenomenological beyond *Dasein* itself or *Dasein* as a phenomenological entity that is responsible for its being. Phenomenology is not a search for transcendental noumena but, rather, a search for what is manifested in beings or phenomena of everyone's ordinary and everydayness life.[98] However, Kierkegaard as an existential religionist brings in something transcendental, resourceful, or pre-phenomenological called the Infinite or the deity or God in his philosophy, as religion involves devoting something transcendental

---

97. *SZ* 284; *BTM* 329; *BTS* 262.
98. *SZ* 27–40; *BTM* 49–64; *BTS* 23–35.

VIEWS OF CONSCIENCE BY HEIDEGGER, KIERKEGAARD, AND PAUL

beyond phenomena. The Infinite or the deity is considered something that "stands above the universal [the world]."[99]

Kierkegaard investigates the voice of the Infinite beyond *Dasein*'s voice in *Fear and Trembling*. His view of authenticity is not to be treated equally with Heidegger's authenticity. Kierkegaard's view involves not only *Dasein* relational to *Dasein*'s self by the call of its own voice of conscience, but also *Dasein* relational to the Infinite by the calling of the voice of the Infinite, who transcends *Dasein* and exists prior to *Dasein*'s thrownness. Kierkegaard's authenticity involves the voice of the divine beyond the voice of *Dasein*'s conscience.

Kierkegaard in *Fear and Trembling* tells Abraham's story. God's voice summons Abraham to sacrifice his son Isaac on Mount Moriah (Genesis 22:1–19), saying, "Take your son, whom you love, and go to the land of Moriah and offer him there as a burnt offering." Abraham might hesitate with anxiety to comply with God's calling. But he cannot resist God's divine voice to sacrifice his son, for Abraham believes that Isaac is ultimately not thrown by him and his wife Sarah but by the Infinite who is something resourceful or something original. Abraham goes to the place of which God has told him. He builds an altar, lays the wood in order, binds Isaac his son, and lays him on the altar, upon the wood. Then Abraham puts forth his hand and takes the knife to slay Isaac. But the messenger (*mal·'ak*) of God calls out to Abraham, saying, "Abraham! Do not lay your hand on him, for now I know that you fear God and you have not withheld your son from me." And Abraham lifts his eyes and beholds a ram caught in a thicket by his horns; and Abraham offers it as a burnt offering instead of his son Isaac.

Although Abraham fails to slaughter Isaac, what he does to kill his son cannot be ethically accepted. Ethical norms that condemn murdering an innocent son by his father are rational, commensurable, and universal. He could be judged as a convicted murderer. On the other hand, he is praised as the father of faith in Judeo-Christianity. Kierkegaard refers to Abraham, who enjoys honor and glory as the father of faith, while he ought to be prosecuted and convicted.[100] For Abraham, the ethical is ignored and is even considered the temptation (*die Anfechtung*) so that he must resist the ethical to join the Infinite. Kierkegaard posits that while typical temptations divert a person from their duties, in this case the ethical itself can become a temptation that prevents one from fulfilling God's will.[101]

99. *FT* 69.
100. *FT* 65.
101. *FT* 70.

Kierkegaard calls such ignorance of and resistance to the universalistic demands of morality a "teleological suspension of the ethical."[102] What Kierkegaard argues in relation to the view of "teleological suspension of the ethical" is that an individual pursues a higher and ultimate *telos*, and the achievement is not carried out by keeping ethical norms and objective values that people or *das Man* observes in publicness. Instead, an individual must suspend or bracket ethical norms and personally aim at relating with the Infinite or deity beyond reasonable thought and universal ethics that Immanuel Kant and Hegel emphasize.[103]

Kierkegaard compares Abraham's attempt to murder his son under the teleological suspension of the ethical with actions by other heroes who also murdered their children. The other stories are referenced in the Old Testament, Greek mythology, and Plutarch. Kierkegaard refers to the story of Jephthah, Agamemnon, and Lucius Junius Brutus, who undertook to sacrifice their children.[104] The three heroes' undertakings to sacrifice their sons or daughters differ from Abraham's attempt to kill his son because Abraham's action to sacrifice his son is grounded on conforming to the voice of the Infinite, while the three heroes conform to the ethical voice, universal norms that everyone in publicness keeps. For instance, Lucius Junius Brutus gains respect from the Roman people and hears their praise in watching the execution on his two sons, Titus Junius and Tiberius Junius Brutus, who conspired to destroy the establishment of the Roman Republic and to return the Roman monarchy, which is considered ethically unacceptable. Kierkegaard maintains that Abraham's relationship to the deity is not understood under the paganism to which the three heroes belong, and they do not enter into any private relationship with the deity, which is called "faith."[105] Although Abraham faced anxiety in the tension between ethics and religious faith, he took religious faith for the sake of a higher individual end, which is to leap into or flee to God, or relate with God. Faith, according to Heidegger, involves the paradox of the individual being higher than the universal, justified against it. The individual is not subordinate to the universal. As long as the individual as the particular stands in an absolute relation to the absolute, which is to be called "faith," the individual is superior to and transcends the universal.[106]

---

102. *FT* 67.
103. *FT* 65–66.
104. *FT* 69.
105. *FT* 70.
106. *FT* 66.

Emphasis on faith and individual relatedness to the Infinite that Kierkegaard argues confronts the question of how individualistic faith is evidenced. Isn't the individualistic faith initiated by hearing the voice of the Infinite regarded as schizophrenic psychosis? Isn't the faith regarded as "a pathological phenomenon"[107]? How can the faith in the Infinite be demonstrated as a highly healthy commitment? In fact, Abraham, whom Kierkegaard mentions in *Fear and Trembling*, is not necessarily to be called the father of faith, unless he fails to slay his son. Fortunately, Abraham hears another voice called "the voice of messenger or angel (*mal·'ăk*) of God (*ĕ·lō·hîm*)," according to Genesis 22:11, saying, "Do not lay a hand on the boy." The voice of the angel from God seems to be the change of God's voice. The voice of messenger sounds like the voice of the ethic that emphasizes the life of individuals. The voice of the messenger seems to tell Abraham that Isaac is proper and worthy to live in himself, not being caged and killed by others, even if he is the son of his father. Because Isaac has his own property and distinctiveness, no one should treat him as his own property. Abraham's hearing of the voice of God that would lead to Isaac's death is again suspended by the messenger of voice which exhorts Abraham to let Isaac live, as Abraham suspends the ethical norm; Abraham finds a ram caught by its horns in a thicket and dedicates it as a burnt offering. Kierkegaard's individualistic and religious faith is dangerous unless he considers other voices significant along with God's voice.

Kierkegaard's use of the voice of the Infinite beyond *Dasein*'s own voice of conscience called his religious faith is to be challenged. Kierkegaard's view of religious faith manifested in suspending or bracketing ethical norms and relating with the Infinite could undermine an individual's distinctiveness and worthiness of one's own being, just as Abraham attempted to murder his son without consideration on the worthiness of his son. While universalistic principles and ethical norms do not entirely acknowledge individual's own-ness and gifts but regulate them in some respects, the entire suspension of ethics could fall into annihilating human dignity and distinction. Instead of completely removing ethical principles, some different way of being toward individuals is demanded to alternate with Kierkegaard's voice of the Infinite. Paul brings in the voice of the Spirit of the resurrected Christ, who recognizes individualistic distinctiveness, others' existence, and relatedness with others, which will be discussed in the next section.

107. Zimmerli, "Word of God," 1.

C. PAUL'S VIEW OF VARIETY IN CONSCIENCE AND THE COMMUNITY OF SPIRIT OR FAITH

Paul's view of the Spirit of the resurrected Christ that transcends Kierkegaard's suspension of the universalistic norms or ethics does not mean that Paul upholds the universalistic principles and discards faith in and individual relatedness to the Infinite that Kierkegaard argues. As Kierkegaard, who was influenced by Paul, puts emphasis on faith and individual commitment to God, so Paul underscores individualistic faith in God. However, Kierkegaard's individualistic faith is to be regarded as the isolate's faith. Karl Löwith in *From Hegel to Nietzsche: The Revolution in Nineteenth-Century Thought* refers to the individualistic faith that Kierkegaard upholds as "the isolated individual."[108] Löwith further says, "Kierkegaard considers 'the 'individual'—who happens to be the basis of Christendom—as the sole salvation of the age."[109] In contrast, Paul is not bound on the isolated faith of an individual, but the cooperative faith engaged with diverse people in the communal world.[110] Heidegger discusses Paul's relationship with the communal world, highlighting how individuals within this world reveal their own voices while cooperating and relating with others, thus contributing to a larger, inclusive community.[111] What is investigated here is how conscience is inherited by Paul from the past, how Paul applies conscience to the Gentiles, and how Paul makes an effort to overcome tensions and chaos due to diverse voices of people in the communal world.

1. The Meaning of Conscience

The word "conscience" (συνείδησις) in Greek to which Paul refers is composed of two terms—"sharing" with (*syn*, συν) and "knowledge" (*eidesis*, εἴδησις)—and thus means "a joint knowledge (συν-είδησις) [*syn-eidesis*] with another," that is, "the ... knowledge shared with one's self ... of one's conduct as one's own."[112] Conscience or *syneidesis* (συνείδησις) is to be understood in conjunction with "the verb σύνοιδα [*synoida*], which means 'I know in common with.' It usually implies knowledge about another person, which can be used in witness for or against him [or her]. Hence, σύνοιδα [*synoida*] came to mean 'I witness bear witness.' Of particular importance

---

108. Löwith, *From Hegel to Nietzsche*, 111.
109. Löwith, *From Hegel to Nietzsche*, 113.
110. Heidegger, *Phenomenology of Religious Life*, 61.
111. Heidegger, *Phenomenology of Religious Life*, 61.
112. Bultmann, *Theology of the New Testament*, 1:216–17. See *GEL* s.v. "συνείδησις."

VIEWS OF CONSCIENCE BY HEIDEGGER, KIERKEGAARD, AND PAUL

is the phrase αὐτῷ [auto] συνείδησις [syneidesis] . . . which means 'to share knowledge with oneself,' 'to know with oneself,' 'to be a witness for or against oneself,' because συνείδησις [syneidesis] . . . is its [substantive] equivalent."[113] Rudolf Bultmann explains that conscience reflects a person's awareness of their own conduct, differentiating it from *nous*, which involves intent. Conscience scrutinizes one's actions against a moral requirement, serving as both a judge of past actions and a guide for future duties.[114] In discussing conscience, Bultmann suggests that it enables a person to constitute their specific self and exercise their freedom. He references 1 Corinthians 10:29, emphasizing that no one else has the right to impose their judgment on an individual's conscience.[115]

The term "conscience" is not cast by Paul. It has its origin from Hebrew tradition[116] and Greek philosophy. Job 27:6 states that Job conscientiously does not do wicked things, as the Law commands him.[117] Ecclesiastes 10:20 also says that anyone shall not condemn the king [God] in one's heart, as God orders Israelites through the Law, because a bird could carry their voice in their heart (conscience) to the king [God].

The term "conscience" is also present in Greco-Roman philosophy, where it is considered a fundamental part of human nature, often linked to divine origin. For example, Xenophon recounts Socrates' belief that those who bear false witness against him would inevitably suffer pangs of conscience. This concept implies that conscience automatically reacts to one's deeds, especially wrongdoings, and this understanding would have been familiar to the writers of the New Testament who were influenced by Hellenistic thought.

While the term "conscience" has come down from Hebrew and Greco-Roman tradition, Paul first brought the term "conscience" to Christian theological-philosophical language.[118] "Among NT writers, Paul first used the term, and most frequently; and perhaps it was he who gave it prominence in Christian usage."[119] Paul especially introduced the term "conscience"

---

113. *IDB* s.v. "conscience."
114. Bultmann, *Theology of the New Testament*, 1:216–17.
115. Bultmann, *Theology of the New Testament*, 1:219.
116. Bultmann, *Theology of the New Testament*, 1:216. C. A. Pierce says, "No recourse can be had . . . to any Hebrew idea in the Old Testament from which material might be forthcoming for an elucidation of its meaning for the New Testament writers, and for St. Paul in particular" (Pierce, *Conscience in the New Testament*, 13).
117. Bultmann, *Theology of the New Testament*, 1:216.
118. Bultmann, *Theology of the New Testament*, 1:216.
119. *IDB* s.v. "conscience."

regarded as power or faculty of humanity "implanted by God"[120] to Gentiles whom he accessed.

2. Advantage of Conscience

In Galatians 2:7–8 Paul states that his responsibility is to preach God's words to the Gentiles or non-Jews, just as Peter is entrusted with the gospel to Jews. The Gentiles in Greek are termed as ἔθνεσιν (*ethnesin*), which means people in contrast to those of the Jewish way of being directed by the Law of YHWH[121] and, thereby, are considered lawless people. Since the Gentiles whose ancestors are not Jews appear to be unfortunate without having the Law, they are not seen as God's children in contrast to Jews whom God offered the Law. Their unfortunateness is not due to their undeserved deeds or morality, but determined by God, for Paul in Romans 9:14–29 states that God elects someone as God's child—just as the potter chooses one vessel for beauty and another for menial use.[122] What Paul discusses of election is understood that God is discriminative and unfair. However, in Romans 9:24–26 Paul paradoxically asserts that God calls God's people those who are not selected and loves the one who is not beloved.

The Gentiles seem to be foolish (*momos*, μῶμος), ignorant, and weak (*atheneo*, ἀσθενέω), for they do not have the Law of God. But Paul 1 Corinthians 1:27–28 states that God chooses those who are foolish and weak but makes them wise and strong, showing that "the Jews are not better than the Gentiles, in spite of circumcision and the proud of possession of the Law."[123] In 1 Corinthians 1:27–28 Paul states that God chose what the world considers foolish to shame the wise; God chose what the world considers weak to shame the strong; God chose what is low and despised in the world—what is considered to be nothing—to reduce what is considered to be something to nothing. What Paul states is similar to what Matthew 1

---

120. Pierce, *Conscience in the New Testament*, 12.

121. *GEL* s.v. "ἐθνικῶς."

122. *Dasein* or human being that Heidegger discusses in his writings is involuntarily thrown into the world. Jean-Paul Sartre also says, "A voluntary deliberation [of *Dasein*] is always a deception, just as the dice are cast (*les jeux sont faits*)" (Sartre, *Being and Nothingness*, 450). See Hoy, "Heidegger and the Hermeneutic Turn," 180. What Heidegger argues is that we cannot discuss why people as Americans or Europeans are born, for they are involuntarily thrown into the world and no one answers the question of why a person is born in the world as a Jew or Gentile, or as a male or a female. As thrown, *Dasein* cannot go back to what and why it is thrown in the world but, instead, projects itself for its future being.

123. Stendahl, "Apostle Paul and the Introspective Conscience of the West," 201.

VIEWS OF CONSCIENCE BY HEIDEGGER, KIERKEGAARD, AND PAUL

introduces the genealogy of Jesus' birth. In 1 Matthew, five women—Tamar, Rahab, Ruth, Uriah, and Mary, who are alien, despised, low—gave birth to the messiah called Jesus Christ.

That the Gentiles are not excluded from God, who is said to be pervasive over the world, implies that they have ability to direct their way of being unbound in Jewish Law. Gentiles' direction is to hear and comply what conscience informs instead of observing the Law. As the Old Testament indicates that the human being as the creature is created in the image of God, conscience is also traceable to God.[124] What Paul emphasizes is that Gentiles as the feature of likeness to God have their direction written (*grapton*, γραπτὸν) in (*en*, ἐν) the (*tais*, ταῖς) hearts (*kardiais*, καρδίαις) so that they are not aimlessly drifting, and are neither to be inferior to Jews who have the Law, nor second-rate people abandoned from God. In Romans 2:14 Paul argues that while Gentiles are outside the Law (*anomois*, ἀνόμοις) and seem to be aimlessly swayed, they are lawful, for they are to be guided by "conscience."

Paul further argues the impracticality of the Law that Jews observe. While observing the Law aims at "'salvation (*e soteria*, ἡ σωτηρία)', finally 'life' (*e zon*, ἡ ζωή),"[125] it is impossible for people fully to follow it. Theologian Krister Stendahl says, "The impossibility of keeping the whole Law is a decisive point in Paul's argumentation in Rom 2:17—3:20."[126] It implies people's obedience to the Law leading to righteousness and salvation is fundamentally unachievable. Paul's disregard of the Law is challenged by many interpreters who accuse Paul of misunderstanding or deliberately misrepresenting the Jewish view of Law and Salvation.[127] They say Paul's access to the Law misses the point so far as to rule out "the Law on the basis that Israel could not achieve the perfect obedience which the Law required."[128] However, Paul emphasizes two points: first, salvation (*soteria*, σωτηρία) and life (*zon*, ζωή) rest on God, not humanity, and observing the Law is carried out by human works and achievements, not God—but salvation depends on God called "God's grace," while God's determination is said to be modified by human efforts. In Romans 9:18 Paul says, "God has compassion and mercy upon whomever God wills," citing Isaiah 29:16: "Shall the potter be regarded as the clay; that the thing made should say of its maker, 'He did not make me';

---

124. *IDB* s.v. "conscience."

125. Heidegger, *Phenomenology of Religious Life*, 48.

126. Stendahl, "Apostle Paul and the Introspective Conscience of the West," 201.

127. Stendahl, "Apostle Paul and the Introspective Conscience of the West," 201. See also Buber, *Two Types of Faith*, 43–50.

128. Stendahl, "Apostle Paul and the Introspective Conscience of the West," 201.

or the thing formed say of him who formed it, 'He has no understanding'?" Faith in God means that salvation leans on God who is reliable, not humanity or human achievements. Second, salvation is open to both Jews whose Laws are bestowed and Gentiles, who are born without the Law.[129]

Conscience is a regulative principle[130] to make *soma*'s resoluteness. Conscience is an "ability" or "power" called "*dynamis* (δύναμις)."[131] As Heidegger argues that *Dasein* forced by *das Man*'s power falls into the inauthentic *Dasein* but the voice of conscience makes it back into the authentic *Dasein*, *Dasein* is freed from subjecting to and being enslaved by *das Man*. Paul in 2 Corinthians 4:2 states that conscience as the power written in people's heart refuses to practice cunning, but opens to truth in the sight of God.

Conscience is the interior voice carrying what *soma* is aware of and sharing what *soma* is experienced with *soma*-self. Conscience introspectively occurs within *soma*. What *soma*'s conscience enacts through sharing knowledge earned by *soma* with *soma*-self indicates that it is internal and "proper (*kathekonta*, καθήκοντα)."[132] Since *soma* in its conscience transmits something aware to *soma*-self, it implies it is informative, directive, regulative to *soma*-self, and thereby is internal and subjective as a condition to make *soma*'s resoluteness. Hence, conscience brings in two issues: while conscience is constituted in *soma*'s inside and conditions its way of being, another law or condition is to come to *soma* to affect the way of conscience; and conscience is to exist in variety, implying conscience does not lie uniformly and symmetrically in the human heart but will be accompanied by chaos and tensions. Paul tells how *soma* unifies different consciences into one.

3. Conscience and Other Conditions

While Paul proclaims that the heathen is a determinative and responsible being because of conscience, he paradoxically states that all people, including Jews and Gentiles, are to fail to be directed by one's own conscience, for all are sinned or corrupted and doomed to death. That all have sinned, apart from whether they have observed the law or not, and have done righteous deeds or not, implies that they are under the power of "sin (*hamartian*, ἁμαρτίαν)," or corruption and the power of sin makes the direction of conscience ineffective and Gentiles lose themselves, and finally come to death.

---

129. Stendahl, "Apostle Paul and the Introspective Conscience of the West," 201.
130. *IDB* s.v. "conscience."
131. *GEL* s.v. δύναμις."
132. Bultmann, *Theology of the New Testament*, 1:71; *IDB* s.v. "conscience."

Paul argues that *soma* ontologically is the being of finitude, which is destined to lose itself, for it is embedded in the tradition of Adam. Paul in Romans 5:12 states that the corruption of humanity and the lostness of itself are transmitted from Adam, the forefather of humanity; Adam transgressed against God's Words and died; his sin and death spread to all humanities. Adam's transgression against God denotes that while Adam's existence is granted by God, Adam pays no heed to his creature and givenness of being by God, but craves to be like God, disconnecting *soma*'s self from God. What Paul mentions of Adam's sin and death that affects all human beings is interpreted by Bultmann. According to Bultmann, there might be a distinction between sin for which humans are responsible and sin for which they are not. From this perspective, one could infer that the concept of inherited sin is rooted in the experience that every person is born into a humanity historically guided by false striving. This understanding applies universally; everyone explicitly aligns themselves with it through their specific transgressions, thus sharing responsibility. Because human life is inherently social, a single lie can destroy mutual trust, establishing mistrust and sin. Similarly, a single act of violence can provoke defensive violence, making law, as organized violence, serve individual interests. These ideas are at least hinted at in 1 Corinthians 6:6, which notes that "a little leaven ferments the whole lump of dough."[133]

While the power of transmittance of the lostness of self and death are preordained to all people from Adam, Paul does not absolutely negate the significance of conscience to orient the way of the heathen's being. What Paul underscores is that the heathen needs to hear the voice of the preacher as the voice by others besides the voice of one's own conscience. Paul preaches two things to the Gentiles who lost themselves because of sin and were destined to death: the voice of the Spirit of the resurrected Christ in the faith community and the resurrection of Jesus Christ. Just as the gander to which Kierkegaard refers proclaims to geese whose authenticity is lost that they are distinctive from other animals and their authenticity is to fly freely through the sky, Paul delivers the good news to the Gentiles that they are proper, worthy, talented, and to be recovered from the loss of themselves as they hear and comply with the voice of the Spirit. The Spirit of the resurrected Christ is concerned with how individuals who lost themselves can be restored in the community of faith, while the view of resurrection of Jesus Christ is about how the heathens who are destined to death has hope for their future being.

133. Bultmann, *Theology of the New Testament*, 1:253.

Since Paul's view on Jesus' death and resurrection is unique and unfamiliar to non-Jewish Christians and the heathen, it is not easy for him to communicate with them. Paul's approach to the heathen concerning death and the resurrection of Jesus is to add what Paul learned from Hebrew-Christian tradition to what the heathen has already believed. Williston Walker in *A History of the Christian Church* argues that the heathen has believed "the immortality of the soul" based on Greek philosophy, saying "Hebrew and Greek ideas were at variance. The Hebrew conception was a living again of the flesh. The Greek, the immortality of the soul."[134] While Greek philosophy of the immortality of the soul is regarded as a preunderstanding as to death and the resurrection of Jesus, Paul's message on the heathen about Jesus' death and resurrection is considered an understanding of it. However, what is already existent and preunderstandingly understood is not easily and compromisingly engageable with and acceptable with what is the newly imported. Heathens might have tensions and struggles in their beliefs and living. As the preexistent view—the immortality of the soul and the newly introduced view—Jesus' death and resurrection encounter in the heathen, tension and conflicts result. As Heathens are born in the world, conscience is already constituted in people. They are also imbedded traditionally and religiously in the idea of the immortality of the soul. Paul gave them the new idea—Jesus' death and resurrection. There will be tension, priority, strife, and compromise among conscience, Greek philosophy, other religious ideas, and the new Christian belief in people's way of being.

4. Variety and Unity of Conscience under the Spirit

In Romans 7:14–25 Paul says that he is torn by two voices, one following his internal conscience, and the other being bound in the law driven from outside. He says the law (*nomos*, νόμος) or the principle is good and directive to his being so that he listens to observe, but he wants to hear his conscience. On the contrary, he does not listen to his conscience despite the demand of the call of conscience, but instead is drawn to what the law directs. While he acknowledges the law is good (*kalon*, καλὸν) and drives him to obey, he cannot and does not want to carry out the (*to*, τῷ) law (*nomo*, νόμῳ). Thus, he cannot call himself, "I," for "I" am torn into two "I"s or selves or personalities. He confesses that he is a wretched man (*talaiporos ego anthropos*, Ταλαίπωρος ἐγὼ ἄνθρωπος!), and asks, "Who will deliver me out of the maze?" "Thanks be to God," He later says, "I [Paul] found who delivers me out of the maze through the Spirit of the Resurrected Christ!"

---

134. Walker, *History of the Christian Church*, 29.

Paul emancipates himself in the Spirit of Jesus' resurrection out of his predicament or wretchedness that he is juxtaposed with his own direction by conscience versus the order by the law. He could not dispense with dipolar powers of both conscience and law, and he does not want to stand on either one or the other. He also confronts priorities between two dipolar positions. As a result, he turns to the third voice that empowers him by abiding in the Spirit; the Spirit cooperates or reconciles two exclusive positions rather than forcing Paul to stand on either one or the other. He settles conflictive, divergent positions into a resolved position by engaging in the attunement of the Spirit. In Romans 8:28 Paul confesses that God works all things together for good for the ones who come to God in the Spirit of Jesus' resurrection.

Conscience is also to be in variety on account of humanity's inner conscience, implying it does not lie uniformly and symmetrically in all human hearts. Disclosed in variety, not sameness, conscience is divergent, depending on what *soma* is conditioned, such as by knowledge, tradition, and culture. Paul in 1 Corinthians 8:1–13 and 10:14–33 refers to variety in conscience manifested in: "solid" or "strong (*stereos*, στερεὸς)," and "weak (*asthenounta*, ἀσθενοῦντα)" conscience as well as "mature (*teleois*, τελείοις)," and "immature (*os nepios*, ὡς νήπιος)" conscience. Such divisions occur in reference to the eating of food sacrificed to idols. Some affirm in their consciences that knowing whether the food was dedicated to idols or not is insignificant and is to be ignored, for they believe in one God who exists in the world, and that idols called as the image of multiple gods are a nonentity. Others allow many gods. If the food that they are supposed to eat is known as the food offered to the idols as a part of the dedication to idols, they are discouraged from eating the food. They are regarded as weak believers. While Paul distinguishes the strong Christian from the weak, he avoids judging the strong as good and the weak as bad. While the strong or weak conscience occurs in daily lives dealing with what and how to eat, the mature or immature conscience arises with the issue concerning how people comport themselves to others who are different. If the strong believer regards the weak believer as unfaithful, they fall into inconsiderate conduct.

Conscience is not an unchangeable substance that constitutes *soma*, but, rather, is changeably conditioned by such knowledge or habit. Paul is not concerned with finding who the strong or the weak believer is, but, rather, with how Christians treat others who are different from them in the way of belief in reference to conscience. As variety in conscience causes tensions, strife, and chaos among people, so different languages, including foreign phonetic languages and extraordinary languages called "speaking (*lalon*, λαλῶν) in tongues (*glosse*, γλώσσῃ)," make people confused and misunderstand each other, which might lead to unfriendliness and exclusivism. Paul did not consider "speaking in tongues" meaningless. Instead, he emphasizes that speaking in tongues is to be intellectually interpreted to people who encounter them. At the same time, Paul brings in the community of faith or love beyond answering the issue of different languages and the issue of variety in conscience.

As people are cast into the world, they are not born in the worldless or community-less world but are dropped into the community of family and friends called "the communal world." If animals such as dogs or cats are thrown into the woods, they might survive. However, human beings might not survive unless they are nurtured in the community, surrounded by people in the communal world. Community of people could be varied, for instance, Sangha, the community of all Buddhists, monks, nuns, and laity, Ummah, the Islam community, and Christian churches. Paul introduces the heathen to the community of faith or the Spirit. He shows how the community of the Spirit, made up of many diverse people, can communicate, relate, and cooperate with each other beyond strife and discord despite distinct and unfamiliar people in the community.

Paul considers a human body filled with many organs the community of faith. In 1 Corinthians 12:12–13 he says that just as the body is one but has many parts, so the Spirit of faith community is one but has many diverse people as members, who have their own talents, regardless of whether they are Jews or Greeks, male or female, the strong or the weak, that exist in the Spirit in the community. First Corinthians 12:14–26 says this about the character of the community of the Spirit: the body does not consist of one member but of many. The foot would not say, "I do not belong to the body, because I am always dirty and am not a hand." If the whole body were an eye, where would the hearing be? If the whole body were hearing, where would the sense of smell be? As it is, there are many members, yet one body. The eye cannot say to the hand, "I have no need of you." While some members of the body seem weaker, the weaker and inferior members of the body are indispensable and should be recognized instead of dispossessed and rejected. While there may be no dissension within the body due to diversity, the members may have the same care for one another. If one member suffers, all suffer together with it; if one member is honored. All rejoice together with it.

Paul presents five points as to the voice of the Spirit. Firstly, the community of the Spirit is like the body of the human being consisting of many different parts or organs. Second, as every organ is unique and valuable in the body, everyone is distinctive and worthy to exist in the community. Third, as every organ is valuable and distinctive, it must acknowledge the value and meaning of other organs. Fourth, while each organ is valuable and unique, its worthiness and uniqueness are manifested as long as it is in the body. Fifth, since each organ is unique and distinct, it should be interactive and cooperative with others, not fall into isolation. The voices that each organ discloses are diverse, distinctive, valuable, and respected. However, the voice in variety could fall into chaos and conflicts. The unity of various distinctions is carried out in the community of faith under the voice of the Spirit which acknowledges one's uniqueness and enhances diversity and unity. Paul shows how the community of the Spirit, made up of many diverse people, can communicate, relate, and cooperate with each other beyond strife and discord despite distinct and unfamiliar people in the community.

So far, we have discussed how the human being called "*Dasein*" or "*soma*" exists in oneself and coexists with others in the world. Conscience that constitutes *Dasein* or *soma*, as *Dasein*'s faculty to direct its way of being, and as a condition or attunement to coexist and relate with others in the communal world, which Heidegger, Kierkegaard, and Paul explored in their writings, is examined. *Dasein* or *soma* is also constituted by death. The next chapter will explore how death—as viewed by Heidegger, Fa-tsang, Kierkegaard, and Paul—leads and conditions its way of being.

IV

Death and Emptiness by Heidegger and Fa-tsang

DEATH IS THE IMPOSSIBILITY of the existence that the human being or *Dasein* has to experience and thereby lies in hopelessness due to anticipating its non-existence. As *Dasein* is thrown into the world, it is unable to get rid of its death and always rests on death. Heidegger refers to the death of the human being from *Der Ackerman aus Böhmen* that as a human being is born in the world, he or she is ready to die.[1] Since death constitutes *Dasein*, whose existence will be no longer soon or later, people have philosophically and religiously searched for ways to manage death and find some vision or hope despite death.

Heidegger in *Being and Time* explores what death is, how *Dasein* anticipates its death called *Angst*, and how it sees the possibility of its existence beyond death. What Heidegger asserts is that while *Angst* brings *Dasein* to experiencing nothingness or emptiness, nothingness directs *Dasein* to project its new possibility of existence, for nothing by anxiety is not a total nothing and the nothing is primordially based on something.[2] *Dasein*, who faces *Angst* and comports itself with emptiness instead of grounding itself, makes its resoluteness to project its new existence. However, *Dasein*'s projection determined by its resoluteness toward its new possibility of existence is not in free-floating potentiality, but in finitude of existence. For this reason, some other views on death and emptiness, which are not bound in *Dasein*'s resolute comportment, are demanded to be searched. We can find a view of

---

1. *SZ* 245; *BTM* 289; *BTS* 228.
2. *SZ* 187; *BTM* 231–32; *BTS* 175.

possibility of the sentient being (*chung-seng*) despite death from Fa-tsang's view of emptiness, which emphasizes its dependence on others. We can also discover *Dasein*'s possibility beyond its death and anxiety from Kierkegaard who discloses the meaning of anxiety and offers relatedness with God. The view of anxiety and relatedness with God discussed in Kierkegaard's writings offers an access to Paul's death, which is called "*kenosis* (κένωσις)" or emptiness and "*parousia* (παρουσία)," the encounter with the resurrected Christ, or presence of divinity in the future beyond the unavoidable hopeless death in a "moment"—which we will discuss in the next chapter.

A. HEIDEGGER'S VIEW OF *DASEIN'S* DEATH

The examination of Heidegger's view of *Angst* and emptiness offers a preunderstanding to comprehend the view of emptiness that Fa-tsang elaborates in his writings; conversely, the comprehension of Fa-tsang's emptiness serves to understand Heidegger's nothingness or emptiness. As nothingness or emptiness directs *Dasein* to see its new existence beyond its death, emptiness that Fa-sang argues serves the sentient being (*chung-seng*) to access *tathagata* (the fully completed = the Buddha).[3] However, emptiness is to be seen as a negative approach to attain Buddhahood for the new existence of the sentient being. In the place of emptiness, Fa-sang introduces *chung-seng*, its relatedness with and dependence on others, called "non-obstruction between principle and phenomenon," and "non-obstruction between phenomena and phenomena as well as *chung-seng*'s emptiness."

Heidegger's view of *Dasein*'s impossibility of existence and its projection toward its new possibility of existence by virtue of *Angst* is similar to death as emptiness and the possibility of union with the Buddha called "Buddhahood," which Fa-tsang claims; Fa-tsang was the third patriarch of Hua-yen school of Mahayana Buddhism (the great vehicle). He states that the wholly detached mind (*hsin*) desires nothing and is emptied and then it comes in Buddhahood manifested in interdependence or non-obstruction between *li* (principle) and *shih* (phenomena), and *shih* and *shih*. This chapter will explore Heidegger's *Angst* and the possibility of existence in reference to Fa-tsang's *sunyata* (emptiness) and Buddhahood.

---

3. Streng, *Emptiness*, 46.

1. Death as Boundary or Limitation

As soon as *Dasein* is thrown into the world, it changes, grows, and projects its future possible being. It does not come to rest, but it, as the being ahead-of-itself, acts and projects toward its future. Since *Dasein* projects its future possibilities,[4] *Dasein* is a possible being, thrown itself for its future, through and through.[5] However, if *Dasein* constantly projects, and exists in an endless way, it would be boundless and unable to be called *Dasein* in its totality. Insofar as *Dasein* is incessantly thrown and projects its possibility through and through, there is something outstanding that keeps us from being able to grasp *Dasein* as a whole. *Dasein* is not conceived in its totality, unless *Dasein* exists as the termination of *Dasein* called "death (*Tod*)." Something that makes *Dasein* as the ending of *Dasein* is death that borders it in totality or wholeness (*die Ganzheit*). Heidegger argues that death is one end of *Dasein* and birth is the other end; *Dasein*'s birth and death comprise *Dasein*'s wholeness.[6]

Death conditions and bounds *Dasein*'s being, free from the expanse of an interminable and indefinite existence. Death limits (*begrenzt*), determines, delineates, and defines (*bestimmt*) *Dasein* as the whole in its totality. Death is a demarcation or mortality of *Dasein*. Death distinguishes *Dasein* A from *Dasein* B.[7] In death, one *Dasein* is distinct from another *Dasein*.[8] Death shapes *Dasein* as *Dasein*'s individual or itself in its totality. Heidegger's discussion of death aims at framing *Dasein* within the being bordered by death.

Death is like a boundary line marked between one state and another state unfolded on a map or like an artist's sketch. Suppose an artist draws a picture on the canvas. He or she has an image and draws a line on the canvas. Of course, it is hard to determine which action is prior to the other between imagining and drawing the line. For instance, a child can first draw the line and later build the image of the line and then continue drawing the line based on the image. Furthermore, the relation between having the image and drawing the line could be simultaneous or consecutive; the picture in its totality could be completed to be drawn instantly or progressively. At the worst the picture could not be created, if only the image, which is indeterminate, boundless, and mysterious, dominates the artist; the velleity

---

4. *SZ* 181; *BTM* 225; *BTS* 170.
5. *SZ* 145; *BTM* 185; *BTS* 136.
6. *SZ* 373; *BTM* 425; *BTS* 342.
7. *SZ* 240; *BTM* 284; *BTS* 223.
8. *SZ* 240; *BTM* 284; *BTS* 223.

could be formless and confused, if he or she only imagines and activates without carrying out hermeneutic action that is equal to boundary action. The artist makes the image hermeneutically explicit, understandable, and interpretable on the canvas. The artist chips away the indeterminate image until it becomes a determinate and beautiful picture such as an elephant; a part of the image has mysteriously gone away by the determinate action. That the part of the image in drawing the picture mysteriously goes away is to be considered the part of the image that is dead, but the dead part can be resuscitated later, for the dead part is not completely annihilated and later is able to be reconstructed. Heidegger argues what is lost and dead in the past in the public does not vanish but is to be remembered or retrieved.[9] The art is carried out by two structural means: hermeneutically delimited, concrete, and narrow directness toward images as well as inexplicable, open-ended, and extensive images.

Life that constitutes *Dasein* is expandable, constructible, and potential in every day. But death that also constitutes *Dasein* makes life simple, rigid, destructible, and limited in its totality, just as an artist determines, defines, and draws on the canvas what he or she unyieldingly imagines. Death is like a trail blazer through which *Dasein* is conditioned to be finite and reduced from its indefinite possibility of being into its definite possibility of being, in contrast to life that is indefinitely expandable in *Dasein*'s being. Death is like a yardstick, while life is like a wide yard. *Death* is a regulatory way to be, as soon as *Dasein* as the being of being-possible (*Möglichsein*) is thrown into the world. Life is thus the possibility of *Dasein* as unboundedness, and death is also the possibility of *Dasein* in the boundedness and concreteness of possibility. Havi Carel in *Life and Death in Freud and Heidegger* argues that life and death are associated in the human being. While death affects a human existence to be in a limited being, life promotes him or her to take an action and project his/her future being every day.[10] Life and death are not separable and isolatable, but mutually workable in human existence.[11] What Heidegger argues is that death is not the event as the end of human breath but a mode of being, that *Dasein*'s being is constituted by death as well as life. Death is constantly present in the life of *Dasein* or *Dasein*'s existence. Death influences, conditions, demarks, and diminishes every day the existence of *Dasein* or the possibility of *Dasein*'s existence as "being-towards-death."

As death conditions *Dasein*'s everydayness and makes *Dasein*' possibility concrete and adequate, death is regarded neither as nothing that

---

9. SZ 385; BTM 437; BTS 352.
10. Carel, *Life and Death in Freud and Heidegger*, 65.
11. Carel, *Life and Death in Freud and Heidegger*, 169.

involves and shapes *Dasein* nor something impossible in *Dasein*. Rather, death is something possible and something affective that conditions the being of *Dasein*, shaping *Dasein*'s being, regardless of whether death makes the being of *Dasein* small or big. Thus, Heidegger characterizes death as "the possibility of *im*possibility of existence [*die charakterisierte Möglichkeit der Un-möglichkeit der Existenz*]."[12] *Dasein*'s possibility of impossibility of existence implies that when death bounds *Dasein*'s indefiniteness of life into its definite existence, there would be possibility for *Dasein*.

Heidegger's view of *Dasein*'s death as the possibility of impossibility of existence, which conditions *Dasein*'s indefinite life into definite existence, is confronted by a question. How can death as "nothingness [*Nichtigkeit*]"[13] be a possibility or condition to affect *Dasein*? Heidegger's view of the possibility of impossibility of existence is challenged by several philosophers who consider death as possibility to be incoherent and irrelevant. They raise a question as to what kind of possibility that is. How can death be a possibility? Heidegger's definition of death as the possibility of impossibility of existence is imperative showing the meaning of possibility.

2. Death as *Angst*

Heidegger's view of the possibility of impossibility of existence is criticized by several philosophers. Jean-Paul Sartre in his *Being and Nothingness* equates death with nothingness, that is, death as the end of possibilities. He asserts that death represents the annihilation of all one's possibilities, an annihilation that does not constitute only a part of one's possibilities. According to him, death is not simply the possibility of ceasing to realize a presence in the world, but rather a complete annihilation of one's possibilities that lies beyond one's control.[14]

Sartre concludes in opposition to Heidegger that death is a contingent fact that does not belong to me or my possibility, but outside of me.[15] Likewise, Paul Edwards argues that death is not possibility in ordinary senses.[16] He complains that Heidegger's term of possibility in relation to death is misleading people, for death is the absence and annihilation of consciousness.[17] In response to the critics, Taylor Carman in his *Heidegger's*

---

12. *SZ* 306; *BTM* 354; *BTS* 283.
13. *SZ* 306; *BTM* 354; *BTS* 283.
14. Sartre, *Being and Nothingness*, 537.
15. Sartre, *Being and Nothingness*, 545.
16. Edwards, "Heidegger and Death," 558.
17. Edwards, "Heidegger and Death," 557–58.

Analytic argues that such criticisms arise from the fact that Heidegger does not mean what is commonly understood about death in ordinary lives;[18] Heidegger's view of death is considered the non-ordinary view of death, which is called the existential view of death ("*das heißt existenzialer Begriff des Todes*"[19]). What is ordinarily understood about death is the perishing (*Verenden*) as the end of the living,[20] that is, the cessation or the end of biological function in an organism of the body. However, Heidegger's view of existential death is something or possibility that conditions *Dasein* to experience its finitude or mortality, or the impossibility of its existence and the meaninglessness of the world.

William Blattner also replies to the criticism that death is not to be regarded as a possibility. Blattner argues that what Heidegger characterizes *Dasein*'s death as a possibility does not mean something that could befall *Dasein*, but is instead a possible way to be.[21] Blattner then distinguishes death (*Sterben*) from demise (*Ableben*), which manifests at the end of *Dasein*'s existence called perishing (*Verenden*).[22] Death (*Sterben*) that Heidegger discuses in *Being and Time* is considered an anxiety-attack that conditions and affects *Dasein*'s being. Blattner interprets Heidegger's concept of "anxiety" (*Angst*) as a pervasive discomfort with the world at large. This attunement or way of being attuned, according to Blattner, is not a discomfort with specific objects or situations, such as the nervousness before a job interview. Instead, it reveals the entire human world in a definite and novel way.[23]

The possibility and the anxiety (*Angst*) attack that Blatter describes concerning Heidegger's view of death is understood as the following: while *Dasein* faces *Angst* as discomfort and uncanniness, the discomfort and uncanniness condition *Dasein*'s way of being and serves it to project its new possible being.

What Heidegger means by *Angst* is to be understood in reference to fear (*die Furcht*). Fear, an emotional feeling of something, is disclosed only in specific oncoming objects and events in the world. Fear is the feeling toward an object. My neighbor was bitten and wounded by a snake. I see a snake in the distance while mowing grass and am suddenly frightened. When I walk on the grass, I feel fearful of the snake without mowing the grass. Fear is an

---

18. Carman, *Heidegger's Analytic*, 276–91.
19. SZ 234.
20. SZ 247.
21. Blattner, "Concept of Death in *Being and Time*," 50.
22. Blattner, "Concept of Death in *Being and Time*," 52.
23. Blattner, "Concept of Death in *Being and Time*," 60.

emotion arisen from an anticipation of some specific danger accompanied by a desire to flee. Heidegger refers to a fear of something threatening and approaching within the scope of the things close at hand and circumstances in everydayness.[24] Kierkegaard, in *The Concept of Anxiety*, differentiates between fear and anxiety (*Angst*). He suggests that *Angst* is distinct from fear and similar concepts that refer to something specific, describing *Angst* as the actualization of freedom through the possibility of possibilities.[25]

In contrast to fear, *Angst* does not have a specific object, but happens in relation to the meaning concerning the world. While fear is the discomfort of something that people have in mind because of something fearful, *Angst* is an existential-ontological mood of rupture of *Dasein*'s being-in-the-world, in which I am nothing. Heidegger states that fear is a fleeting experience, which does not belong to the primordial constancy of existence.[26] Because of this he claims that his task is to exhibit the ontological structure of mood called *Angst* in *Dasein*'s existential constitution.[27] David Farrell Krell in *Ecstasy, Catastrophe: Heidegger from Being and Time to the Black Notebooks* distinguishes fear (*die Furcht*) from *Angst* by an illustration: when the house is in flames, the resident of the house is confused in a chaotic situation and is full of fear, and he or she wants to grab whatever presents itself to him/her and carry it out to a secure place.[28] By contrast, Heidegger describes *Angst* as a state that brings *Dasein* back to its most authentic ability, which is to be the foundation of a nullity.[29]

Heidegger discusses *Angst*, which does not come upon one with something definite or objective. He refers to *Angst* that does not arise from the specific threat that *Dasein* encounters in everydayness. Instead, *Angst* arises from the fact that *Dasein* has a mood or state of mind of the irrelevance to the world in which *Dasein* exists. *Dasein*, which has *Angst* in the state of mind, falls into the insignificance of the world (*Unbedeutsamkeit der Welt*), which reveals the nothingness or nullity (*die Nichtigkeit*) of what *Dasein* is concerned about and takes care of.[30]

By *Angst* Heidegger means the mood (*die Stimmung*) of discomfort that *Dasein* reveals in the world. In a psychological sense, *Angst* is anxiety, dread

---

24. *SZ* 341; *BTM* 391; *BTS* 313.

25. Kierkegaard, *Concept of Anxiety*, 42, hereafter referred to as *CAC*. See also Humbert, "Freedom and Time," 75.

26. *SZ* 340; *BTM* 391; *BTS* 313.

27. *SZ* 340; *BTM* 390; *BTS* 313.

28. Krell, *Ecstasy, Catastrophe*, 49–50.

29. Krell, *Ecstasy, Catastrophe*, 49–50.

30. *SZ* 343; *BTM* 393; *BTS* 315.

or depression. Phenomenologically, *Angst* is a mood of uncanniness ("*In der Angst ist einem unheimlich*") or unsettledness (*die Unheimlichkeit*), of "not being at home" (*das Nicht-zuhause-sein*)[31] or groundlessness—nothingness (*die Nichtigkeit*).[32] In *Angst*, acquaintances, and familiarity in which *Dasein* has been used in everydayness collapses ("*Die alltägliche Vertrautheit bricht in sich zusammen*"),[33] leaving *Dasein* alienated. In *Angst*, every ground on which *Dasein* relies is destructive and becomes nothingness or groundlessness, or nullity. In *Angst Dasein's* world becomes lacking in significance.[34]

Angst is *Dasein's* own being-toward-death ("*Das Sein zum Tode ist wesenhaft Angst*").[35] Being-toward-death or dying (*das Sterben*) is not something that drives *Dasein* to its end, but a condition that has some bearing on the way of *Dasein's* being. Heidegger says, "*Das Sterben ist keine Begebenheit, sondern ein existenzial zu verstehendes Phänomen* [Dying is not an event, but a phenomenon to be understood existentially]."[36] The event of death does not occur during the lifetime of the entity but happens at the end of the entity's liveliness. The event of death could be the consequence that the function of the lively body is terminated and transformed into the lifeless body. However, dying or being-toward-death in the existential concept does not mean the absence of life, but something phenomenal from the being reveals as far as *Dasein* exists. Dying or *Angst* in the existential mood is a directing possibility that impels *Dasein* to see the world on which it relies as strange and uncanny (*unheimlich*). While the world in which anxious *Dasein* exists has fallen into insignificance, the insignificance of the world directs *Dasein* not to be dependent on the world and thereby makes it free, and serves *Dasein* to take care of itself, apart from what it is bound, that is, the impossibility of projecting oneself upon a potentiality-of-being for its future.[37]

As *Angst* as *Dasein's* own being-toward-death ("*Das Sein zum Tode ist wesenhaft Angst*")[38] makes *Dasein* see the world empty and unfamiliar, it takes *Dasein* back from its "worldly" possibilities and finds freedom from bounding on the world. While *Angst* impels *Dasein* to be no longer dependent on the world on which *Dasein* counts, it releases itself from

31. SZ 188; BTM 233; BTS 176.
32. SZ 285; BTM 331; BTS 263
33. SZ 189.
34. SZ 186; BTM 231; BTS 174.
35. SZ 266.
36. SZ 240; BTM 284; BTS 223.
37. SZ 343; BTM 393; BTS 315.
38. SZ 266; BTM 310; BTS 245.

being bound up with the world and thereby "illuminates all other possibilities as being part of a finite structure."[39] Thus, Kierkegaard in *The Concept of Anxiety* refers to anxiety as "the possibility of possibility,"[40] which not only holds out the meaninglessness of the world, but also the possibility for the vision of the meaningful something for *Dasein*. Hubert Dreyfus, in his work *Being-in-the-World*, argues that accepting *Angst* leads to fearlessness. He suggests that accepting *Angst* can be seen as a positive form of existential reduction, illuminating both *Dasein* and its world in their entirety while exposing their lack of foundation.[41]

Thus, *Angst* looks like the moment of enlightenment when *Dasein* is aware of itself and frees itself from attachment to the world and becomes a disclosedness, such as Buddhahood, which means the enlightened one through detachment from the world. Of course, *Angst* does not necessarily mean a religious awakening but awareness of *Dasein* itself and liberation from what *Dasein* was bound in everydayness. David Farrell Krell discusses the role of anxiety (*die Angst*) in revealing our being. He asserts that it is not intellectuality that disrupts our dogmatic slumber, but a remarkable attunement or mood that can suddenly overtake us, leading to a new paradigm and shifting away from previously significant beliefs.[42] Hence, Krell considers *Angst* a remarkable openness and disclosedness for *Dasein*, offering this new paradigm.[43]

Angst directs *Dasein* to see the world emptiness, that is, discloses the nothing,[44] called "nothingness (*die Nichtigkeit*)." Heidegger in "What Is Metaphysics?" argues that *Dasein* releases it from the world "into the nothing, . . . [and] liberates itself from those idols everyone has . . . cringing . . . so that it swings back into [the state of mind] which the nothing itself compels."[45] Nothingness is openness or disclosedness (*die Erschlossenheit*), and openness provides for *Dasein* a new eye toward the world and thereby has the projection toward the new possibility of its existence. *Die Erschlossenheit* or disclosedness comes from its verb *"zu erschliessen"* or "to open up," or "to explore," and *"zu erschliessen"* is based on *"zu schließen"* or "to close" or "to shut." Nothingness is emptiness or "nihilation,"[46] and

---

39. Carel, *Life and Death in Freud and Heidegger*, 74.
40. CA 42.
41. Dreyfus, *Being-in-the-World*, 182.
42. Krell, *Ecstasy, Catastrophe*, 47.
43. Krell, *Ecstasy, Catastrophe*, 48.
44. Heidegger, "What Is Metaphysics?," 103.
45. Heidegger, "What Is Metaphysics?," 112.
46. Heidegger, "What Is Metaphysics?," 105.

nihilation liberates *Dasein* from the world to which it is attached, and thereby helps it freely see the world.[47] Kierkegaard also argues that anxiety is to be conceived in the direction of freedom.[48] Heidegger argues that to be in *Angst* discloses, primordially and directly, the world as world ("*Das Sichängsten erschließt ursprünglich und direkt die Welt als Welt*").[49] *Angst* impels *Dasein* to project the new possibility of the impossibility of existence of the world (*die Möglichkeit der Unmöglichkeit der Existenz*). What *Dasein* releases itself from the attachment to the world implies that *Dasein* becomes authentic; when it becomes the authentic one,[50] it is followed by projecting the new possibility of the impossibility of existence.

That *Dasein* frees itself from being bound on the world, becomes the authentic one, and projects the new possibility of its existence does not mean that the possibility of its existence is not limitless. The term "possibility" that Heidegger argues does not refer to unbounding potentiality or free-floating potentiality of being (*das freischwebende Seinkönnen*) in the sense of the "liberty of indifference [*libertas indifferentiae*]."[51] Heidegger explains the possibility of its existence ensued by emptiness does not mean unlimitedness, but finitude by discussing *Dasein* with time. Just as *Dasein* is bordered by death or finitude of existence, *Dasein* is bounded by the temporality of time. *Dasein*'s limited possibilities are disclosed in time conceived as "temporality" in which *Dasein* lies and engages; the primordial ontological basis for *Dasein* is in temporality.[52] Heidegger's discussion of *Dasein*'s impermanent time is comparable to Kierkegaard's notion in *The Sickness unto Death*. Kierkegaard remarks that as time available for existence diminishes, everything becomes increasingly instantaneous.[53] *Dasein*'s groundlessness is manifested in the temporality, not eternity of its existence (impermanent time) as well as impossibility of its existence (finite existence).

Dasein's emptiness, detachment, and openness to the world that Heidegger argues is releasement (*die Gelassenheit*). *Die Gelassenheit* is the sense of "'composure,' 'calmness,' and 'unconcern,'" in which *Dasein* keeps its comportment open, "letting the world go."[54] *Die Gelassenheit* involves "waiting" in which *Dasein* does not await anything that it purposely craves,

47. Heidegger, "What Is Metaphysics?," 112.
48. *CA* 66.
49. *SZ* 187; *BTM* 232; *BTS* 175.
50. *SZ* 344; *BTM* 395; *BTS* 316.
51. *SZ* 144; *BTM* 183; *BTS* 135.
52. *SZ* 234; *BTM* 277; *BTS* 216.
53. *SD* 169.
54. Heidegger, *Discourse on Thinking*, 54.

but "In waiting we leave open what we are waiting for, not expecting, and not waiting for anything in particular, but waiting 'for [auf]' the openness."[55] That *Dasein* does not wait for anything in particular, but wait for the openness, implies time does not belong to *Dasein*, but *Dasein* is appropriate to time. Just as *Dasein* lets the world go in its comportment of releasement (*Gelassenheit*) due to the impossibility of existence, so *Dasein* lets time properly come to itself instead of the time that it desires and anticipates. That time comes to *Dasein*, not vice versa, shows time conceived as temporality lets *Dasein* be formulated in being temporalized in contrast to being eternal, which is said to be attributed to God.

3. Time as Temporality instead of Eternity

Just as *Dasein* exists as itself, so too does it exist with others, which is called "being-with-others" or "*Mitsein*." While *Dasein* exists individualistically, responsibly, and freely, its existence is conditioned by and conditions others, that is, is constituted with the community in which *Dasein* is thrown. The others that constitute *Dasein* involve not only the community of people, but also time (*die Zeit*). Heidegger emphasizes that as *Dasein* exists along with others as *Dasein*'s being-in-the-world (*In-der-Welt-sein*), it has to exist with time as "*Dasein*'s being-in-time (*In-der-Zeit-sein*)."[56] In *Der Begriff der Zeit/The Concept of Time* he states that *Dasein* is determined as being-with-one-another so that in everydayness *Dasein* is not that being that I individually am, but, rather, the everydayness of *Dasein* is that being is with one another and that being exists there or here, and that being exists now, or existed in the past, which means one's time (*die* "*Man's*" *Zeit*) and shows the time of being-with-one-another-in-the-world.[57] *Dasein* is not understood without time; apart from *Dasein*, time is to be considered nothing. Heidegger emphasizes the significance of time, which brings light to *Dasein* to grasp something as the being of entities under a perspective or standpoint of time.[58]

Heidegger radically departs from the traditional view of time advocated by such as Plato, Aristotle, and St. Augustine of Hippo. The time that Heidegger argues is involved in humans and is characterized as impermanence and temporality, but the time that traditional philosophers and theologians affirm is engaged with God, and in this manner is it envisaged

55. Heidegger, *Discourse on Thinking*, 23, 68.
56. BTM 497.
57. Heidegger, *Begriff der Zeit/Concept of Time*, 17E.
58. SZ 17; BTM 39; BTS 15.

as eternity and permanence which lies among God's attributes. Plato in *Timaeus* refers to time that belongs to eternity of the creator.[59] Just as the father begets his children, so the creator (He) created the universe and rejoiced and was well pleased. The universe is created in the act of ordering by Him, not by chance. The universe that He created is constituted by days, nights, months, and years, which did not exist before the creation of universe. He then devised the generation of them along with the fashioning of the universe. While progress and sequences, including the change of the present, past, and future, are portions of time, according to Plato, we cannot ascribe them to the eternal essence, which belongs to the creator, who is not bent on change and progress. "Time itself is a phase of the timeless, or, . . . 'an eternal image of eternity.'"[60]

Augustine, who was influenced by Plato's view of eternity of time, argues that time did not exist before the creation of the universe. Bertrand Russell in *A History of Western Philosophy* refers to Augustine's view of time: "Time was created when the world was created. God is eternal, in the sense of being timeless; in God there is no before and after, but only an eternal present. God's eternity is exempt from the relation of time; all time is present to Him at once."[61] Augustine regarded time as an endless series of *now*. Time is conceived as successive moments of now or the eternity of an enduring present, for the past is no longer present and the future is not yet present. The present can never be a moment of time because it makes the flow of time possible; the non-flowing or timeless moment from which time moves away is called eternity. Augustine in *Confessions* discusses how people might understand that time derives its length from numerous successive movements into the past, as they cannot all persist simultaneously. He contrasts this with eternity, where nothing transitions into the past and everything exists in an ever-present state. Unlike time, which is never entirely present at once and is driven by the future and past, both of which have their origins and terminations in the eternal present, eternity encompasses neither past nor future but governs both.[62] Thus, time as viewed by Plato and Augustine adheres to a vision that transcends the unstable, sensible, and phenomenal world but leads to the non-changing, immutable, and timeless of the eternal realm.

Heidegger seeks to find time in the mutable, phenomenal world, and time with *Dasein* who is in finitude and mortality different from God, who is traditionally said as the eternal, unchanging, undying being. Heidegger

---

59. Archer-Hind, *Timaeus of Plato*, 119–21.
60. Archer-Hind, *Timaeus of Plato*, 41.
61. Russell, *History of Western Philosophy*, 353.
62. Augustine, *Confessions*, 261–62.

did not absolutely ignore the significance of Plato, Aristotle, and Augustine despite criticizing them but felt that their views are theological, not philosophical. He is concerned with philosophy in which the human being is the essential issue and humanity is in finitude distinct from eternity and God, which belongs to theology. Heidegger in *Pathmarks* addresses the common juxtaposition of theology and philosophy, where theology is tied to faith and revelation, while philosophy is perceived as detached from faith and revelation.[63] He suggests that the theological view of time is perplexed because God's eternal time differs vastly from the mortal time experienced by humans.[64] Heidegger argues that if time's meaning is derived from eternity, it must be understood from the perspective of eternity. Thus, if faith is the means of accessing God, then philosophy, lacking this faith, cannot methodologically employ eternity to discuss time. Consequently, theologians are considered the legitimate experts on time.[65]

Heidegger discusses time related to *Dasein*, who exists as a finite or dying entity. If the issue of time is exempt from the finite humans or the existence of *Dasein*,[66] it is "meaningless (*sinnlos*)."[67] Seeking time in relation to *Dasein*'s existence is to find how time conditions *Dasein* to make its decision or resoluteness for the care of *Dasein* itself, for time characterized as change and temporality is engaged with *Dasein*'s existence manifested in birth, growth, resoluteness, and death. Heidegger is not concerned with what time objectively is and what is eternity of time belonging to God, but what time is for *Dasein* and how time works with *Dasein* in the world in contrast to Newtonian understanding of time, according to which it had an existence independent of the knowing *Dasein*.[68] Thus, he emphasizes that time does not exist without human existence. However, what he refers to time that does not exist without humanity does not mean that time does not go on unless *Dasein* exists. Heidegger acknowledges the continuation of time despite *Dasein*'s no longer being.[69] Heidegger further elaborates on how time conditions *Dasein*'s being. He posits that the essential question is not about the occurrences in ongoing time or the encounters from time, but about the fundamental nature of coming-toward-oneself.[70] He asserts

---

63. Heidegger, *Pathmarks*, 40.
64. Heidegger, *Begriff der Zeit/Concept of Time*, 1E.
65. Heidegger, *Begriff der Zeit/Concept of Time*, 1E.
66. Heidegger, *Begriff der Zeit/Concept of Time*, 21.
67. Heidegger, *Begriff der Zeit/Concept of Time*, 21.
68. Humbert, "Freedom and Time," 29.
69. SZ 330; BTM 378; BTS 303.
70. SZ 330; BTM 378; BTS 303.

that "*Dasein* is time" because time fundamentally conditions *Dasein* in its temporal existence.[71]

Time is *Zeit* in German. *Zeit* or time has the adjective *zeitlich*, which means "temporal" or "transitory" and the noun *die Zeitlichkeit* or temporality.[72] Heidegger seeks to find what time is from time itself and how time works with *Dasein* instead of God. As *Zeit* has its adjective as "temporal," and its noun "temporality," time is characterized as the temporal or temporalization, making others transitory and temporal. What we define time as temporality seems to be tautological, for the noun time already has temporality in it. Heidegger also explains that "time is temporal," emphasizing that this assertion is not a tautology since temporality signifies non-identical actuality. He argues that time, as temporality, is not a tangible thing even if people perceive it as such.[73] Instead, temporality manifests and shapes possible ways of itself.[74]

While time as temporality is not to be defined as something such as a chair or table, time exists with entities and conditions them, making them temporalized and transitory. Time conditions *Dasein* to be transitory. Moreover, Heidegger contends that it is not that "time is," but rather that "*Dasein*, as time, temporalizes its being." Time is not an external framework for world events, nor is it an internal mechanism within consciousness. Instead, it is what enables the state of being-ahead-of-itself-while-already-being-involved-in, which is the essence of care. Being in the world with others and discovering the shared world is a particular kind of temporality. Natural movements, which are defined in spatio-temporal terms, are encountered in time only because their being is discovered as pure nature, even though they are inherently time-free.[75]

4. Time as *Augenblick* (the Moment of Insight)

Time engages *Dasein* to temporalize instead of perceptualizing or eternalizing it. Time as temporality participates in *Dasein*'s projection or resoluteness after seeing the insignificance of the world in *Angst* through providing *Dasein* to experience the moment of vision or the moment of insight called "*Augenblick*." *Augenblick* literally means the glance of the eye or the moment. But *Augenblick* is not simply translated as the moment or instant,

---

71. Heidegger, *Begriff der Zeit/Concept of Time*, 20–21E.
72. Inwood, *Heidegger Dictionary*, 220.
73. *SZ* 328; *BTM* 376; *BTS* 302.
74. *SZ* 328; *BTM* 376; *BTS* 302.
75. Heidegger, *History of the Concept of Time*, 319–20.

but is philosophically translated as the moment of insight. Carel, in *Life and Death in Freud and Heidegger*, translates *Augenblick* as "the moment," following Dreyfus; Albert Hofstadter as "the instant"; John Macquarrie and Edward Robinson as "the moment of vision";[76] Joan Stambaugh as "the Moment." The moment of insight comprises that suddenly (*exaiphns*, ἐξαίφνης)[77] something comes to enlighten *Dasein*.[78] *Augenblick* as the moment of insight that I translate rather than being translated as the moment or instant implies unaccountable moments of the past, the present, and the future in the unity. Heidegger explains that the phenomenon of *Augenblick* cannot be clarified merely in terms of the present moment.[79] He describes the concept of "*Augenblick*" as a moment that presents something as part of a resolved decision, revealing the situation upon which this resolution is based. In this instant as an ecstasis, the being (*Dasein*) is carried away into the factical possibilities and contingencies of its current situation of action.[80] He refers to *Augenblick* that must be understood in the active sense as an ecstasy (*Ekstase*)[81] in order to understand the moment of insight.

A Greek word ἔκστασις (ecstasy) is constituted by two terms, *ek* (εκ) or out and *stasy* (στασις) or a stand. Ecstasy (ἔκστασις) literally is defined as "'standing outside, forth,' hence 'removal, displacement,' and, later, 'being beside oneself, or out of one's mind.'"[82] Ecstasy (ἔκστασις) means "distraction, confusion, astonishment," and biblically means "trance, a state of being brought about by God, in which consciousness is wholly or partially suspended."[83] Heidegger uses ecstasy in German terms, "*entrücken, resoluteness*, [entailing] 'to carry away, transport, enrapture; transport, carrying away, being carried away, rapture' . . . 'shaking, rocking,' and then 'moving,' 'away [ent-],' and also a heightened emotional state."[84]

---

76. "'The moment' (Dreyfus) is a translation of *Augenblick*, which is also translated as 'the instant' (Hofstadter), or 'the moment of vision' (Macquarrie and Robinson). I shall follow Dreyfus in using 'the moment,' because this formulation lends itself nicely to such expressions as 'being in the moment' and 'the moment of transformation,' as well as being consistent with the English translation of Kierkegaard's *Oieblik*, which is the source of Heidegger's term (Dreyfus, 1991, x)" (Carel, *Life and Death in Freud and Heidegger*, 89). Joan Stambaugh also translates *Augenblick* as the Moment.

77. GEL s.v. "ἐξαίφνης."

78. Krell, *Ecstasy, Catastrophe*, 35.

79. SZ 338; BTM 387; BTS 311.

80. Heidegger, *Basic Problems of Phenomenology*, 287–88.

81. SZ 338; BTM 387; BTS 311.

82. Inwood, *Heidegger*, 90.

83. GEL s.v. "ἔκστασις."

84. Inwood, *Heidegger Dictionary*, 221.

Since time itself temporalizes, people are not aware of the process of temporality. Temporality should be ex-temporalized to be made aware of it by people. Time's ex-temporalization is in a mode of being called "*stasy* (στασις)" and "ex (εκ)" or *ek-stasy* that time stands outside or out-of-itself toward, back, and among stances or positions revealed in future, present, and past. The three ecstases—future, present, and having-been (past)—interplay in the unity of temporality. Heidegger states that the unity of the horizonal stances of future, having-been, and present is established in the ecstatic unity of temporality.[85]

As *Dasein* is not a single, individualistic entity, but instead the entity of being-with-others in-the-world, it thereby determines its existence as together and with one another, so the moment of *Augenblick* is not a single, present moment. The moment is arisen from what it was beforehand and what it was in advance and might be constituted by many other moments. What it was beforehand for the present moment is considered a primary source. It is like seeing a piece of paper in one's hand. People who see the product of paper in a moment can imagine many previous moments involved by various people such as the woodcutter, truck driver, manufacturer, and seller. Hence, *Dasein*'s resoluteness entails many previous instants, despite being seen at an instant. Michael Inwood says, "Resolute *Dasein* runs ahead to its death, and reaches back into the past, before deciding what to do in the present, the authentic present or *Augenblick*, the moment of vision."[86]

Jacques Derrida argues that a single moment of now or present is like a metaphysical substance, which is in-self and for-itself inaccessible by others.[87] The self-identical moment of the presence needs nothing else to be understood.[88] Then, the moment as the self-presence is not conceived, because it is claimed to be "within the sameness"[89] of itself. Rather, every present or the point of now is already comprised of a trace or previous suppliers, that is, "the 'present' is [already] itself constituted, produced, and derived from a more primordial [in advance] source of nonpresence."[90] For instance, Hubert Dreyfus in *Being-in-the-World* refers to Heidegger's view of *Augenblick* as handed down from Paul's "the twinkling of an eye" (*en*

---

85. SZ 365; BTM 416; BTS 334.
86. Inwood, *Heidegger*, 88.
87. SZ 94; BTM 126; BTS 82.
88. Derrida, *Speech and Phenomena*, 68.
89. Derrida, *Speech and Phenomena*, 68.
90. David B. Allison, "Translator's Introduction," in Derrida, *Speech and Phenomena*, xxxvii.

atomo, en rhipe ophthalmou, ἐν ἀτόμῳ, ἐν ῥιπῇ ὀφθαλμοῦ)[91] in 1 Corinthians 15:52 of the New Testament; Luther's translation of it; Kierkegaard's use of it as *Øieblikket* in Danish, which is the primordial source to make Heidegger's *Augenblick*;[92] Kierkegaard in *Philosophical Fragments* says, "*Øieblikket* (the Moment) . . . is really decisive for eternity"[93] of God. The moment of present "goes back to the past, since it cannot fully grasp its present situation or decide how to act in it unless it understands how it reached its present situation."[94]

As *Dasein*'s moment of insight does not mean the present or single moment but extends to going back to the past and forward to the anticipation of its future, how far does the resolute *Dasein* of *Augenblick* find primordial or in advance sources of nonpresence? Heidegger describes factical *Dasein* as existing in a state of being that is born and simultaneously oriented towards death, with both the beginning and the end, as well as the period in between, defined by *Dasein*'s existence and grounded in the being of *Dasein* as care.[95]

The term *facticity* that Heidegger uses implies that *Dasein* as an entity within the world or being-in-the-world can understand itself as bound up in its destiny with the being of those entities which it encounters in its familiar world, not beyond the world.[96] What constitutes *Dasein*'s moment of insight reaches *Dasein*'s birth of the past and death of the future anticipated by it. Since Heidegger does not consider *Dasein*'s primordial sources going beyond the world of its birth and death, he as a philosopher, not theologian, does not discuss where and what world was before *Dasein* was born and where and what it would be like after its death apart from within the world.[97] In a sense, Heidegger limits the possibility of existence between the birth and death within the world.

However, since *Dasein* exists as the being-with-others as well as the being-in-itself (*eigen*)-in-the-world, *Dasein*'s moment of insight is

---

91. Paul first referred to the moment of vision (ἐν ἀτόμῳ—in an instant, ἐν ῥιπῇ ὀφθαλμοῦ—in the twinkling of an eye) in 1 Corinthians 15:52 of the New Testament.

92. Dreyfus, *Being-in-the-World*, x.

93. Kierkegaard, *Philosophical Fragments*, 72.

94. Inwood, *Heidegger*, 88–89.

95. SZ 374; BTM 426–27; BTS 343.

96. SZ 56; BTM 82; BTS 52.

97. Some Buddhists believe that a human being has his/her former or previous existence prior to this life and would become something else after death beyond the world. "If one lives like an animal, one is liable to reborn as an animal; if one lives like a human being, one will be reborn as a human being; if one lives like a god, one will be reborn as a god" (Buswell, *Encyclopedia of Buddhism*, 186).

constituted not only by itself extemporalized by its past (birth), present, and future (death), but also by other *Dasein*s of the world such as Plato, Aristotle, St. Paul, Augustine, Meister Eckhart,[98] Martin Luther, Schleiermacher, Kierkegaard, and Eastern religious thoughts historically handed down from the past. They are past, but they are not dead in publicness and are remembered by *Dasein*s. They condition and participate in *Dasein*'s moment of insight to help *Dasein* make its resoluteness. Heidegger holds that if *Dasein* exists as being-in-the-world in being-with others, its happening (*das Geschehen*) is an existence with them as destiny (*das Geschick*).[99]

Dasein's moment of insight is not simply a collection of transient experiences that follow one another and then vanish.[100] Rather, *Dasein*'s moment of insight belongs to *Dasein*'s resolute determination on what is in advance offered to it as possibilities and make them fit the situation of its existence. Experiences of birth and death as anticipation and other *Dasein*s, which have been beforehand to *Dasein*, are "past possibilities."[101]

Past possibilities are considered indefinite, indeterminate, neutral, and non-circumstantial until *Dasein* acts them out for its resoluteness. *Dasein* makes them definite and determinate "*in der Entschlossenheit für bestimmte Möglichkeiten*"[102] [in the resoluteness for definite possibilities] for its own sake. If *Dasein*, by anticipation, lets death become powerful in itself, that is, empties itself, it then becomes free, but the power of its freedom is limited. *Dasein* does not choose all that has been offered to it, but limits some things as a choice, and can have a clear vision about the chance elements in the situation disclosed.[103] Hence, Heidegger suggests that *Augenblick* involves a resolute engagement of *Dasein* with possibilities and circumstances that must be managed within a given situation, and held in a state of resoluteness (*in der Entschlossenheit gehaltene Entrückung des Daseins an das, was in der Situation an besorgbaren Möglichkeiten, Umständen begegnet*).[104]

Dasein's visional, insightful resoluteness is particularly undertaken and served by heroes whom *Dasein* historically encounters such as Zarathustra's prophecy (Übermensch) that Friedrich Nietzsche interpreted in *Thus Spoke Zarathustra: A Book for All and None*.[105] Heidegger refers to a hero as a

---

98. Zimmerman, "Heidegger, Buddhism, and Deep Ecology," 250.
99. *SZ* 385; *BTM* 436; *BTS* 352.
100. *SZ* 374; *BTM* 426; *BTS* 343.
101. Dreyfus, *Being-in-the-World*, 330.
102. *SZ* 384; *BTM* 436; *BTS* 352.
103. *SZ* 384; *BTM* 436; *BTS* 351–52.
104. *SZ* 338; *BTM* 387; *BTS* 311.
105. *SZ* 396.

"model"[106] who is able to contribute to *Dasein*'s anticipatory resoluteness (*in der vorlaufenden Entschlossenheit*). Heroes did not vanish despite the being of past, and are possibilities to make them historical and alive in the new era through "*Dasein*'s soul"[107] to make its resoluteness. Thus, world-history (*Weltgeschichte*) is to be caught up in *Dasein*'s existential happening and puts the world-history into *Dasein*'s history. *Dasein* in its *Augenblick* chooses its hero to make its resoluteness circumstantially fit to what *Dasein* is positioned.[108] Dreyfus in *Being-in-the-World* speaks of the possibility that *Dasein* may choose its hero, but it "might be more fitting to say that *Dasein*'s hero chooses *Dasein*."[109] What he says is that *Dasein* has its comportment to let heroes openly and inclusively come to *Dasein*'s mood and repeat[110] what heroes have historically displayed, which is called "historicality (*die Geschichtlichkeit*)" or "historicity." Macquarrie and Robinson translate *die Geschichtlichkeit* as historicality; Stambaugh as historicity.

Historicality (*die Geschichtlichkeit*) is like the new interpretation of what has already been for the here-being and living being, for interpretation is considered an attempt to fit what is distant and alien to the interpreter. Historicality is understood as a re-possessive discovery that what has occurred in the past and what has been alien should not be excluded and did not come to an end but is open, repetitive, renewable, and resourceful to revision and has the effect of bringing the past alive in the present for *Dasein*'s resolute transaction. As commonly understood about time under the view of the physical or clock time, the past seems to be past and forgotten and is considered something inauthentic that *Dasein*'s own or authentic resoluteness does not involve. However, the past is neither nothing nor dead as the impossibility of existence but effective and revivable. For instance, someone who is struggling with depression because of abuses in their childhood might not be aware that these experiences are the cause of his/her depression until being revealed by psychoanalysis or counselling; they are part of his/her history and are constitutive of his/her present state of being. The psychoanalyst helps the client bring the past fault to the present and encourages him/her to have a new vision of its existence and resoluteness beyond the past. The psychoanalyst makes three stances unified into one moment. Heidegger elaborates that temporality manifests itself through the unity of its ecstatic dimensions, where *Dasein* temporalizes itself in the

---

106. SZ 385; BTM 437; BTS 352.
107. Heidegger, *Kant and the Problem of Metaphysics*, 111.
108. SZ 371; BTM 422; BTS 339.
109. Dreyfus, *Being-in-the-World*, 330.
110. SZ 385; BTM 437; BTS 352.

unity of future, past, and present. Authentic historicality is the foundation for uniting these three temporal dimensions, grounded in temporality as the existential meaning of the being of care.[111] What *Dasein* makes its resoluteness by means of repeating the past and anticipating its future in the moment of insight (*Augenblick*), which unifies the past, the present, and the future, is not symmetrical to what the past has handed over to *Dasein*, but renews the past and unifies three stances into one moment for the care of *Dasein*.

So far, we have discussed death as the impossibility of the existence that always rests on *Dasein* and the anticipation of the impossibility of *Dasein*'s existence called *Angst* or despair, which makes *Dasein* see the world where it exists uncanny and benumbed, and thereby takes *Dasein* back from its worldly possibilities. While *Dasein* in *Angst* makes everything of the world view nothingness or emptiness, emptiness liberates *Dasein*, which lies in "*being-ahead-of-itself*,"[112] from the world to which it is attached, and thereby directs it to project the possibility of its new existence. However, the possibility that Heidegger argues is not infinite, but finite due to time as temporality engaged in *Dasein*'s existence as no-longer or not-eternal existence. Hence, *Dasein*'s death is thought of not only as the impossibility of existence, but also its existence within temporality, not in eternity, in disparity to God whose attribute is said as eternity that implies neither birth nor death.

However, *Dasein*'s finitude of existence and temporal existence that Heidegger claims is challenged by Fa-tsang whose essential views are "emptiness" and "Buddhahood." While Fa-tsang's emptiness encourages *chung-seng* or the sentient being to attain Buddhahood by means of emptiness, Buddhahood is not juxtaposed to the sentient being, but rather they relate, cooperate with, and depend on each other, in contrast to the severance between God and *Dasein*. Buddhahood is not transcendent being like God but an interactive and relative with *chung-seng*. In addition, *Dasein*'s finite existence, no-longer existence, and emptiness that Heidegger asserts are questioned by Kierkegaard whose ideas are that *Dasein*'s anticipation on the impossibility of its existence does not cause *Dasein* to have its resoluteness toward the projection of its new possible existence, but to flee to God who saves *Dasein* from its despair and to have a relatedness with God. Kierkegaard transcends *Dasein*'s impossibility of existence and temporality of existence through engaging with and depending on God[113] which we will discuss in the next chapter.

111. *SZ* 396–97; *BTM* 448; *BTS* 362.
112. *SZ* 337; *BTM* 386; *BTS* 310.
113. Humbert, "Freedom and Time," iii.

B. FA-TSANG'S EMPTINESS AND BUDDHAHOOD

Michael Zimmerman, in the article "Heidegger, Buddhism, and Deep Ecology," contends that Heidegger has an interest in Buddhism and Taoism, saying, "Heidegger spent most of the summer in 1946 working with a Chinese student, Paul Shih-yi Hsiao, translating portions of the Tao Te Ching [and studying Buddhism]."[114] Both Buddhism and Taoism in which Heidegger has an interest is synthetically revealed in Hua-yen Buddhism. While Hua-yen Buddhism is based on the Avatamsaka sutra (flower garland scripture) known in Chinese as the *Hua-yen Ching* transferred from India in which Buddhism is founded by Sakyamuni or the Buddha, it was developed and established by hermeneutically interpreting the sutra in reference to Taoism.[115] The concept *li*[116] of the non-obstruction of *li* (principle) and phenomena or *shih* in Chinese (*artha* in Sanskrit) called "*li-shih wu-ai*," which is an essential idea of Hua-yen Buddhism advocated by Fa-tsang, is founded on Taoism. Since *li* and *shih* are not Chinese translations of Sanskrit Buddhist terms, both are to be understood in reference to a history of the Chinese philosophy.[117] Hua-yen Buddhism is considered a synthetic, totalistic Buddhism that involves the Abhidharma, Madhyamika, Yogacara schools, Taoism, and Chinese tradition. "Hua-yen, as the inheritor of Madhyamika, Yogacara, and tathagatagarbha traditions, quite naturally received all necessary doctrinal elements from them."[118] Hua-yen Buddhism is said to be founded by Tu-shun (557–640), formulated by Chih-yen (602–668), systematized by Fa-tsang (643–712), and elucidated by Ch'eng-kuan (737–838) and Tsung-mi (780–841).[119] Hua-yen Buddhism is concerned with the issue how the sentient being called "*chung-sheng*" exists in a family, school (*tsung*), society, and the world, and how *k'ung* or *sunyata* (emptiness), which is regarded as the *tao* or way of *chung-sheng*, works in and by the being to attain Buddahood; the *tao* as the principle of Buddhahood is identified with *k'ung* or emptiness.

---

114. Zimmerman, "Heidegger, Buddhism, and Deep Ecology," 250.

115. Oh, "Study of Chinese Hua-Yen Buddhism," 116. See also Williams, *Mahayana Buddhism*, 130–31.

116. Chinese transliteration will follow the Wade Giles romanization system.

117. Wright, "Emptiness and Paradox," 114.

118. Oh, "Study of Chinese Hua-Yen Buddhism," 222.

119. Oh, "Study of Chinese Hua-Yen Buddhism," iv.

1. *Chung-Seng* (the Sentient Being) with Others in the Community

As *the Dasein* that Heidegger examines is thrown, it is cast into the world where other *Daseins* exist. *Dasein's a priori* condition of existence is *Dasein's* being with others in the world, i.e., *Dasein*-being-with-others-in-the-world,[120] in contrast to the traditional subject-object/observer-observed duality of metaphysics. Nevertheless, *Dasein* itself is thrown as itself in the world, and thereby unavoidably enters it into "the existential mode of '*not-being-at-home*,'"[121] called uncanniness (*die Unheimlichkeit*), unsettledness, uneasiness, and non-familiarity in which *Dasein* collapses. Heidegger states that *Dasein* is authentically itself in the primordial individualization of reticent resoluteness and thereby expects it *Angst* of itself.[122] Since *Dasein* itself is the fundamental entity that Heidegger explores in his philosophy, others are to be conditions and provision for the sake of *Dasein's* constancy of existence. However, *chung-seng* (the sentient being) or a human being that Fa-tsang refers to becomes nothing without being surrounded by other sentient beings, relating and depending on each other in the world.

As Heidegger describes *Dasein* as "the being with others" or *Mitsein* besides *Dasein* itself, he puts *Mitsein* on the term "*Dasein*-with-others-in-the-world." The way in which Heidegger hyphenates *Mitsein* implies *Dasein* does not exist by itself, but is connected to something else like a net of jewels that someone holds in one's hand. Hua-yen of Hua-yen Buddhism literally means "wreath"[123] or "circlet," which indicates sentient beings do not exist in themselves, but circularly are connected to, coexist with, and depend on others like several beads threaded together on a string. Fa-tsang depicts Hua-yen or wreath by using "*wu-ai*" or the non-obstruction, which is the essential view of Fa-tsang's Hua-yen Buddhism. The Hua-yen or circlet to which Fa-tsang refers is revealed in two ways. The first is that one *dharma* or phenomenon is interconnected with other *dharmas* in the universe. The second circlet is that the sentient being (*chung-seng*) is related and depends on others in the community of family, sangha, and society.

One *dharma* or phenomenon interconnected with other phenomena in the universe is based on the idea that Buddha-nature pervades the universe and participates in all the sentient beings and phenomena; interestingly, Plotinus (204–270) refers to the One or the Sun which emanates light

---

120. *SZ* 53; *BTM* 78; *BTS* 49.
121. *SZ* 189; *BTM* 233; *BTS* 176.
122. *SZ* 322; *BTM* 369; *BTS* 297.
123. Fung, *History of Chinese Philosophy*, 340.

indiscriminately to the world.[124] Thus, one *dharma* reflects all others in the universe, which is disclosed in the image of Indra's net. As Fa-tsang was invited to preach Hua-yen Buddhism in particular and Buddhism in general by Tang's empress Wu (624–705), he explained the mystery of Indra's jewel net,[125] which is a metaphor of Mahayana Buddhism. Far away in the heavenly realm, there is a vast net that stretches infinitely in all directions in the universe. In each eye of the net is a single brilliant, perfect jewel, and the net itself is infinite in dimension, the jewels are infinite. Each jewel reflects every other jewel, infinite in number, and each of the reflected images of the jewels bears the image of all the other jewels, so that there is an infinite reflecting—infinity to infinity. Whatever affects one jewel affects them all. "The Hua-yen school has been fond of this image [which is originated from Hinduism], mentioned many times in its literature, because it symbolizes a cosmos in which there is an infinitely repeated interrelationship among all the members of the cosmos."[126] For that reason, Buddhism is considered pantheism despite the insufficient definition of it. "Everything is seen, in this [Indra net], as infinitely related to other things. Apart from this relatedness, nothing has an existence of its own. Every *dharma* finds its existence only in its relationship to others."[127] The Indra net that Fa-tsang mentioned is a cosmological relationship of phenomena in the universe.

Fa-tsang uses the analogy of the ten coins on a string like the beads of a rosary in order to interpret the way of the sentient being (*chung-seng*), who is related to and depends on others in the community of family, sangha, and society, for Fa-tsang's perspective on being and time is circular, not lineal. Fa-tsang in *Hua-yen Wu Chiao Chang* says:

> The ten [coins] are the ten within the one [on a string]. Why? Because if one coin does not exist, ten coins would not be formed. Because one has complete power, it includes the ten. However, [the ten coins] are ten, not one. The remaining nine are also like this; each one [of the remaining nine coins] possesses ten. You can understand this in the same way [as the original coin and its inclusion of ten]. [On the other hand], there are also ten coins. Ten coins include one. Why? If there were no ten, one would not be formed. Because one is completely without power, it is included in the ten.[128]

124. Russell, *History of Western Philosophy*, 287–97.

125. Chang, *Buddhist Teaching of Totality*, 22–23.

126. Cook, "Jewel Net of Indra," 214.

127. Oh, "Study of Chinese Hua-Yen Buddhism," 217.

128. Fa-tsang, "*Hua-yen i ch'eng i fen ch'i chang*," known by the briefer title "*Hua-yen Wu Chiao Chang*," hereafter referred to as *HYWCC*, in Takakusu and Watanabe, *Taisho*

Imagine that there are ten coins which are in a loop. One can call the ten coins 1, 2, and so on. In the loop of ten coins, each coin has its value of existence. If one coin is missing in the set of ten coins, the loop would not exist, and then all of them would be meaningless. Each coin possesses its power and ability called "being (*yu*)." However, when one says that coin 1 possesses its power, it does not mean that it only has power without relating to the other nine coins in the loop. By saying that coin 1 possesses its power, it means that the other nine coins also have power and support coin 1. Insofar as coin 1 joins the other nine coins, mutually interacts with them, is supported by them, and connects it to them in the loop, it has power. Otherwise, a coin apart from the loop surrounded by many other coins is valueless and could be disposed. We can assume that a coin has the value of $1. But if the coin is donated and used for a social community with other donated coins, the collection of coins constitutes one fund and can be valued more highly.[129]

Yet, the value of mutual relatedness or interaction in an organic body like the loop does not correspond to the arithmetic addition: "1 + 9 = 10." Instead, the value of relatedness could imply "1 + 9 = 20," or "1 + 9 = 100," for the totality of the string of coins cannot be captured by analytic examination. Imagine a red apple on the table. The apple can be chemically analyzed into many elements such as vitamins, water, and minerals. Yet, one cannot say that each element is the apple and the amalgamation of the elements is the apple. In order to be called an apple, all elements must be organically related to other elements in the apple. Likewise, Fa-tsang's mutual connection and dependence or *hsiangju* on others implies that every individual as an element must exist in dynamic interaction with other individuals and depend on each other in an organic community. Otherwise, every individual outside of the organic community could be weak, ignored, and become nobody.[130] However, mutual connection and dependence are not a "mixture" of existences analyzed into many elements such as vitamins, water, and minerals, but an "interconnected synergy" joined by many others or manyness.[131] Fa-tsang's *hsiangju* is manifested in the community.

While each coin (1, 2 . . .) joins the other nine coins in the loop and mutually interacts with them in the community, each is identified with itself and exists in itself, as coin 1 is different from coin 2. Then, an issue is raised

---

Shinshu Daizokyo, 45:503b–c, hereafter referred to as *TD*. See Cook, "Fa-tsang's *Treatise on the Five Doctrines*," 476, hereafter referred to as *FD*.

129. The view of Fa-tsang's Hua-yen Buddhism that I discuss is based on the view that I revealed in my dissertation. See Hwang, "Process and Harmony."

130. Cook, "Jewel Net of Indra," 215.

131. Hwang, "Process and Harmony, 197–99.

by asking how a sentient being (*chung-seng*), who is identified with itself, connects, and depends on others without losing its identification, uniqueness, and independence in the community, and exists with other entities who are different from the sentient being itself. Fa-tsang brings in *k'ung* or emptiness to respond to the question. He focuses on how a sentient being turns (*yuan*) to depend on and relate to different entities through suspending its identity called *sunyata* or *k'ung* in the community. Fa-tsang refers to a sentient being's dependence and relatedness through *k'ung* (*sunyata*) or detachment divergent from emphasizing its substantiality. If *k'ung* is carried out by the sentient being (*chung-seng*), what and how could *chung-seng* be?

2. Dharmas and Sunyata (Emptiness) or K'ung

Kierkegaard's anxiety (*Angest*) and *Øiebliket* (moment), and Paul's emptiness or "kenosis (κένωσις)" and "an instant in the twinkling of an eye (*atomo en rhipe ophthalmou*, ἐν ἀτόμῳ ἐν ῥιπῇ ὀφθαλμοῦ)" are the source of Heidegger's *Angst* and *Augenblick* or the moment of insight. Early Buddhism's *dharmas* and *sunyata* (emptiness) related to the concept of *anatta* (the doctrine of none-self) are the source of phenomena (*shih*) and *k'ung* that Fa-tsang maintains in Hua-yen Buddhism. Death that Heidegger argues brings about *Angst* or the anticipation of death, and *Angst* directs *Dasein* to face nothingness (*die Nichtigkeit*) or groundlessness or emptiness, and helps it project its new possibility of existence. As *k'ung* that Fa-tsang discusses gives directions to the sentient being (*chung-seng*) to negate *chung-seng*'s self-substantiality, so the *k'ung* serves *chung-seng* to undergo Buddhahood manifested in "*li-shih-mu-ai*" and "*shih-shih-mu-ai*." While the *k'ung* implies the meaning of negation and annihilation of self-substantiality inherited from *sunyata* of Indian Theravadan Buddhism (the small vehicle), *sunyata* is developed into *k'ung* of Hua-yen Buddhism, and *k'ung* directs *chung-seng* to see its *mu-ai* or non-obstruction of interrelatedness and interpenetration with other *dharmas* rather than emphasizing the negation of selfhood. Nothingness (*die Nichtigkeit*) or emptiness that *Dasein* encounters impels it to project its future possibility of existence despite its limited possibility. In contrast, *k'ung* (*sunyata*) that Fa-tsang claims, which is considered a meditative state of the sentient being or an ontological feature of *chung-seng*'s reality, serves it to gain the enlightenment manifested in non-prejudicious interrelatedness with and interdependence on others in the universe. Fa-tsang's *k'ung* (*sunyata*) is similar to Husserl's epoché, which is a suspension of judgment to free from the influence of prejudices in phenomenological inquiry and clarification.

DEATH AND EMPTINESS BY HEIDEGGER AND FA-TSANG 131

Dasein that Heidegger elaborates in *Being and Time* is constituted by *Dasein* itself and its death; *Dasein* itself is revealed and makes its resoluteness for the care of itself by means of its conscience. *Chung-seng* (the sentient being) that Fa-tsang examines in his writings consists of *dharmas* or phenomena and *sunyata* (emptiness) or *k'ung*; *chung-seng* itself is constituted by *dharmas* and determines itself based on the innate nature or mind (*hsin*) that *chung-seng* bears. While the term *dharma* or *fa* is generally described as an element and a regulator or norm of the universe, Fa-tsang defines *fa* in three ways: that which upholds, keeps, or maintains *chung-seng* itself, that which regulates the universe, and that which constitutes the world.[132] The mind or *hsin* is considered a capacity or faculty like Heidegger's conscience to let *chung-seng* make its determination prior to speculative thought.[133]

Dharmas, according to the teaching of Abhidharma Buddhism, which is considered a form of religious praxis and mode of interpreting the teaching of the Buddha after his death in the early centuries, are known or cognized as "ultimate realities [constituents of reality] in the sense that they cannot be reduced further to other constituents"[134] in terms of the reality of entities. The Abhidharma school is raised by a question, "Do things or entities really exist?"[135] When the Abhidharma school contends that "everything is," it means that all elements called *dharmas* exist. In other words, "everything exists" means that everything is composed of existing elements or *dharmas*. *Dharmas* are similar to actual entities that Alfred North Whitehead in *Process and Reality*[136] discusses. According to Whitehead, the actual entities, which the world consists of and which are considered a vast number of microcosmic entities, are conceived as constituents that constitute *chung-seng*.

As *Dasein* is constituted by death and conscience, so *chung-seng* or the sentient being consisted of *dharmas* or phenomena is formed by *sunyata* (emptiness) and mind (*hsin*). *Chung-seng* is shaped by *sunyata* under the thesis that all things in the phenomenal world are empty.[137] Just as death that constitutes *Dasein* conditions and bounds the possibility of *Dasein's* existence and expansion, so *sunyata* that constitutes *chung-seng* conditions *chung-seng's* existence to be groundless, but instead impels it to relate to

---

132. See *TD* 44:63b; Liu, "Teaching of Fa-tsang," 392; de Bary, *Buddhist Tradition in India, China, and Japan*, 6; Hwang, "Process and Harmony," 116.

133. *TD* 32:576a; Hakeda, *Awakening of Faith*, 32–33; Gregory, *Tsung-mi and the Sinification of Buddhism*, 139–40.

134. Williams, *Mahayana Buddhism*, 15.

135. Stcherbatsky, *Central Conception of Buddhism*, 61; Conze, *Buddhist Thought in India*, 1–61.

136. Whitehead, *Process and Reality*.

137. Chang, *Buddhist Teaching of Totality*, 64, 107.

others in the world. The term *sunyata* is literally composed by two words, "*sunya*," or "void or empty," and a participle suffix, *ta*, as 'ness.' *Sunyata* is translated as "voidness or emptiness"; *sunya* was originally derived from the root *svi*, "to swell," so that *sunya* implies "swollen."[138] A *Sanskrit-Chinese Buddhism*[139] describes *sunyata* as illusoriness, dream, bubble, and shadow, which implies unreality and groundlessness. What *dharmas* in the phenomenal world are constituted by *sunyata* means that *dharmas* are empty, unfounded, impermanent, and non-self-sufficient.

As soon as a human being comes to life, he or she is at once old enough to die;[140] as soon as *Dasein* exists in the world, it is in such a way that its existence would be non-existence at any time. Death that *Dasein* necessarily faces causes *Dasein* to anticipate its own death called *Angst*. *Angst* is a mood of uncanniness ("*Angst ist einem unheimlich*"), unsettledness, uneasiness, and non-familiarity in which *Dasein* collapses and becomes void. However, *Angst* leads *Dasein* to emptiness that serves to free it from attachment to the world, that is, detachment or emptiness. As *chung-seng* is born in the world, its being will soon be non-being or empty. *Chung-seng* in its life unavoidably experiences sorrow, suffering, and affliction, which is called *duḥkha* in Sanskrit or *dukkha* in Pali, as well as happiness, joy, and pleasure. *Duḥkha* is translated as "being painful, disagreeable, unpleasant, uneasy, unsatisfactory, and sorrowful."[141] *Duḥkha* is the mood of anxiety, distress, frustration, unease, un-satisfactoriness similar to the mood of uncanniness or uneasiness of *Dasein* when *chung-seng* does not have what it wants but it has what it doesn't want. As *chung-seng* is endowed in the world, *duḥkha* is unavoidable to *chung-seng*, for it is ontologically constituted by *duḥkha* based on death or impermanence of existence that it inescapably confronts. Nevertheless, *seng-chung* has desire, craving of impermanent phenomena called "attachment," that leads to worldly bondage, for it is in ignorance (*wu-ming*) that gives rise to its attachment to or holding onto that which is inherently impermanent and ungraspable.[142] Fa-tsang claims that all forms of *dharmas* are impermanent and any form of attachment to them leads to *duḥkha*[143] but emptiness or detachment of *dharmas* is *chung-seng*'s truthful path to the enlightenment (*ju*) or "the attainment of Buddhahood

---

138. Chang, *Buddhist Teaching of Totality*, 60.
139. Eitel, *Sanskrit-Chinese Buddhism*, 164.
140. SZ 245; BTM 289; BTS 228.
141. Apte, *Practical Sanskrit-English Dictionary*, 819.
142. Wright, "Emptiness and Paradox," 51.
143. Wright, "Emptiness and Paradox," 52.

(*ch'eng-fo*),"¹⁴⁴ which is considered soteriological salvation free from *chung-seng*'s ignorance (*wu-ming*) that it is constituted by *duḥkha*. The attainment of Buddhahood is carried out by making the impermanence of all existences empty and internalizing it in the mind (*hsin*) that *chung-seng* bears.

The path to the enlightenment (*ch'eng-fo*) that Fa-tsang claims brings about two questions: what teaching (*chiao*) helps *chung-seng* access the enlightenment (*ch'eng-fo*) and what *ch'eng-fo* looks like. The moment of insight or *Augenblick* that Heidegger asserts in *Being and Time* involves that suddenly (*exaiphns*, ἐξαίφνης)¹⁴⁵ something comes to enlighten *Dasein*. However, *Dasein*'s moment of insight does not signify only the present or single moment but extends to going back to the past. Jacques Derrida claims that every present or the point of now is already comprised of a trace of previous suppliers; the present is constituted, produced, and derived from a source of the past despite nonpresence of the past.¹⁴⁶ The enlightenment (*ch'eng-fo*) to which Fa-tsang refers is considered the enlightenment in an instant moment advocated by the sudden teaching (*tunchiao*) similar to *Augenblick*. Fa-tsang says that "sudden" means that enlightenment is revealed suddenly, not gradually.¹⁴⁷ He also says, "'Sudden doctrine' means that the teaching through words is suddenly stopped, the nature of ultimate principle is suddenly revealed, comprehension and practice are suddenly perfected."¹⁴⁸ However, the enlightenment in a suddenness does not mean simply the present, single moment, but extends to going back to the enlightenment handed down from the gradual teaching or school (*chienchiao*) of the past. People cannot fully grasp the enlightenment in the suddenness unless they understand how the earlier teaching, namely, the gradual teaching, turns the enlightenment over the sudden school with which Fa-tsang and other Hua-yen Buddhists engaged.

While Fa-tsang is influenced by the sudden teaching to systematize Hua-yen Buddhism, he did not symmetrically repeat what is handed down from the sudden teaching. Fa-tsang introduces three ways of the practice (*hsing*) or teaching (*chiao*) to access Buddhahood: the gradual teaching (*chienchiao*), the sudden teaching (*tunchiao*), and the totalistic or comprehensive teaching (*yŭanchiao*).¹⁴⁹ Hua-yen teaching to which Fa-tsang

144. Gregory, *Tsung-mi and the Sinification of Buddhism*, 202.
145. *GEL* s.v. "ἐξαίφνης."
146. Allison, "Translator's Introduction," xxxvii.
147. *HYWCC* 481b; *FD* 175.
148. *HYWCC* 481b; *FD* 174–75.
149. *Yŭanchiao* (Hua-yen Buddhism) is translated as the perfect teaching. However, I translate *yŭanchiao* as the totalistic or comprehensive teaching, for the term *perfect* implies the faultless. Fa-tsang's *yŭanchiao* entails synthetic, totalistic, and interactive

refers assumes that the two different teachings are unified into one teaching (Hua-yen teaching) or *yŭanchiao*. He renews the past through unifying the gradual and sudden stances into one Hua-yen stance. The term *yŭan* is derived from "*yŭan-man*, i.e., *paripurna*"[150] (in Sanskrit), which means integrity, totality (*chuan*), or completeness.[151] Fa-tsang's Hua-yen's teaching is not simply the assemblage of two different teachings, the gradual and sudden. Rather, the totalistic teaching is a wholistic teaching beyond the simple mixture of the gradual and sudden teachings. Fa-tsang develops a creative and holistic teaching which subsumes both gradual and sudden teachings through proposing the view of dynamic relatedness as manifested in his doctrine of "mutual nonobstruction (*wuai*)," and "interpenetration (*hsiangju*),"[152] which makes antithetical teachings to be constructive to each other in a hermeneutically appropriate fashion.

3. Emptiness and Buddahood by Two Different Teachings

a) The Gradual Teaching

What makes the gradual and sudden teachings discriminative is Buddhanature (*fo-hsing*).[153] While both teachings aim at "the attainment of Buddhahood (*ch'eng-fo*),"[154] they disagree on the way to the attainment of Buddhahood. Etymologically, "Buddha" (*fo*) means the person who lived in India about 2,500 years ago and has awakened.[155] What Fa-tsang raises as a question is whether Buddhanature is existent only in a particular figure such as Gautama Buddha or the Buddha Sakyamuni ("sage of the Sakya tribe") or not. While the gradual teaching limits Buddhanature to a particular being, the sudden teaching that Fa-tsang describes considers the pervasion (*man*) of Buddhanature throughout the universe. The pervasion of Buddha-nature is similar to the universal salvation that Karl Rahner in *On the Theology of Death* claims and we will discuss at the last chapter of this book. Fa-tsang says:

---

teaching that includes both the gradual and sudden teachings rather than the flawless teaching.

150. Gimello, "Chih-yen," 380.

151. Hwang, "Process and Harmony," 157.

152. Hwang, "Process and Harmony," 157–58.

153. *HYWCC* 488a.

154. Gregory, *Tsung-mi and the Sinification of Buddhism*, 202.

155. See Ch'eng-kuan, "*Hua-yen fa-chieh hsuan-ching*," TD 45:672b; Reynolds and Hallisey, "Buddha"; Soothill and Hodous, *Dictionary of Chinese Buddhist Terms*, 225.

> Buddhanature is existent only in the Buddha, according to the small vehicle. [Buddhanature] is possessed by all beings except grass and trees, according to the later school [the Yogacara school]. According to the earlier school . . . some have it and others do not [that is, it depends on the beings' attitude]. . . . According to the sudden school, we cannot say that one has it or lacks it, because it is beyond characteristics.[156]

The distinction between the gradual teaching that limits Buddhanature to a particular being and the sudden teaching that emphasizes the pervasion of Buddha-nature extends to realms of dissimilarity between the holy (*sheng*) and the profane (*su*). While the gradual teaching stresses two discriminative realms, namely, the realm of the holy and the profane, the sudden teaching avoids two discrepant realms, but underscores mutual interconnection between two realms like the theory of interaction between *yin* and *yang* of Chinese cosmology. The realm of the holy is that-world where worldly bonds are released or enlightened (*chiai-t'o*); the realm of the profane is this-world where worldly bonds are unenlightened.[157] The holy realm is also considered pure (*ching*), while the profane realm is considered impure (*jan*).[158] The goal of the gradual teaching is to shun the profane, the impure and to terminate worldly-bonds, but to achieve the holy state (*nirvana*).

While the gradual teaching emphasizes that-world, which worldly-bonds are liberated from this-world, which profane and impure matters are dominated, this-world is not the world that *chung-seng* could get rid of and consider it exclusively meaningless. Rather, the profane or this-world realm is the starting point, and the holy or that-world realm is the ending point. This-world is a preparatory stage prior to that-world as a fruitful stage in order to attain Buddhahood. The preparatory stage is regarded as the efficient conditions for aiming and attaining at Buddhahood.[159] Fa-tsang describes the preparatory and fruitful stages by illustrating the growth of an amala tree, which is expressed in the Yogacara sutra.[160] The seed of the tree is first planted in the ground as a tiny (*wei*) existence. This tiny existence puts forth its bud and grows big (*chu*). Finally it bears its fruits. What Fa-tsang points

---

156. *HYWCC* 488a.

157. Fa-tsang, "Hua-yen yu-hsin fa-chieh chi," *TD* 45:644a, hereafter referred to as *HYFC*. For a brief survey concerning two distinctive realms, the realm of the holy or that-world and the realm of the profane or this-world, see Gimello, "Chih-yen," 214–56.

158. *HYWCC* 485b, 495c.

159. Hwang, "Process and Harmony," 164.

160. *HYWCC* 481b; *FD* 174. "'Gradual' as the amala-fruit ripens gradually not suddenly."

out in this analogy of the growth of a tree is that the growth of the tree occurs in sequential succession from a tiny seed to a large fruit-bearing tree. The process of growth occurs gradually, not suddenly. Second, the succession of the growth includes the relation of cause and effect: cause as the tiny seed is antecedently planted in the ground, and the tree bears its fruit as effect. Fa-tsang says, "[Because] the stages are performed in sequence, cause and effect are in succession, and because one proceeds from the tiny to the big, they are called 'gradual.'"[161]

The access to Buddahood demands at least two ways of deeds in the gradual teaching: the learning (*hsueh*) of doctrines and meditation (*kuan*) on the attainment to Buddahood. According to the gradual teaching, this-world realm is tainted by defilements and trapped in ignorance. The defilements (*klesa* in Sanskrit) consist of desire, detestation, pride, doubt, biased views, and perverted views.[162] These defilements are the obstacles to prevent *chung-seng* from attaining Buddahood. The learning of doctrines serves *chung-seng* to eliminate the obstacles or defilements in consciousness.

The meditation (*kuan*) on the attainment of Buddahood seeks to achieve a vision of Buddahood through meditative insight.[163] This vision leads to liberation from cyclical, worldly bondage. To meditate on Buddahood means to existentialize and internalize the impermanence of all existences so that the meditator becomes free from attachment to existence.[164] The character, *kuan*, "meditation," allows one to see external things in ordinary usage. Yet, the Buddhist term *kuan* means internally to have an insight into the nature or the ultimate essence of things. *Kuan* means to contemplate, concentrate on, and realize the ultimate truth or reality (*ch'ing ching*) in *chung-seng*'s mind (*hsin*), which is free from self-attachment and the release from the endless, worldly bondage.[165] Since the goal of the gradual teaching is to avoid the profane, impure, or worldly bonds and to achieve the holy state or *nirvana*, it is to be regarded as a negative way of access—as the cessation of suffering and the absence of delusion or defilements. Yet, the ideal goal is pictured in a positive way by stressing the

---

161. *HYWCC* 481b; *FD* 174.

162. *HYWCC* 492b, 495c–496a.

163. While these two processes, which include (a) learning of doctrines, which leads to the elimination of defilements, and (b) meditation on ultimate reality, are said to develop gradually, Fa-tsang does not explicitly describe which way is prior to the other between the learning of doctrines and meditation.

164. Schumacher and Woerner, *Encyclopedia of Eastern Philosophy and Religion*, s.v. "meditation."

165. Lai, "Meaning of 'Mind-Only' (*Wei-hsin*)," 66–72.

qualities of emancipation, bliss, and peace beyond the conventional world. Fa-tsang describes the attainment of *nirvana* in the following way:

> Defilements do not happen [*in nirvana*]. . . . The mind is tranquil like the sea. Erroneous thoughts are all extinguished, and there is no compulsion. One gets out of bondage and is free from obstacles, and forever cuts off the source of suffering. This is called entry into *nirvana*.[166]

The gradual teaching faces at least two questions—what kinds of, and how many, sentient beings achieve Buddhahood, which brings about the issue of universal salvation. The second question is what the attainment of Buddhahood transcendent over the thisworld realm involves.[167] As has been shown, the gradual teaching, according to Fa-tsang, limits Buddha-nature (which is considered a potentiality for Buddhahood) to a particular being. The attainment of Buddhahood is earned by some limited sentient beings but not by all beings. Since the attainment of Buddhahood, namely, soteriological salvation, is emphasized as being limited to some sentient beings, the gradual teaching is considered the small vehicle (Theravada Buddhism) in contrast to the great vehicle (Mahayana Buddhism).

That limited sentient beings attain Buddhahood according to the gradual teaching is questioned by what kinds of sentient beings are allowed to attain Buddhahood and which sentient beings are excluded from this attainment. The question could be extended by asking why particular sentient beings are included or excluded from the attainment of Buddhahood. According to Fa-tsang, the gradual teaching or the small vehicle does not give clear answers to these questions. The sudden teaching, according to Fa-tsang, considers the pervasion (*man*) of Buddhanature throughout the universe. The sudden teaching maintains that even the *icchantinka* (the one who has no desire for Buddhahood and who is devoid of the root of goodness) has Buddha-nature.[168]

As the gradual teaching emphasizes distinction (*ch'apieh*) and separation between the realm of Buddhahood (thatworld) and the profane

---

166. Fa-tsang, "*Chin shih-tzu chang*," TD 45:666, hereafter referred to as *CSTC*. The translation is based on Chan, *Source Book in Chinese Philosophy*, 413–14; Fung, *History of Chinese Philosophy*, 358.

167. Hwang, "Process and Harmony," 168.

168. The term "*icchantika* . . . is meaning 'desire,' 'to wish' and 'to long for.' This explains the variant Chinese renderings of the term '*icchantika*' as 'a being of many desires' (*to-yu*),' 'a being cherishing desires' (*lo-yu*) and 'a being full of greed.' . . . [The term is] . . . associated with people [who are described] . . . as 'devoid of good roots' and as 'the most wicked being'" (Liu, "Problem of the *Icchantika*," 58). See also Liu, "Doctrine of the Buddha-Nature."

(thisworld), thatworld is the transcendent world, blissful and free from suffering (*k'u*) and thisworld is dominated by defilements, delusions, and worldly bonds. Yet, the two realms are not absolutely alienated from each other, for this-world is regarded as the preparatory or methodological realm prior to the fruitful realm and thereby that-world cannot exist without thisworld. The attainment of thatworld is caused by the learning of doctrines and meditation by practitioners who live in thisworld, not in thatworld. If this is the case, thatworld is not a transcendent world. Instead, thatworld is connected with thisworld. The sudden teaching even considers mutual interconnection instead of exclusive dichotomous worlds. Thus, the sudden teaching points out that the thatworld advocated by the gradual teaching is a speculative postulation; apart from thisworld, which is filled with suffering and defilements, the gradual teaching postulates a thatworld emancipated from thisworld. The sudden teaching eliminates the opposition between *nirvana* and *samsara*, denying that *nirvana* is an emancipation from the realm of *samsara* dominated by suffering and delusion.

b) The Sudden Teaching

As the sudden teaching averts the distinction between thatworld (*nirvana*) and thisworld (*samsara*), it seeks a nonobstructive, inclusive single realm of existence into which all things are fused and wherein all discriminations cease. Such a unitary and ultimate realm of existence is the total (*ch'uan*) interfused existence.[169] Fa-tsang explains that no dual existences divisible into the pure and the impure, and *nirvana* or *samsara* are teachable, because all pure and impure characteristics are no longer in reality divisible into two things.[170]

The sudden teaching affirms that Buddhanature exists embryonically within all sentient beings. That Buddha-nature exists in all sentient beings implies that Buddha-nature is already present as innate nature in them.[171] Buddhanature, in the sudden teaching, is considered as preveniently and universally given to the world. Since Buddhanature already exists in all sentient beings, the focus in the sudden teaching is not on difficult practices including many stages to attain Buddhahood. Instead, the sudden teaching emphasizes direct meditation on enlightenment or Buddhahood.

---

169. *HYWCC* 501c.

170. *HYWCC* 485b; *FD* 223; Gregory, *Tsung-mi and the Sinification of Buddhism*, 139.

171. *HYWCC* 495b–486a.

The sudden teaching neither accentuates the learning of doctrines[172] nor requires the eradication of defilements.

Instead, the sudden teaching emphasizes direct meditation on Buddhahood since Buddhahood is already immanent in the world. The teaching through meditation is considered mindonly (*wei-hsin*) meditation.[173] *Hsin* (mind) has two aspects. The first aspect is that *hsin* pervades the universe. The second aspect is all sentient beings have *hsin*. Fa-tsang says, "Whatever there is in the world is only the pervasion of one mind. Outside of mind there is not a single thing that can be supposed";[174] "all things or existences arose from mind."[175] Mind is not believed to be possessed by some limited people such as Arhats, who have gained insight into the true nature of existence, Pratyeka-buddha, who independently achieves liberation, and the Buddha, but all sentient beings.

Hsin (mind) is considered a capacity or potentiality to achieve Buddhahood in the sudden teaching.[176] Mind is considered ultimate and universal in its scope and is the ultimate source of all existences.[177] Mind (*hsin*) as a capacity or potentiality is prior to speculative thought to sentient beings. The mind is distinguished from consciousness (*shih*)—the intellectual and cognitive action called "thought" or speculative thinking for grasping external objects. Thought, the knowledge of external things,

---

172. Chih-yen, "*Hua-yen ching nei chang men teng tsa k'ung mu chang*," TD 45:586a. See also TD 15:36c; 16:509c. "If someone hears of the true nature of all things and diligently practices accordingly, then he will not advance stage-by-stage, and, if he does not advance stage by stage, then he will not abide in either *samsara* or *nirvana*. Since there are no [stages] that exist, how could there be a sequence [of stages]?" (Gregory, *Tsung-mi and the Sinification of Buddhism*, 141).

173. Many Chinese scholars, such as W. Lai, distinguish mind-only meditation (*wei-hsin*) from consciousness-only meditation (*wei-shih*). The difference between the two meditations is expressed in the two different terms *hsin* and *shih*. *Hsin* is considered feeling or mind prior to intellectual or epistemological knowledge (*shih*). Lai maintains that mind-only meditation is characteristic of Chinese Buddhism and that consciousness-only meditation, which is especially emphasized in the Yogacara school, is typical of Indian Buddhism. To have a brief survey of the relation between mind-only and consciousness-only, see Lai, "Meaning of 'Mind-Only' (*Wei-hsin*)."

174. Fa-tsang, "*Hsiu hua-yen ao-chih wang-chin huan-yuan kuan*," TD 45:640a, hereafter referred to as HHWK. Whether mind exists in all things including inanimate beings or not is a controversial issue for Hua-yen Buddhists. Yet, that is not the issue for Hua-yen Buddhism, for Buddhahood like God's grace of Christianity is inherent in the world. "In several Sino-Japanese traditions not only sentient beings but also the vegetable and mineral kingdoms are said to possess [mind]" (Williams, *Mahayana Buddhism*, 112).

175. Fa-tsang, "*Ta-sheng ch'i-hsin lun i-chi*," TD 44:252b.

176. HYWCC 485b. See also Lai, "Meaning of 'Mind-Only' (*Wei-hsin*)."

177. Fung, *History of Chinese Philosophy*, 359.

is easily deluded.¹⁷⁸ Mind is regarded as something primordial or generic beyond thought in the sudden teaching. For instance, if a mother chances to see her baby fall into water, the mother, regardless of what might happen to her, immediately jumps into the water to save the baby. The mother's jump is not preceded by speculative thinking. The reason she jumps into water is that her love, or feeling of compassion, compels her to do so.

Since *hsin* is considered prior to speculative thinking, it is like feeling. Since the feeling is understood beyond expression of words, the sudden teaching avoids verbal expression. The practitioner of the sudden teaching believes that the verbal expression fails to have a directive awareness. The sudden teaching asserts that all forms of verbalization, description, and conceptualization are provisional and without reality. It further claims that reality transcends all words.¹⁷⁹ This assertation can be made because "what one expresses is itself a thing, which means that by so doing one remains in the state of being linked with things."¹⁸⁰ "To be without words, without speech, without indication . . . is entering the *Dharma* [ultimate truth] of nonduality."¹⁸¹ Thus,

> All explanations by words are provisional and without validity, for they are merely used in accordance with illusions and are incapable [of denoting Suchness]. The term Suchness likewise has no attributes [which can be verbally specified]. The term Suchness is, so to speak, the limit of verbalization wherein a word is used to put an end to words. . . . It should be understood that all things are incapable of being verbally explained or thought of; hence, the name Suchness.¹⁸²

In a sense, the sudden teaching "demands abandonment of conceptual or intellectual faculties in favor of some higher and noetic experience."¹⁸³ But the sudden teaching calls attention to practical action (*hsiu*), which cannot be depicted by words.

---

178. *TD* 32:576a; Hakeda, *Awakening of Faith*, 32–33; Gregory, *Tsung-mi and the Sinification of Buddhism*, 139–40.

179. *HYWCC* 481c; *FD* 176–77. See also *TD* 32:576a; Hakeda, *Awakening of Faith*, 32–33; Gregory, *Tsung-mi and the Sinification of Buddhism*, 139–40.

180. Fung, *History of Chinese Philosophy*, 393.

181. *TD* 14:551c, quoted from Gregory, *Tsung-mi and the Sinification of Buddhism*, 138.

182. Hakeda, *Awakening of Faith*, 33; Gregory, *Tsung-mi and the Sinification of Buddhism*, 140.

183. Gimello, "Chih-yen," 36.

Mind (*hsin*) as a practical faculty runs through both "quiescence" or "cessation" (*chih* in Chinese; *samatha* in Sanskrit) and "insight" or "contemplation." Quiescence or cessation is the silencing, or putting to rest, and realizing that "all things are devoid of any nature of their own and undergo neither production nor destruction."[184] Fa-tsang discusses quiescence, saying, "If you would practice, stay in a quiet place, sitting straight with proper attention; do not rely on the breath, do not rely on physical form, do not rely on space, do not rely on earth, water, fire, or air, do not rely on information, perception and [speculative] knowledge."[185] He also refers to contemplation, saying, "The contemplation is on true emptiness, returning objects to mind. This means that whatever there is in the world is only the creation of one mind; outside of mind there is not a single thing that can be understood. Therefore, it is called returning to mind."[186] The sudden teaching stresses one mind, which is filled with Buddhanature that pervades all things throughout the world. The practitioner becomes immersed in one totality (or mind) through the practice of both quiescence and meditation, which involves concentration. The sudden teaching emphasizes nostages, one realm, and one mind.[187]

While Fa-tsang considers the gradual and the sudden teaching equally significant to systematize Hua-yen Buddhism, he leans to the sudden teaching. He claims that the sudden teaching is superior to the gradual teaching.[188] He believes that the sudden teaching fundamentally serves as a preamble to his Huayen teaching. Yet, he is not fully satisfied with the sudden teaching and does not completely follow it. He raises at least two questions about the sudden teaching: how the sudden teaching is possible if it avoids all forms of verbalization and how individuation occurs if all things throughout the world are manifested by mind (*hsin*), which is equivalent to Buddhanature. Fa-tsang supposes that the sudden teaching overstates the totalistic view of reality, while the gradual teaching emphasizes the distinctive realms (the holy and the profane and that-world and this-world). Fa-tsang proposes an organic relationship between the holy and the profane and between the ultimate and the conventional. He also proposes a dynamic identification or interpenetration between the two realms. Fa-tsang's technical terms for such identification are "the derivative in the fundamental" and "the fundamental

---

184. Fung, *History of Chinese Philosophy*, 375.

185. *HHWK* 639c. I have adapted the translation of Cleary, *Entry into the Inconceivable*, 164.

186. *HHWK* 640a. I have adapted the translation of Cleary, *Entry into the Inconceivable*, 165.

187. *HYWCC* 490b–c; *FD* 284–91.

188. Gregory, *Tsung-mi and the Sinification of Buddhism*, 141.

through the derivative,"[189] or "one in all" and "all in one."[190] Another term for these views is mutual nonobstruction (*wuai*) and interpenetration (*hsiangju*). The essence of Fa-tsang's religious philosophy is, in a word, the infinite interrelationship between the holy and the profane or the primary and the secondary.[191]

4. Fa-tsang's *Wu-ai* (Non-obstruction) and *Hsiangju* (Interpenetration)

When Fa-tsang attempts to synthesize the preceding two teachings in his Huayen system, he does so in two ways. First, Fa-tsang replaces *dharmas* and *sunyata* driven from Indian Buddhism with phenomena (*shih*), *k'ung*, and principle (*li*) fit to Chinese Buddhism. Then, he illuminates his view of synthesis beyond antithetical aspects of teachings through the view of mutual nonobstruction (*wuai*) and interpenetration (*hsiangju*).

a) Mutual Non-Obstruction Between Phenomena (*shih*) and Principle (*li*)

The term *li* (principle) was not extant in the Indian tradition but is a new term introduced into Chinese Buddhism from Confucianism and Taoism. The term *shih* (phenomenal things) is derived from *artha* (phenomenal affairs) in Indian Buddhism. Phenomena (*shih*) developed from the term *dharma*. Fa-tsang reconstructed the view of *dharmas* and replaced the term with phenomena (*shih*) so that it would be suitable in the Chinese context. *Shih* is the term designating all phenomenal events in Chinese civil society, socio-political relationships, and Chinese families.[192] *Dharmas* (*fa*), on the other hand, are the subpersonal elements of the universe. Phenomena (*shih*) are considered actual or empirical events or things, as forms of activity arising from sentient beings (*chungsheng*) in society. Conversely, *dharmas* (*fa*) are considered neutral elements apart from concrete situations.[193] *Sunyata* or emptiness of *dharmas* is considered the norm to which all existing things belong.[194] *Sunyata* of Indian Buddhism is replaced by *k'ung* and principle or *li*,

189. *HYWCC* 482b.
190. *HYWCC* 503c.
191. *HYWCC* 498b; *FD* 394.
192. Williams, *Mahayana Buddhism*, 118.
193. *HYWCC* 481c.
194. Wright, "Emptiness and Paradox," 46.

which is rooted in Chinese Taoism and Confucianism.[195] While phenomena (*shih*) exist as forms, they are neither unprocessed nor substantial things, but empty and non-substantial beings, that is, *k'ung*, which means not only emptiness, but also mutual dependence and interaction instead of substantial and unchanging being. What Fa-tsang refers to *li*, *shih*, and *k'ung* is that while *li* and *shih* is exclusive from each other, both are mutually dependent, which is called *k'ung*,[196] like mutual interaction between *yin* and *yang*, which is called *Tao*. It is similar to the interaction between life and death in *Dasein*'s existence that Heidegger discusses in *Being and Time*.

When Fa-tsang refers to the mutual dependence between principle (*li*) and phenomena (*shih*), namely, *li-shih-mu-ai*, he uses the analogy of the Golden Lion statue. When one sees the statue of a golden lion, one can imagine that the statue was made by a skilled craftsman. The craftsman molded the gold. The gold metal and its skillful sculptor are the cause (*yin*) or seed (*chung*) of the golden lion, according to Fa-tsang. He explains that the gold and the sculptor are the primary and secondary causes, respectively, of the golden lion. The gold is the essential cause that enables the creation of the lion, while the artisan's work in shaping the gold serves as a contributing cause.[197] The gold metal is manifested through the shape of the lion which includes eyes, nose, and ears, and is not simply a lump of gold. There can be no golden lion statue without a lump of gold. On the other hand, the statue is no more than a shapeless lump unless it is manifested through its figure. "Gold only exists as having some form or another, in this case that of a lion. There is no gold without form which then takes on, as it were, some form or another."[198] Thus there must be a connection, that is, non-obstruction (*wu-ai*) between gold metal and its shape by the deeds of the artisan.

Paul Williams interprets Fa-tsang's analogy of the Golden Lion statue by explaining that the gold represents "li," which stands for principle or noumenon, and the lion represents "shih," which stands for phenomenon. He relates "li" to the Tao and Buddha-nature as the absolute principle.[199] The Buddha-nature is translated as *li* or the principle. This approach is understood by the interaction between Buddhism and Taoism that encourages sentient beings to live in harmony with nature.[200]

---

195. Oh, "Study of Chinese Hua-Yen Buddhism," 241, 250–52, 255.
196. Williams, *Mahayana Buddhism*, 131.
197. Fung, *History of Chinese Philosophy*, 342.
198. Williams, *Mahayana Buddhism*, 131.
199. Williams, *Mahayana Buddhism*, 130.
200. Williams, *Mahayana Buddhism*, 130–31, quoted in Lai, "Chinese Buddhist Causation Theories," 252–53.

The term *wuai* (mutual non-obstruction) that Fa-tsang refers to is a compound word composed of *wu* or "nothing" and *ai* or "hindrance/obstruction." "Mutual nonobstruction" (*wuai*) is equivalent to fusion, relatedness, or interaction.[201] Fa-tsang maintains that the view of mutual nonobstruction of principle and phenomenal things (*lishih muai*) does not simply indicate the fusion of principle and phenomena. Instead, the view of mutual nonobstruction of principle with phenomenal things is a dynamic relatedness between principle and phenomena. To illustrate a dynamic relatedness, Fa-tsang uses the analogy of water and waves to illustrate the relationship between noumenon (li) and phenomenon (shih).[202] Water symbolizes the mind, while waves represent human affairs. The ocean, with its water and waves, is dynamic and interactive, influenced by the wind.[203] Calm wind leads to a pleasant voyage, while stormy wind creates disturbance, symbolizing ignorance. To achieve tranquility, it is necessary to quell the stormy wind, which represents overcoming ignorance through quiescence and meditation. This process restores the dynamic interaction between principle and phenomena.[204]

Thus, mutual nonobstruction between principle and the phenomenal, namely, the dynamic interrelatedness or the participation of Buddha-nature-principle in phenomenal things-various worldly things is "not a matter of '*is*' but a matter of '*ought*.'"[205] Besides this view, Fa-tsang focuses on how sentient beings dynamically interact in society through the view of interpenetration (*hsiang-ju*). Fa-tsang's term for interpenetration is *shihshih wuai* or mutual nonobstruction of phenomena. The view of the mutual nonobstruction of phenomena focuses on how sentient beings relate to each other. Specifically, it focuses on how sentient beings in actual society relate to each other and share their power. The technical term for such sharing of power is "interpenetration" (*hsiangju*).

b) Interpenetration (hsiangju)

In the compound *hsiangju*, the *hsiang* means "mutuality" and the *ju* means "to enter," or "to penetrate." Thus, *hsiangju* means "mutual penetration" or "interpenetration." When Fa-tsang discusses interpenetration, he points

---

201. HYWCC 485b, 489c, 491a, 498b, 507a.

202. Fa-tsang, "*Ta-sheng ch'i-hsin lun i-chi*," TD 44:260a, hereafter referred to as TSCL; CSTC 666a.

203. HYWCC 494b–c.

204. Gregory, *Tsung-mi and the Sinification of Buddhism*, 161.

205. TFM 395.

out two aspects. The first is the recognition of an individual sentient being's capability. In this aspect, every sentient being is individual (*i*) and powerful (*li*).[206] The second is how an individual's power or capability is actualized and performed. This second aspect assumes that an individual has to empty or suspend its own substantiality and cooperate with others for the existence of the organic body. Fa-tsang figuratively illustrates the metaphor of a house for two aspects. He poses a rhetorical question about the necessity of various components to make a house. He argues that if rafters alone were considered sufficient to make a house, they would not truly be rafters without tiles and other components, thereby emphasizing the interdependence of all parts in creating a complete structure.[207] The house is constituted of many elements, and each element stands for a phenomenon (*shih*) and the house stands for principle (*li*). Each component is not the same as others in the house, as rafters are different from tiles. Each element has to connect and depend on others for the existence of the house (*shih-shih-mu-ai* and *li-shih-mu-ai*).

As the above passage shows, the view of interpenetration is concerned with the fact that every individual is insignificant (i.e., weakly powerful or *shao-li*). A house is built with individual materials, and cannot be built unless many individual materials are provided. In terms of the significance of individual materials, Fa-tsang holds that every individual being is weakly powerful. Yet, an individual is not always weakly powerful. There is a time when an individual functions powerfully and creates something. There is also a time when it is only weakly powerful.[208] An individual is said to be alternatively powerful and weakly powerful. An individual is considered a nonfixed being but gravitates toward power or weakly power. Weakly power is considered potential power. Thus, although he/she has power, his/her power as an individual is considered potential energy.[209] Then, when, and how is an individual powerful or potentially powerful? The answer depends on how various individuals' powers are exercised or actualized.

According to the second aspect, no individual gains complete power or cannot exercise his/her power, until he/she is given some context. Specifically, not until an individual is in an organic unity and relates with other individuals in the unity is his/her power displayed. Where an individual is given in some context, it is said to be powerful. That an individual

---

206. Fa-tsang, "*Hua-yen ching ming fa p'in nei li san pao chang*," *TD* 45:620a–b.
207. *HYWCC* 507c–508a; *FD* 530.
208. *HYWCC* 503b.
209. Potential power is contrasted to complete power (*chuan-li*). See *HYWCC* 503b–c.

is given in the context of society implies that the individual does not exist independently or substantially. Instead, an individual exists interdependently with other individuals in organic society. Francis H. Cook, in "The Jewel Net of Indra," even insists that an individual outside the context would be a powerless nonentity.[210] An individual meaningfully and powerfully exists insofar as he/she exists interdependently in the organic house. Where an individual exists independently and substantially, it is called an imaginary or weak existence. Where an individual participates in organic unity with other individuals, it is called powerful existence. The way of individuals' participation in the organic house is to bracket and empty its own power, and instead, to comport to join the organic house or *li* to relate to and depend on others.

Fa-tsang avoids the separateness between the two aspects, namely, (1) the mutual nonobstruction and the relatedness between principle and phenomena, and (2) the relatedness among phenomena. Fa-tsang's Huayen teaching is the synthesis of both "mutual nonobstruction of principle with phenomena" (*lishih wuai*) and "mutual nonobstruction among phenomena" (*shihshih wuai*). The view of mutual nonobstruction of principle with phenomena might be considered as primary or originative, while the view of mutual nonobstruction among phenomena is secondary or derivative. Fa-tsang does not regard one aspect as more important than the other. Instead, he maintains dynamic interrelationship between the primary and secondary nonobstruction[211] like the cosmological and dynamic interrelationship between *yin* and *yang* or life and death with which *Dasein* has deal in its existence.

Fa-tsang's philosophy is a family philosophy or community philosophy. His philosophy emphasizes a whole body or community rather than individuals who constitute the community. Reality exists in the totality (*ch'uan*) of the whole. His goal is to overcome the weakness of the individual through the community. All phenomena are relative, and they are all dependent upon and related to each other. Nothing can have an isolated existence or fixed value of its own. His philosophy is challenged by critics that one's responsibility and ability is ignored, for oneself has to empty or suspend one's substantiality for the existence of the community to which individuals belong. The Hua-yen Buddhist view is often criticized as deterministic, non-free, and uncreative, because an individual has to sacrifice one's own possibility or talents to connect and depend on others in the community. Charles Hartshorne, in "Sankara, Nagarjuna, and Fa Tsang,

---

210. Cook, "Jewel Net of Indra," 215.
211. *HYWCC* 498b.

with Some Western Analogues," points out the deterministic tendency of Buddhism as reflected in Nagarjuna and Fa-tsang.[212] He points out that Hua-yen Buddhism is based on an assumption of symmetry which implies the interdependence between causing and being caused without considering what the cause and its effect are and the significance of revelation of individuals' uniqueness and talents in society. Robert C. Neville in *The Tao and the Daimon* argues that interrelatedness, interpenetration, and mutual correspondence of Fa-tsang are "not in the Western imagination,"[213] which elevates one's own possibility, value, and talents.

When one individual confronts difficult situations, including depression and despair, Fa-tsang's Hua-yen point is to empty one's ownness and unsubstantiate one's desires and will, and run to the community, for the community is considered to constitute individuals. However, we can ask the question if there is a perfect and healthy community able to take care of individuals' despair. If it is, how many communities and what kinds of communities, including sangha and churches, are there in the world? According to Heidegger, *Angst*, in which *Dasein* sees the world as unfamiliar and meaningless, directs *Dasein* to make its resoluteness and to project its new possibility of existence through nothingness (*die Nichtigkeit*) or emptiness. However, Kierkegaard challenges Heidegger's view of *Angst* and emptiness. He argues that the human being tries to flee from despair and to find the possible being or God who can provide familiarity and possibility for the despaired. Kierkegaard seeks God, who is regarded as the being of unlimited possibility and infiniteness,[214] for the sake of *Dasein*'s continuous existence of possibility. Kierkegaard in *The Sickness Unto Death* elaborates how the human being, whose possibility of existence in despair becomes void or *nichtig*, is restored by means of relatedness with God, who is considered all things possible.[215] The next chapter will discuss Kierkegaard's view of anxiety and God's possibility.

---

212. Hartshorne, "Sankara, Nagarjuna, and Fa Tsang."
213. Neville, *Tao and the Daimon*, 184.
214. *SD* 168.
215. *SD* 169.

V

Death and God by Kierkegaard and Paul

HEIDEGGER IN *BEING AND TIME* defines *Dasein*'s death as the impossibility of existence, which implies *Dasein*'s boundary of existence, apart from unlimited possibility of its existence. As *Dasein* anticipates its death as its no-longer existence, it is occupied by the mood of *Angst*, in which *Dasein* views the world nothingness (*Nichtigkeit*) and insignificance. What Heidegger explores is that *Dasein*, as the finite being due to its unavoidable death and its anticipation of death, searches to find its meaning of existence despite its temporality, finiteness, and limitedness, and its valuableness of existence in temporality, finiteness, and limitedness. While *Dasein*, which faces the issue of death in its existence and anticipates its own death, falls into a mood of not-being-at-home called "uncanniness (*die Unheimlichkeit*)" or unfamiliarity, it does not undertake to get more and to possess abundantly for its own sake in searching for its meaning of existence. Rather, it turns itself to release what it is occupied and captivated, and to detach or empty what it is attached. Releasement or emptiness provides freedom and openness for *Dasein*. Then *Dasein* in the anticipation of death called *Angst* learns how to exist limitedly, and tries to find finitude from infiniteness, temporality from eternity called "the moment of insight (*Augenblick*)" with ecstasy (ἔκστασις, *Entrückung* in German), which means rapture or displacement or astonishment; three stances of past, present, and future are made into a unity of temporality called "ecstasy."

Kierkegaard, who affected Heidegger to explore and build the view of *Angst*, nothingness (*Nichtigkeit*), temporality, and *Augenblick*, conceives the human being as the limited, temporal existence constituted by psyche and body.[1] In *The Concept of Anxiety* and *The Sickness Unto Death*, he investigates humanity's finite existence manifested in anxiety (*Angest*),[2] time of impermanence and eternity, and *Øieblikket*[3] (the moment or instant), in which humanity's finitude and temporality is overcome through "a relationship with God."[4] As Kierkegaard searches for having a relationship with God for humanity, he discloses alienation, absurdity, illogicality, paradox and contradictoriness of humanity, and synthesis beyond paradox through the spirit.

To examine Kierkegaard's view of anxiety (*Angest*), temporal existence of the human being, and *Øiebliket* helps us not only understand how Heidegger established his view of *Angst*, emptiness, time, and *Augenblick* in reference to Kierkegaard's views of paradox or absurdity, *Angest*, and *Øieblikket*, but also how Heidegger's view regarded as the preunderstanding discussed in the preceding chapter works to identify Kierkegaard's own *Angest*, time, and *Øiebliket*. Furthermore, to explore Kierkegaard's *Angest* (anxiety), and *Øiebliket* provides a preunderstanding for comprehending Paul, whose essential views are death, *kenosis* (emptiness), time, and resurrection, *parousia* (the presence of divinity), and "the twinkling of an eye (*en atomo, en rhipe ophthalmou*, ἐν ἀτόμῳ, ἐν ῥιπῇ ὀφθαλμοῦ)" in 1 Corinthians 15:52 of the New Testament.

A. KIERKEGAARD'S VIEW OF ANXIETY (*ANGEST*)

As *Angst* that Heidegger examines directs *Dasein* to see the world insignificant, empty, null, and uncanny and makes it unbound in the world, that is, free and releases it from the attachment to the world, *Angst* as emptiness operates to make *Dasein* open to see and project its new existence for the sake of itself. However, *Dasein*'s projection by virtue of *Angst* is neither free nor unlimited, but is explicit and conditioned into finite possibilities. For that reason, *Dasein*'s *Angst* that Heidegger argues is, for Kierkegaard, not considered meritorious and advantageous absolutely to direct *Dasein* to project its new possibility. Kierkegaard claims that those who are attacked by *Angest* are neither strong nor free enough to get rid of the assaults of

---

1. CA 43.
2. *Angest* in Danish, which is equitable with *Angst* in German, is translated into anxiety, despair, and dread.
3. The term *Øieblikket* in Danish is equitable with the term *Augenblick* in German. As I use *Augenblick* without translating it into English, I also use the term *Øieblikket* without translating it into English.
4. SD 162.

Angest, and the *Angest* becomes a spirit to be against their will that they wish to go.[5] *Angest* enters into one's soul and searches out everything and anxiously torments everything finite and petty.[6] Those who are under *Angest* need some power to rescue them from it. Kierkegaard seeks God, who is regarded as the being of unlimited possibility and infiniteness,[7] in response to the *Angest* (anxiety) that makes the human being fall into nothing. Kierkegaard says, "God is that all things are possible";[8] "God is not finite as the human being is . . . and . . . God is infinite."[9] Kierkegaard argues that *Angest* of nothing goes away when the individual is formed to faith in God.[10]

Kierkegaard brings in three spheres of existence that the human being is to comport: the aesthetic, the ethical, and the religious[11] in response to how to deal with the finite existence of the human being. The aesthetic sphere is characterized as a person living in one's passions and fashions, the ethical sphere is that a person lives and acts according to the moral imperative, and the religious sphere epitomizes the ideal of the individual standing before God. Kierkegaard does not emphasize which sphere is the most desirable among the three despite considering the religious sphere the highest passion.[12] The religious sphere is disclosed in relation with the issue of *Angest* that the human being has to confront in its being and tries to overcome the attack of anxiety by virtue of God's power and possibility. Kierkegaard begins to examine the issue of *Angest* psychologically in *The Concept of Anxiety: A Simple Psychologically Orienting Deliberation on the Dogmatic Issue of Hereditary Sin*. He shifts the issue of *Angest* from psychological examination to Christian religious understanding, which is examined in *The Sickness unto Death: A Christian Psychological Exposition for Edification and Awakening*. While Kierkegaard brings about the issue of anxiety from Adam of the biblical narrative of the Old Testament in *The Concept of Anxiety*, *The Sickness unto Death* discloses a response or answer to the issue from the religious sphere with Lazarus of the narrative of the New Testament, saying, "'This sickness is not unto death' (John 11:4), and yet Lazarus died; for when the disciples misunderstood the words which

5. CA 159.
6. CA 159.
7. SD 43–65.
8. SD 171, 172, 173, 205.
9. SD 252–53.
10. CA 159.
11. See Dreyfus, *Being-in-the-World*, 283–340.
12. Walter Lowrie, "Translator's Introduction," in *FT* 9–10, 15.

Christ adjoined later, 'Lazarus our friend is asleep, but I go to wake him out of his sleep' (11:11), He said plainly, 'Lazarus is dead' (11:14)."[13] The religious sphere through standing before God is considered "faith."[14]

1. Heidegger vs. Kierkegaard

Heidegger does not cite what Kierkegaard refers to.[15] Thomas Sheehan, in "Heidegger's 'Introduction to the Phenomenology of Religion,' 1920–1921," argues that Heidegger paid his debt to Kierkegaard, but adjudged Kierkegaard to be inadequate.[16] Instead, Heidegger shows in *Being and Time* how his view is different from Kierkegaard's in several points.

First, Heidegger argues that his view is ontological, while Kierkegaard's is ontic, saying that ontological inquiry is more primordial than the ontical inquiry in philosophy.[17] The ontic study is primarily concerned with beings, entities, things, facts, but the ontological study with the being of entities or beings. The ontical inquiry typically has to do with discerning attributes of a thing, e.g., the size, weight, and color of an entity, which are to be considered quantitative characteristics. If we apply the difference between ontic and ontological inquiry to human existence, Kierkegaard's view on human existence is ontic, limited to its individual self, and interested in itself as the particular entity. Instead, Heidegger maintains that his view of existence is not only related to *Dasein*'s individuality, but also its relationship with others as the being of entity in the world. Heidegger notes that in the nineteenth century, Kierkegaard delved into the issue of existence in a deeply insightful manner concerning ontic being or thing. However, Heidegger observes that Kierkegaard was so unfamiliar with the ontological problem of existence that he was heavily influenced by Hegel and his perspective on ancient philosophy. Heidegger suggests that Kierkegaard's 'edifying' writings offer more philosophical insight than his theoretical work, except for his treatise on the concept of *Angst*.[18]

Second, Heidegger maintains that when Kierkegaard speaks of "temporality," he does not discuss the primordial temporality, for Kierkegaard ignores the significance of *Augenblick* based on a moment (ecstasy). Heidegger observes that Kierkegaard perceived the existentiell phenomenon

---

13. *CA* 144.
14. *FT* 23–24, 33.
15. See Magurshak, "Concept of Anxiety"; Geter, "Missed Appropriations."
16. Sheehan, "Introduction to Phenomenology of Religion," 40.
17. *SZ* 11; *BTM* 31; *BTS* 9.
18. *SZ* 235; *BTM* 494; *BTS* 407.

of *Augenblick* in an exceptionally profound way. However, he notes that Kierkegaard did not achieve the same level of success in the existential interpretation of it. According to Heidegger, Kierkegaard remained entangled in the ordinary concept of time, defining *Augenblick* with reference to both the now and eternity. Kierkegaard's notion of "temporality" refers to human beings' existence in time. Heidegger argues that while time, as within-time-ness, recognizes only the now, it never acknowledges a moment. He suggests that experiencing the moment in an existentiell manner presupposes a more primordial temporality, even if it remains existentially inexplicit.[19]

Third, Heidegger argues that Kierkegaard's view is theological, while his view is philosophical. Heidegger believes that theology is an ontic science. Heidegger comments that it is no coincidence that the phenomena of *Angst* and fear, which have never been thoroughly distinguished, were significant for Christian theology both ontically and ontologically, though within very narrow limits. This occurred particularly when the anthropological problem of human beings toward God took precedence, with phenomena such as faith, sin, love, and repentance shaping the questions.[20]

Heidegger further criticizes Kierkegaard's view of anxiety in *The Concept of Anxiety: A Simple Psychologically Orienting Deliberation on the Dogmatic Issue of Hereditary Sin*. Heidegger states that Kierkegaard made the most progress in analyzing the phenomenon of *Angst*, particularly within the theological context of a "psychological" exploration of the problem of original sin.[21]

Apart from whether Heidegger's criticism of Kierkegaard is valid or not, what is certain is that Heidegger is influenced by Kierkegaard.[22] Heidegger says, "Impulses were given by Kierkegaard, and Husserl opened my eyes";[23] "strong impulses for the hermeneutical explication presented here stem from the work of Kierkegaard."[24] Hubert Dreyfus, in *Being-in-the-World*, believes that the essential view of existence, death, time as temporality, and *Augenblick* that Heidegger explores is to be understood in reference to Kierkegaard's issue of existence, time, death, temporality, *Angest* (anxiety), and *Øieblikket* (the moment). Kierkegaard's views on such issues are disclosed in *The Concept of Anxiety: A Simple Psychologically Orienting Deliberation on the Dogmatic Issue of Hereditary Sin*, and *The*

19. SZ 338; BTM 497; BTS 412–13.
20. SZ 190; BTM 492; BTS 404.
21. SZ 190; BTM 492; BTS 405.
22. See Geter, "Missed Appropriations," 1–12.
23. Heidegger, *Ontology*, 4.
24. Heidegger, *Ontology*, 25.

Sickness Unto Death: A Christian Psychological Exposition for Edification and Awakening. Joakim Garff in Kierkegaard: A Biography says "the work [*The Concept of Anxiety*] was originally to have been entitled 'On / the Concept of Anxiety. /A Pure and Simple Psychological Reflection with Respect to / the Dogmatic Problem of Original Sin / by S. Kierkegaard / MA.'"[25] *The Concept of Anxiety* and *The Sickness Unto Death* are to be considered a two-stage illumination of human existence, which is constituted by anxiety (*Angest*), sin, and death. The first stage is to be aware of what the human being is and how the human being struggles with anxiety or alienation in its existence, which is examined in *The Concept of Anxiety*. The second stage is a response or solution to the issue of anxiety through having the relationship with God, which is explicated in *The Sickness Unto Death*.

2. *Dasein's* Lostness of Self and Adam's Lostness of Self

a) *Dasein's* Lostness of Self

As *Dasein* is thrown into the world, it is already surrounded by *das Man* (anyone or the they) in publicness. *Dasein* is a free, responsible, and independent being; *das Man* is forceful to condition *Dasein*. *Das Man* is not regarded as a specific entity but, rather, as anyone unnamed and indefinite who exists along with *Dasein* in the world. *Das Man* has its own ways to be and presents every judgment and decision as its own. Insofar as *Dasein* exists in the world, it cannot avoid encountering and engaging *das Man*. As *Dasein* engages *das Man*, *Dasein* is conditioned by *das Man*'s force to follow what *das Man* sees, fashions, and determines, and then *Dasein* loses itself, and falls into *das Man-Selbst* (the anyone-self) in everydayness as an inauthentic being.

While *Dasein* makes no choices, gets carried along by *das Man*, and thus ensnares itself under *das Man*, *Dasein* is neither absolutely captivated in *das Man* nor entirely subject to *das Man*. *Dasein*, as a self-responsible being, brings itself back (*das Sichzurückholen*) from *das Man* for its own existence, decision, and sake. The way that *Dasein* brings itself back to itself from its dominance of *das Man* is called the "existentiell modification"[26] under the force of *das Man* into *Dasein's* authentic, responsible being-one's self. *Dasein's* turning back from the *das Man*-self to the authentic *Dasein*-self

---

25. Garff, *Kierkegaard*.
26. *SZ* 268.

is to hear *Dasein*'s voice of conscience, which is called "wanting to have a conscience (*Gewissen-haben-wollen*)."²⁷

The voice of conscience that calls *das Man*-self to come out of *das Man* and to return to the *Dasein*-self is challenged by the question whether the voice is strong and effective enough to pull *das Man-self* (inauthentic *Dasein*-self) out of the force of *das Man* in which *Dasein* is already factically webbed with others-in-the-world. How does *Dasein* come out of *das Man-self*, who is used to being amid *das Man*? Does *Dasein* fully recover or retrieve its "self" from *das Man-self* by wanting to have a conscience? From the perspective of Kierkegaard, *Dasein*'s *das Man*-self to come out of the force of *das Man* is not fully possible without hearing some voice from without called God. Kierkegaard in *Fear and Trembling*, *The Concept of Anxiety*, *The Sickness unto Death*, and *Philosophical Fragments* examines the lostness of the human self, and discuss the release of the lost-self.

b) Adam's Lostness of Self

Kierkegaard as an existential religionist brings in something transcendental, or pre-phenomenological called the Infinite or God who is viewed as something that "stands above the universal [the world]."²⁸ He raises a question where the meaninglessness or groundlessness of the world called *Angest* (anxiety) comes to humanity.²⁹ Kierkegaard in *The Concept of Anxiety* examines the origin of existence, the origin of anxiety, and the lostness of self with Adam of biblical narrative disclosed in Genesis chapters 2–3.

As Adam (Ἀδὰμ) is presented by God to the world, he is surrounded by other beings or entities. According to Genesis 1, other beings or things were created prior to Adam's existence. Adam cannot avoid encountering and engaging other beings, which are created by God, so that Adam is placed in "seduction"³⁰ by them. Adam is conditioned by following what they see and determine, and then Adam falls into an inauthentic or selfless being. Others, as conditions or power that make Adam fall into no-self or inauthenticity, fallenness or sin, are to be considered "sensuousness."³¹ While the term "sensuousness" is relating to the senses, suggesting passionate affectedness, it implies affectedness by objects which powerfully influence the mode of

27. *SZ* 288; *BTM* 334; *BTS* 265.
28. *FT* 71.
29. *SD* 149.
30. *CA* 43.
31. *CA* 58.

Adam and makes him fall into fallenness. Sensuousness is not sinfulness, but by Adam' deed and lostness of himself sensuousness became sinfulness.[32]

God planted a garden in Eden and put Adam in the garden as its gardener to tend and care for it. God made to grow every tree in the garden that is pleasant to the sight and good for food: the tree of life was also in the midst of the garden, and the tree of the knowledge of good and evil. God commanded Adam, saying, "You may freely eat of every tree of the garden; but of the tree of the knowledge of good and evil you shall not eat. In the day that you eat of it, you shall die." God's command to Adam is to distinguish what he is freely able to do from what he is not supposed to do. What Adam is freely able to eat is fit to him, but what he is not supposed to eat, that is, the tree of the knowledge of good and evil, is considered not fitting to him and does not belong to Adam. Adam does not discern the difference between himself and others until God commands what he is able to eat and not to eat.

Although God's command restricts Adam not to cross his boundary, God's voice also gives Adam an encouragement on displaying Adam's ability, freedom, property, and talents. Since Adam is situated to engage with others like *das Man*, which seduce Adam to follow them, God's voice warns Adam not to lose his ability, gifts, and possibility. Kierkegaard refers to voices beyond one's own voice that calls the hearer not to lose oneself through introducing the parable story titled "The Tame Geese: A Revivalistic Meditation." In the parable, there are geese which enjoy their lives. But they fall into the comfortable zone and lose their ownness and distinctiveness, which is the flying over the sky.[33] One gander preaches to geese that their freedom, uniqueness, and ability is to fly freely in the sky.

Eve, the wife of Adam, was tempted by the serpent to eat the fruit that God prohibited. Genesis 3:1–6 tells about the seduction of the serpent and Eve's response to the seduction. The serpent said to Eve, "Did God say, You shall not eat of any tree of the garden"? Eve said to the serpent, "'I may eat of the fruit of the trees of the garden; but God said, 'You shall not eat of the fruit of the tree, which is in the midst of the garden, neither shall you touch it, lest you die.'" The serpent said to Eve, "You will not die. For God knows that when you eat of it your eyes will be opened, and you will be like God, knowing good and evil." When Eve saw that the tree was good for food, and that it was delightful to the eyes, and that the tree was to be desired to make one wise, she took of its fruit and ate. Eve also shared some with Adam, and he ate. Both transgressed God's words. The eyes of both were opened,

---

32. *CA* 63.
33. Kierkegaard, "Tame Geese," 433.

and they knew that they were naked so they sewed fig leaves together and covered them to conceal their fallenness and shame. However, God later made leather clothing for Adam and Eve and covered them.[34] "If nakedness has to do with shame, exposure, and vulnerability, and they already had made clothes for themselves, God's act of clothing them may relate to issues of salvation. . . . God acts to cover their shame and defenselessness. . . . This act recognizes continuity in their estranged relationship; this is something with which they must now live."[35]

Genesis 3:24 tells that God drove out Adam and Eve whose selves were lost by others, particularly, by the serpent, which offered ungrounded words like gossip to Eve, and apples which looked good. Both fell into sin and death, which is the destruction of eternity, and into the lostness of selves, and were expelled from the garden. Kierkegaard argues that sin leads to humanity's destruction, suggesting that only sin's corrosion can eternally destroy the soul. He emphasizes that sin is not a phase to be passed through but an eternal fall from eternity itself, making it impossible for sin to be a one-time occurrence.[36] What Kierkegaard asserts is that Adam's sin did not incur instantly once, but is continuously inherited in his descendants' "hereditary sin" despite Adam's personal, unique, and momentaneous act.

3. Dispersion and Inheritance of Adam's Sin to His Descendants

While the particulars between the "Catholic," "Orthodox," and "Protestant" understandings of the origin of sin differ, two polemic ideas have been disputed: one idea advocated by Augustine of Hippo and the other advanced by Pelagius.[37] Augustine emphasizes humanity's total corruption inherited from Adam and no redemption except the irresistible divine grace by Christ. In contrast, Pelagius finds more strenuous ethical standards, moral earnestness, and the freedom of the human will. "Pelagius did not reject grace, but to him grace was remission of sins in baptism and general divine teaching."[38] When Reidar Thomte translates the original sin in *The Concept of Anxiety* from Danish to English, he uses the Danish term, "*Arvesynd*," as "hereditary sin," instead of "original sin."[39]

---

34. Meeks, *HarperCollins Study Bible*, 9–10.

35. Keck, *New Interpreter's Bible*, 1:364, hereafter as *NIB*.

36. Kierkegaard, *Christian Discourses*, 108.

37. Tennant, *Sources of the Doctrines of the Fall and Original Sin*, 326. See also Walker, *History of the Christian Church*, 168–69.

38. Walker, *History of the Christian Church*, 169.

39. "This translation is intended to highlight the paradoxical meaning of hereditary

Kierkegaard defines Adam's sin based on Augustine as "*peccatum originale* [original sin], because it has been *quia originaliter tradatur* [transmitted from the origin],"[40] which designates the guilt of Adam that all humans inherit from birth. Kierkegaard points out that the Protestant Church's strongest and most definitive expression of hereditary sin in humans is that individuals are born with concupiscence or *concupiscentia* (*Omnes homines secundum naturam propagati nascuntur cum peccato h.e. sine metu dei, sine fiducia erga deum et cum concupiscentia*), meaning they are born with sin, lacking the fear of God, without trust in God, and with concupiscence.[41] *Peccatum originale* (original sin) to which Augustine refers is that Adam's sin does not remain in himself, but is transmitted to his subsequent generation by concupiscence. Since humanity is already constituted by Adam's sin and death, the reversal of sin and death can be accomplished by "Christ" who has made satisfaction for Adam's sin.[42] Kierkegaard raises several questions about Adam's role in hereditary sin: Did Adam bring hereditary sin into the world? Was hereditary sin an actual sin in Adam, and does it signify the same for him as for everyone else in the human race? He also wonders if Adam's entire life was an embodiment of hereditary sin and if the first sin led to other actual sins in him.[43]

Pelagius contrasts with Augustine. Kierkegaard describes Pelagius, who denied any original sin inherited from Adam and maintained that every man, as Adam before the fall is innocent, is born without sin.[44] Pelagius often begins discussions on the principles of virtue and a holy life by highlighting the capabilities and characteristics of human nature, showing what humans are capable of achieving.[45] Paul Lehmann in "The-Pelagian Writings" describes Pelagius in three ways. First, he maintained that the nature of human willing had to do with the power and the possibility of choice. Second, there was no denial of the grace of God and the saving grace of Christ in the view of the freedom of the will. Third, his position only could comprehend the ways of God with humanity.[46] He taught that humans were free of Adam's

---

sin which is of great importance to Kierkegaard. It stresses that sin is inherited (not a product of the individual will) and yet still a sin (a product of human action, for which the individual is 'guilty')" (Humbert, "Freedom and Time," 284).

40. *CA* 27.

41. *CA* 41. Kierkegaard quotes the passage from Augustine, *Confession* 2.1.

42. *CA* 28.

43. *CA* 28.

44. *CA* 231; Walker, *History of the Christian Church*, 168.

45. Walker, *History of the Christian Church*, 168, quoted from Ayer, *Source Book for Ancient Church History*, 458–59.

46. Lehmann, "Anti-Pelagian Writings," 211–12.

sin, for it would be unjust for any person to be blamed for someone else's action. According to him, the human being was created in the image of God and God granted humans a capacity called conscience that discerns right and wrong. In Pelagius' view, Augustine's concept of original sin thus let the individual ignore responsibility. All beings have fallen by their own guilt, not by Adam' original sin, but they are guilty because they have all acted like Adam and Eve.[47] Pelagius' view makes Adam's original sin nothing or a fantasy. In Pelagius' view, Adam's sin was considered historical-fantastic and Adam's appearance is regarded as a plenipotentiary for the whole race.[48] Kierkegaard raises questions: is Adam's sin that Genesis introduces nothing significant for humanity? Kierkegaard suggests that Adam's sin is more than merely something in the past, indicating a significance beyond the pluperfect tense.[49]

Augustine's view is that Adam's sin is transmittable to the existence of humanity; all human beings are already corrupted and sinned because of Adam's sin. In contrast, Pelagius' view emphasizes human ability, morality, and will beyond Adam's sin. Kierkegaard does not side with one or the other, but comprehensibly understands both views and replaces it with his own interpretation.

The hereditary sin that Kierkegaard examines in the first chapter of *The Concept of Anxiety* indicates that Adam's sin does not remain in himself but is transmitted to his descendants—but this brings about questions. The first question is how and why Adam's sin matters to us now. What is the relation of Adam's sin to the sins that his descendants commit? If sin is inherited, how can the individual descendant be responsible for one's own sin? Kierkegaard's answer to the question is worded into, "Adam is himself but, Adam is also a race." Thus, Kierkegaard claims, in *The Concept of Anxiety* that Adam is not different from the race, that he is himself *and* the race.[50] What Kierkegaard asserts—that as Adam is himself, so Adam simultaneously is the race—is similar to what Heidegger in *Being and Time* maintains that *Dasein* is itself, and at the same time, *Dasein*'s self is dispersed into publicness. Heidegger remarks that *Dasein* is fragmented into various things that occur daily, saying, "Everyday *Dasein* has been dispersed into the many kinds of things which daily 'come to pass.'"[51] Dreyfus asserts that, similar to Kierkegaard, Heidegger believes *Dasein* is typically dispersed, and achieving

---

47. Tennant, *Sources of the Doctrines of the Fall*, 231, 294, 296, 298, 313.
48. CA 25.
49. CA 26.
50. CA 29.
51. SZ 389–90; BTM 441; BTS 356.

continuity involves imparting constancy to one's otherwise scattered life.[52] That *Dasein*'s self is dispersed into publicness of the world is similar to what Fa-tsang argues, that one *dharma* or phenomenon is connected with other phenomena in the universe. The term "*genos* (γένος)" or "race" that Kierkegaard uses is defined as "descendants of a common ancestor," "family, relatives," and "nation, people."[53] Adam, tainted by sin, is dispersed to his descendants despite his individual and unique commitment to transgression. Adam's sin is distinctively committed by him but his unique act is connected to the race of the world.

Adam's self—tainted by sin—is dispersed to his descendants but is not symmetrically copied by the race or his descendants. When Adam's sin as the original or unique sin is dispersed, the original sin or his particular sin becomes the state of sin to his descendants, and implies the original, existentiell physical or quantitative sin is transformed into a quality of sin, which is a condition for his descendants. The way of transformation from Adam's particular or existentiell sin to common, qualitative, or existential sin of the race is considered to be the "qualitative leap" in suddenness, like spiritual DNA. Kierkegaard notes that a new quality emerges suddenly and enigmatically with the first leap. He argues that if the first sin were merely a single numerical sin, it would not lead to a historical narrative, and sin itself would lack historical presence both individually and collectively.[54] When a particular sin is dispersed into its race, that is, the qualitative change from Adam's sin to the sin of the race, it does not mean that there is a qualitative difference between Adam's sin and his progeny. Kierkegaard posits that the difference between Adam's sin and the first sin of any subsequent individual is established by the individual's own actions. He emphasizes that everything revolves around this concept, allowing each person to understand qualitatively concerning themselves what they comprehend quantitatively concerning others.[55]

That Adam's sin is dispersed to his descendants, that is, his particular sin's transmittance to his race means Adam's participation in the world where his descendants exist. That Adam's descendants are hereditary from their forefather means conversely that they participate in Adam's sin, which is traditionally handed down to them. Kierkegaard views Adam as an individuum, simultaneously representing himself and the whole human race. This suggests that the entire race participates in the individual, and the individual

52. Dreyfus, *Being-in-the-World*, 324.
53. GEL s.v. "γένος."
54. CA 30–31.
55. CA 232.

partakes in the whole race.[56] The existence of a self is an act of relating itself to itself in such a way that it relates itself to the other. Kierkegaard refers to the human self, saying it is "a relation which relates itself to its own self, and in relating itself to its own self relates itself to another."[57] What Kierkegaard explains as the hereditary sin by referring to the relation between the particular sin inaugurated by Adam and the inherited sin participated by the race of the world is similar to what Heidegger refers to *Mitsein* (the being of being-with). *Dasein* or the human being that Heidegger examines in *Being and Time* not only exists as an individual (being-in) and responsible being in the world, but also as the being of being-together-with or being-with-others-the world, in which *Dasein* is connected to other entities, and thereby conditions it others and is conditioned by them.

Kierkegaard in *The Sickness unto Death* expands on the relation between God and the human being, the infinite and finite, possibility and necessity, and the eternal and the temporal, and a synthesis between two factors.[58] He states that the self is the conscious synthesis of infinitude and finitude, the eternal and the temporal, which relates itself to itself, whose task is to become itself; the task can be executed by means of a relationship to God.[59] Before he in *The Sickness unto Death* goes to examine the relation and synthesis between two factors, in *The Concept of Anxiety*, he describes from the Genesis narrative more about the origin and concept of anxiety as the precondition to understand the relation.

4. The Origin and Concept of Anxiety from the Genesis Narrative

Kierkegaard begins with innocence and ignorance which are the cause of anxiety. As Adam (Ἀδὰμ) to which Kierkegaard refers is innocent and ignorant,[60] prior to falling into the lostness of Adam's self. He says, "Innocence is ignorance."[61] That innocence is equitable with ignorance does not mean Adam is in the state of pure being, but is regarded as someone who without concern, has no direction of knowledge, or lack of knowledge.[62] Adam's innocence is especially ignorant of good and evil.[63] Ignorance like

56. CA 28.
57. SD 146.
58. SD 149.
59. SD 162.
60. CA 35.
61. CA 37.
62. CA 37.
63. CA 45.

tabula rasa, which is a condition that the human mind is blank before it is filled with experiences and knowledge carried by the senses, gives birth to anxiety, for ignorance implies vagueness and nothing of good and evil. The self in its ignorant conditions under vagueness suffers a form of anxiety.

Kierkegaard says, "Anxiety may be compared with dizziness."[64] The Genesis narrative introduces how Eve was in dizziness. The serpent said to Eve, "Even if you eat the fruit, you will not die. When you eat it, you will be like God." When she sees the tree that God prohibits, the tree looks valuable, flavorful, nice, delightful, harmless, and makes her a wise person to know good and evil as the serpent seduces her. Eve is in dizziness, between temptation and innocence, ability and restriction, and attraction and repulsion, which are called in words as "sympathetic antipathy and an antipathetic sympathy."[65] Kierkegaard describes how Eve, whose gaze accidentally falls into the abyss, becomes dizzy. He interprets this dizziness as anxiety, arising from the confrontation with freedom.[66] Kierkegaard refers to Eve or Adam as a child. He explains that observing children reveals this type of anxiety, particularly as a quest for the adventurous, the monstrous, and the enigmatic. Kierkegaard believes this anxiety is essential to the child, stating that its absence is not significant, as it is also absent in beasts; the less spirit there is, the less anxiety. He concludes that this anxiety is so fundamental to the child that they cannot do without it. Although it causes them distress, it also captivates them with its pleasing anxiousness (*Beængstelse*).[67]

Anxiety arisen from innocence or ignorance is like a "dreaming spirit." Kierkegaard characterizes anxiety as a condition of the dreaming spirit.[68] The dreaming spirit involves Adam's spirit in the state of innocence that is not yet present but is "dreaming." The spirit is the same as the self, as Kierkegaard says, "[The human being] is spirit. But what is spirit? Spirit is the self."[69] Spirit in dreaming has an awareness of vague self and does not fully realize itself in relation to others, which is similar to the lostness of self. That Adam's spirit is dreaming implies that he has not fully matured into a human being, but potentially in the human being whose spirit or self exists in his mode of being.

When Adam is potentially in the spirit, he hears some voice from God. Genesis 2:17 states that Adam shall die if he eats the tree of knowledge

64. CA 61.
65. CA 42.
66. CA 61.
67. CA 42.
68. CA 41.
69. SD 146.

of good and evil. God's voice is prohibition. Kierkegaard contends that prohibition induces anxiety in an individual by awakening the possibility of freedom alongside its restriction.[70] Adam might not grasp what it means to die, for he did not experience someone's death before him in the garden. Nevertheless, Adam might be terrified, for even animals are aware of a mimic expression and movement in the voice of the speaker without fully understanding the word.[71] In this case, the prohibition is regarded as awakening the possibility and impossibility of desire.[72] In conclusion, Kierkegaard adheres to the Biblical narrative, assuming the prohibition and the voice of punishment as external impositions.[73] Kierkegaard is concerned with a solution to the anxiety with the voice from without. He refers to the voice from without in the parable of "The Tame Geese: A Revivalistic Meditation" and Abraham's hearing a voice from God, which is elaborated in *Fear and Trembling*.

5. Anxiety as Alienation

Anxiety or alienation that Heidegger discusses in *Being and Time* arises from tension, friction, and disrelation between *Dasein*'s self and *das Man-Selbst*, who fled from *Dasein* and became *das Man-self* under the force of *das Man*. *Dasein* calls *das Man-Selbst* by its own voice of conscience to come back to *Dasein*-self to relate itself (*das Man-Selbst*) to itself (*Dasein-Selbst*). However, a question is raised if *das Man-Selbst* is able to come out of the force of *das Man* to return to *Dasein*-self, for *Dasein* is already embedded in the world where *das Man* strongly directs and rules. Adam and Eve, who are in dreaming spirit, are not able to come out of the force of anything which surrounds them beyond their own ability or conscience. For that reason, Kierkegaard concludes the issue of *Angest* in reference to the voice coming from without[74] despite the significance of the inside voice or the call of conscience. The issue that the voice coming from without confronts is that it is not one unified voice, but multiple voices, which are mutually exclusive and juxtaposed to each other, and thereby are in tension and disrelation among different voices and one's own voice. Kierkegaard discusses how differing and conflicting voices relate to one another, and synthesize in the self and by the self.

70. *CA* 44.
71. *CA* 45.
72. *CA* 44.
73. *CA* 45.
74. *CA* 45.

Kierkegaard uses Genesis 2:17 and 3:5 to illustrate dissenting voices from without.[75] Genesis 2:17, as God's voice to Adam, says that he shall die in the day when he eats the tree of knowledge of good and evil. Genesis 3:5, from the voice of the serpent to Eve, tells that she will not die, even though she eats the tree of knowledge of good and evil, but instead, her eyes will be opened and be like God. Referring to the serpent, Kierkegaard acknowledges it as a myth. He explains that although the serpent, described as more cunning than other animals and responsible for seducing the woman, can be seen as a myth, but this does not disturb rational thought or confuse the concept. The myth allows internal events to manifest outwardly.[76] The identity of the serpent is debatable. "The serpent presents a metaphor, representing anything in God's good creation that could present options to human beings, the choice of which seduce[s] them away [from] God. The tree itself becomes the temptation, while the serpent facilitates the options the tree presents."[77]

Genesis 2:17—that Adam shall not eat the tree of knowledge of good and evil—implies that Adam's freedom is limited and has nothing to do with his ability. The prohibition reminds him of his ability and possibilities that are not infinite, but finite. The prohibition alerts him that he is neither a self-perpetual being nor self-grounded being. Adam is not the creator, but created and presented to the world by God. He neither comes from himself nor is a determinant for his existence, but is released (*entspringt*) to himself[78] by God's creation. The prohibition manifested in "not doing something" entails that Adam is not through himself, but to himself by God.

On the other hand, in Genesis 3:5 the serpent, "representing anything in God's good creation," tempts Eve to eat the tree of knowledge and to make her to be a self-grounded being. What the serpent says—if Eve eats the tree of knowledge, she will not die and she will be like God—connotes that she will be infinite and eternal, knowing good and evil. She followed what the serpent directed, and ate the fruit. This narrative is assumed that the woman is more sensuous and weaker in spirit than the man. However, Kierkegaard discusses the derivation of woman, suggesting it provides insight into why she is considered weaker than man, a notion accepted throughout history by figures ranging from a pasha to a romantic knight. However, he emphasizes that despite differences, man and woman are essentially alike. He explains that anxiety is more reflected in Eve than in Adam, not as an empirical

---

75. *CA* 41, 235.
76. *CA* 46.
77. *NIB* 1:360.
78. *SZ* 284–85; *BTM* 330–31; *BTS* 262.

observation or average, but to illustrate that her guilt is not greater than Adam's and that anxiety signifies the potential for perfection.[79] If Eve's guilt is greater than Adam's guilt because of her first transgression prior to Adam, her guilt paradoxically increases more grace by God, as Paul in Romans 5:20 refers to sin, saying, "sin increased, grace paradoxically abounded all the more." What Kierkegaard argues is equality between man and woman. He asserts that in the relationship with God, where distinctions such as man and woman disappear, both men and women achieve selfhood through devotion.[80]

Adam is thrown or presented to the garden or the world where God, anyone (like *das Man*), and anything surround and convey. He is engaged with what God utters or God's words that he is not allowed to eat the tree of good and evil. As God's voice directed him, Adam's self becomes God's voice-self like *das Man-Selbst*. Then Adam encounters Eve, whose self is already directed and determined by the serpent and became the serpent-self. Adam has to face two opposite and contradictory selves, God's voice-self and Eve's voice-self, which is ensnared by the serpent, namely, antinomy (etymologically, *an-ti*, ἀντί-against and *nomie*, νόμος-law) to which Immanuel Kant refers as the mutual incompatibility of two laws, or contradictoriness. Both are juxtaposed to each other. God's words-self is "the eating of not," while the serpent words-self is "the eating of yes." God's words-self is Adam's limited freedom and the serpent's words-self is Adam's unlimited possibility. After Adam hears two clashing voices, he has to relate himself to two conflicting selves and make his resoluteness for his care and future.

As Kierkegaard regards Adam as himself and race, Adam, who confronts two paradoxical selves or antinomy, is to be considered representable and equable to all humans, who are shaped by opposite constituents in their existence. Kierkegaard defines the human being as a compound and paradoxical being, who is constituted by contradictory factors such as the infinite and the finite, the temporal and the eternal, of freedom and necessity, and soul and body.[81] The infinite and finite, the temporal and the eternal, the soul and body are not mutually compatible to the human self of being or existence. While the human being is an ironically constituted being, the human existence has to relate or synthesize two opposite factors. Otherwise, the human being will fall into estrangement or alienation and "the self in its alienated condition suffers a variety of forms of despair

---

79. *CA* 64.
80. *SD* 184.
81. *SD* 146, 158.

[anxiety]."⁸² Anxiety results from the self's alienated condition.⁸³ If people do not synthesize and reconcile contrasts in their existence, they will be in unhealthiness or sickness and sickness is finally unto death, as Kierkegaard's *The Sickness unto Death* literally indicates.

When Adam confronted contradiction between God's words and Eve's words affected by the serpent, he did not synthesize two opposite laws in himself. Rather, he made his resoluteness in an imbalanced position manifested in being away from God's words. Kierkegaard mentions that if there is an excess in one part of the synthesis, the result is a deeper cleft when the spirit asserts itself, allowing anxiety to expand within the realm of freedom's possibilities.⁸⁴ Adam did not make his resoluteness related to God's words, but leaned on the serpent's words. He attached himself to Eve's-self snared by the serpent and made his relationship with Eve's serpent words-self, and ended up by the disrelationship with God. Since Adam is deficient in the God-relationship, which is the ground of relationship of any other things, he falls into the position of self-slaughter.⁸⁵

While the human being, who is constituted by paradoxical antinomies in existence, makes an effort to relate and synthesize opposite and alienated selves, relationships, reconciliations, and syntheses are not carried out by themselves. Instead, the self "constituted and sustained by spirit"⁸⁶ synthesizes paradoxical opposites. Kierkegaard argues that the human being as the self is the synthesis of opposite antinomies and self, and the self synthesizes antinomies by virtue of spirit in its existence.⁸⁷ While Kierkegaard did not define exactly what the spirit is, the spirit to which Kierkegaard refers is divergent from what Hegel deals with as the spirit or *Geist*. Kierkegaard's spirit is to relate itself to itself by means of "a relationship to God";⁸⁸ the remedy to sickness of anxiety or alienation is, for Kierkegaard, sought in religion that involves God.⁸⁹ Hegel's spirit (*Geist*) is Reason or mind, which is a human faculty or instrument characterized as the essence of humanity

---

82. Bernstein, *Praxis and Action*, 101.
83. Bernstein, *Praxis and Action*, 101.
84. CA 64.
85. SD 179.
86. CA 81.
87. SD 162; CA 43.
88. SD 162.
89. Walter Lowrie, "Translator's Introduction," in *SD* 144.

to draw a logical consequence,[90] and is to unify the discrepancy between it and itself.[91]

Geist, the fundamental concept in Hegel's philosophy, is translated as spirit instead of mind.[92] While Geist is translated into the spirit, it is identical in content with the mind, reason, or *nous* (νοῦς), in humanity's essence.[93] Geist is translated into Reason. According to Hegel, Reason governs the world. Reason is similar to the universal law that reigns over the individual, and thereby asserts Hegel "the unity between reason and reality, and between universal essence and individual existence."[94] But Kierkegaard emphasizes faith instead of Reason through expressing that faith is justified and paradoxical when the individual as the particular is higher than the universal.[95] In *From Hegel to Nietzsche: The Revolution in Nineteenth-Century Thought* Löwith argues Kierkegaard finds the ground of reality in "interest" instead of "speculative reason" advocated by Kant and Hegel, saying, Kierkegaard contrasts the interest he calls 'passion' or 'ardor' with speculative reason. He states that passion, unlike the conclusive nature of Hegel's system (reason), necessitates a determination that requires decisive action—either one way or another. This decision, epitomized by the leap, serves as a decisive protest against dialectical reflection.[96] Hegel in *the Philosophy of History* states that the movement of the solar system does not take place randomly, but is reflected by unchangeable laws. These laws are to be reflected by Reason, implicit in the phenomena in question. Neither the sun nor the planets, which revolve around it according to these laws, can be said to have Reason.[97] Instead, the laws show themselves in the light of humanity's self-cognizant idea that is actualized in human reason or *Nous*, which reflect the laws.[98] "*Nous* (Νοῦς) as the faculty of thinking implicit in the human being initiates one's thoughts and plans.[99]

The issue that Hegel brings in his philosophy is alienation or estrangement (*Entäusserung*). While Hegel's concept of alienation owes much to previous thinkers such as Jean-Jacques Rousseau and Johann Gottlieb

---

90. Bernstein, *Praxis and Action*, 15.
91. Inwood, *Hegel Dictionary*, 36.
92. Bernstein, *Praxis and Action*, 14.
93. Bultmann, *Theology of the New Testament*, 1:203.
94. Löwith, *From Hegel to Nietzsche*, 145.
95. *FD* 65–66.
96. Löwith, *From Hegel to Nietzsche*, 150.
97. Hegel, *Philosophy of History*, 55.
98. Hegel, *Philosophy of History*, 53.
99. *GEL* s.v. "νοῦς."

Fichte, Hegel's concept of alienation is substantially original.[100] Alienation (*Entäusserung*) "corresponds to *entäussern*, 'or [to] make outer or external (*ausser*),' and means 'surrender' or 'divestiture.'"[101] At the same time, alienation entails "*Entzweiung* (from *zwei*, 'two'), 'bifurcation,' 'disunion'; *Zerrissenheit* (from *zerreissen*, 'to tear, rend, dismember, disconnect'), 'dismemberment,' 'disjointedness'; *Zwiespalt* (also from *zwei*), 'discord,' 'conflict,' 'discrepancy'; Diremtion; and Trennung, 'separation' (from *trennen*, 'to separate')."[102] *Nous* or Reason, which constitutes the human being as the essence of being, according to Hegel, mediates the self's alienation.[103]

Adam's self from the Biblical narrative was awakened when he heard a warning from God who spoke to him not to eat the tree of good and evil, and his-self becomes God's words-self. Then Adam encounters Eve, who fell into the seduction of the serpent to eat the fruit and became the serpent-self. Adam is juxtaposed or torn between two different kinds of selves: God's words-self and Eve's words-self or the serpent's words-self. Adam suspended God's words, and made his resoluteness on the basis of his reason or *nous* in contrast to understanding (*Verstehen*), which involves the access to religion[104] called "faith." Adam disrelated God's words-self, but related Eve's words-self, and stubbornly became himself on the basis of Eve's self. Adam's determination to eradicate alienation is rooted in *nous*, not faith, which primarily demands God's words. Kierkegaard describes a state where the self is entirely free from anxiety, noting that this represents the condition of the self when anxiety is fully eradicated;[105] by relating itself to its own self and by willing to be itself, the self by the mediation of *nous* is formulated and identified as itself[106] away from discrepancy or dismemberment (*Zerrissenheit*). However, according to Kierkegaard, the self achieves sound health and freedom from anxiety only by being rooted transparently in God, having experienced anxiety.[107] What he argues is that Adam fled from *Angest* through relating itself to itself by the mediation of *nous*, suspending God's words but leaning to the serpent's words, to suggest "a stage beyond 'when despair [*Angest*] is completely eradicated.'"[108] The stage means that Adam has to accept the fact

100. Inwood, *Hegel Dictionary*, 36.
101. Inwood, *Hegel Dictionary*, 36.
102. Inwood, *Hegel Dictionary*, 36.
103. Bernstein, *Praxis and Action*, 101.
104. Inwood, *Hegel Dictionary*, 36.
105. *SD* 147.
106. *SD* 147.
107. *SD* 163.
108. Bernstein, *Praxis and Action*, 101.

that there is God, and to exist before God beyond the stage where alienation is removed by virtue of the implementation of *nous* (νοῦς).[109]

While Kierkegaard was influenced by Hegel, who brought about the issue of alienation and overcame the inner contradictoriness by mediation of *nous* that resolves discords or dissentions,[110] Kierkegaard does not follow Hegel's Reason (*Nous*), but faith. "Faith stands in radical opposition and is an offense to Reason [*nous*]."[111] Kierkegaard contrasts his views with Hegel, asserting the paradoxical nature of Christian truths, which involve a transcendence beyond the grasp of reason.[112] Humanity discovers a stage of self-consciousness in which the self is aware of its alienation or discrepancy by *nous*, and *nous* participates in the discrepancy to have unification or reconciliation (*Versohnung*) of alienated selves. While the stage of *nous* makes humanity relate itself to its own self, *nous* does not serve humanity fully to identify itself, for human-selves distinct from the beast consist of contradictory factors: "the infinite and the finite, of the temporal and the eternal, of freedom and necessity."[113] Kierkegaard argues humanity needs a second stage to synthesize contradictory factors through a relationship with God or faith beyond the first stage of the mediation of *nous*. Kierkegaard characterizes the self as a synthesis of the infinite and finite, or the eternal and temporal, whose task of becoming itself can only be accomplished through a relationship with God.[114] If the human being struggles to synthesize contradictory factors by means of faith instead of *Reason* or *nous*, his/her effort is very absurd and empty, for contradictory factors through faith are regarded as illogical and paradoxical constituents that identify humanity, but *nous* or *Reason* works for logical and rational consequences. Bernstein, in *Praxis and Action*, explains that the union and reconciliation of concepts such as freedom and necessity, the infinite and the finite, and the universal and the particular—a mediation seen as the work of Reason—are considered impossible. He suggests that the Absolute Paradox, which Hegel identifies as the hallmark of Reason, involves the eternal becoming temporal and the infinite becoming finite, an idea that contradicts logical reason.[115] In contrast, Kierkegaard, distinct from Hegel, argues that humanity as the paradoxical or contradictory being needs to

109. SD 159–60.
110. Bernstein, *Praxis and Action*, 101.
111. Bernstein, *Praxis and Action*, 102.
112. CA 233.
113. SD 146.
114. SD 162.
115. Bernstein, *Praxis and Action*, 105.

choose faith in God instead of Reason in humanity to understand human paradox. Kierkegaard's philosophy fundamentally is to synthesize humanity's temporality and finiteness with God's eternity and infiniteness in its existence, which is called the "Moment" or "Øieblikket."

Webster's Dictionary defines the moment as a minute portion of time in duration without separating two states or a point of time present or regarded as present in respect to a particular context. "The Danish word *Øiblikket* (the moment) is figurative in the sense that it is derived from *Øiets Blik* (a blink of the eye)."[116] The "Moment" or "*Øieblikket*" that Kierkegaard brings in his philosophy means the synthesis between the temporal and the eternal, or the finite and the infinite, or "time [temporality] and eternity [God's time] touch each other."[117] Following the meaning of *Øiblikket* (the moment), Kierkegaard's departure point for the idea of the Moment (*Øiblikket*) is based on 1 Corinthians 15:52, which we will discuss in the following section of this book. Kierkegaard refers to a poetic paraphrase in the New Testament, where Paul indicates that the world will pass away in a moment, thus showing that a moment of destruction is commensurable with eternity.[118] This verse of 1 Corinthians 15:52 describes "*parousia* (παρουσία)," the encounter with the resurrected Christ, or presence of divinity in the future beyond the unavoidable hopeless death in a "moment, in the blink of an eye," which is a momentous event of dramatic transformation for humanity.

B. PAUL'S VIEW OF DEATH BY ADAM AND RESURRECTION BY JESUS TOWARD *PAROUSIA*

Heidegger views time as temporality in contrast to eternity advocated by Plato, Aristotle, and St. Augustine of Hippo whose time is bent on God. According to Plato, time itself is a phase of the timeless with an eternal image of eternity.[119] Time that Augustine argues was created when the world was created by God who is eternal; God's eternity is exempt from temporality of time.[120] Time as eternity relying on God transcends the unstable, sensible, and phenomenal world and belongs to the non-changing, immutable, and timelessness of eternity.

---

116. *CA* 245.
117. *CA* 87.
118. *CA* 110.
119. Archer-Hind, *Timaeus of Plato*, 41.
120. Russell, *History of Western Philosophy*, 353.

On the other hand, Heidegger seeks to find time in the mutable, phenomenal world, and time with *Dasein*, who is in finitude and mortality different from God as the eternal, unchanging, undying being. Heidegger argues that the understanding of time based on eternity of God is carried out by a theological approach, but time in the mutable, sensible, and phenomenal world where *Dasein* exists is considered a philosophical relevance. Heidegger observes that common understandings tend to oppose faith and knowledge, and revelation and reason, when considering the relationship between theology and philosophy.[121] He shows not only the different perspective of time between eternity and temporality, but also a discrete access to time by philosophy or theology.

In contrast, Kierkegaard did not discriminate theology from philosophy, apart from whether time is to be understood as temporality or eternity in philosophy or theology, for time as eternity rises from the Christian Bible as well as Greek philosophy that Plato and Aristotle discussed. While Greek philosophy is metaphysical, metaphysics is not symmetrically to be considered theology. At the same time, what Kierkegaard searches for in time is reconciliation, synthesis, and relationship through mediating the spirit[122] instead of *Reason* (*nous*) between temporality and eternity, and further, contradictory, and paradoxical components of humanity such as soul and body,[123] sin and grace, and mortality and immortality.[124] The synthesis and relationship between the temporal and the eternal is called "Moment (*Øiblikket*)." Since the argument that Kierkegaard discloses is theological and philosophical, his view is considered a preunderstanding for Paul's theological issues of *parousia*, sin, grace, death and resurrection.

1. Kierkegaard's the Moment (*Øiblikket*)

Heidegger argues that time as temporality temporalizes itself in the future and the having been (past), which are united in the present.[125] *Dasein's* present moment does not mean the present or single moment but extends to going back to the past and forward to the anticipation of its future, while time is ordinarily conceived as the present, the past, and the future. Derrida states that every present or the point of now is constituted, produced, and

---

121. Heidegger, *Pathmarks*, 40.
122. *CA* 43.
123. *SD* 146, 158.
124. *SD* 153, 190, 241.
125. *SZ* 396–97; *BTM* 448; *BTS* 362.

derived from the previous process of time as the source of nonpresence.[126] While time is extemporalized into the present, the past, and the eternal, Kierkegaard argues that no real distinction between the present, the past, the future, and the eternal is recognized.[127] He argues that dividing time into present, future, and past is incorrect because every moment is a process. He suggests that time should be thought of as a continuous flow rather than being spatialized into discrete segments.[128] In *Philosophical Fragments*, he explains that in the moment, a person becomes conscious of being born, experiences a new birth, and recognizes their previous state of non-being.[129] Kierkegaard emphasizes that the moment and eternity touch together. This instant with eternity is called Øiblikket (the Moment). He finds beauty in the concept of the moment as the blink of an eye, which is commensurate with the eternal.[130]

The Moment (Øiblikket) to which Kierkegaard refers is the synthesis of the temporal and the eternal. The synthesis does not occur by itself. The synthesis of the temporal and the eternal is "constituted and sustained by spirit."[131] Kierkegaard posits that a synthesis is unthinkable unless the two components are united in a third, which he identifies as spirit.[132] The spirit constitutes and synthesizes the temporal and the eternal. Kierkegaard's spirit that constitutes the synthesis between the temporal and the eternal is understood in reference to God who is the ground of all beings[133] beyond humanity, for the temporal is engaged in the human being but the eternal belongs to God. Kierkegaard claims that every human existence which is not conscious of itself before God as spirit, but serenity in some abstract universal ideas like *Geist*, falls into anxiety.[134] He believes that any existence not grounded in God but instead in abstract universality or obscure self-awareness tends to rely on its faculties merely as active powers without understanding their deeper origin. Such existences, regardless of their accomplishments or enjoyment of life, fall into spiritlessness and paganism.[135]

---

126. Allison, "Translator's Introduction," xxxvii.
127. CA 94.
128. CA 85.
129. Kierkegaard, *Philosophical Fragments*, 25–26.
130. CA 87.
131. CA 81.
132. CA 43.
133. SD 179.
134. SD 179.
135. SD 179; CA 93–96.

Spiritlessness and paganism do not help people in anxiety or alienation to synthesize two opposite factors.

a) Spiritlessness

The term "spiritlessness" means the lostness of self, and paganism is about pagans who are not conscious of themselves before God as spirit. Kierkegaard suggests that in a state of spiritlessness, there is no anxiety due to an excessive contentment and lack of spiritual engagement. He differentiates paganism from spiritlessness, noting that paganism is characterized by an absence of spirit but still oriented toward it, making it preferable to spiritlessness.[136]

The Adam that Kierkegaard explores in *The Concept of Anxiety* is offered to the garden or world surrounded by many things, including the serpent and anyone like *das Man*. While Adam is an individual and responsible for his existence, he is affected by anyone, loses himself, and becomes anyone-self, that is, falls into spiritlessness. He first heard a voice from God who said that he was not able to eat the fruit of good and evil in the garden. He followed God's Words, became God's Words-self, and was filled with God's spirit. The self of Adam was primitively grounded on God's Words. But later anyone or the serpent regarded as a mysterious being accessed Eve, and she was seduced by the snake, which determined that the forbidden fruit by God was available to any beings and would make the eaters of the fruit be like God. She ate the fruit, lost herself, and became the serpent-self, that is, she was spiritless. Adam met Eve, who convinced Adam to eat the fruit to be like God. He ate the fruit, became the serpent-Eve-self, and fell into spiritlessness.

Adam's anxiety, according to Kierkegaard, consists in the lack of primitiveness, which is primarily given to Adam by God's words or Spirit, or of the fact Adam has deprived his spirit of his primitiveness; "it consists in having emasculated oneself, in a spiritual sense."[137] While Adam is primitively planned to be a self, appointed to become oneself, he was defrauded by the serpent.[138] While the serpent is not identified with precision from the narrative, it implies a symbol of passion and sensual pleasure of the world.[139] Kierkegaard argues that those who engage excessively in worldly affairs like *Dasein*'s involvement in *das Man* that Heidegger holds in *Being and Time*

136. CA 95.
137. SD 166.
138. SD 166.
139. IDB s.v. "serpent."

lose their ownness or selves. Such individuals forget their divine identity and find it easier to conform to the crowd, becoming mere imitations. By doing so, they achieve success in the world but lose their true self, becoming smooth and indistinguishable, like a well-used coin.[140]

b) Paganism

While spiritlessness is the lostness of self, paganism is about those who are not conscious of themselves before God as spirit. Ephesians 2:12, which Kierkegaard uses to define pagans,[141] says, "Remember that you Ephesians were separated from Christ, alienated from the commonwealth of Israel, and strangers to the covenants of promise having no hope and without God in the world." Kierkegaard argues that pagans measure themselves by purely human standards and their sin lies in their unawareness of God and of existing before God, which means being "without God in the world."[142]

As Adam was affected by others to follow what they show and sway, he lost himself and became spiritless. He subjected himself to the serpent's words through Eve. Despite Adam's spiritlessness under the force of the serpent and its idle or ungrounded words, Adam ontologically constituted by conscience or his wanting to have a conscience (*Gewissenhavenwollen*)[143] conscientiously was aware of what he did. Adam and Eve realized they were naked. They sewed fig leaves together, made themselves aprons, and covered themselves. Then they hid from the presence of God; God called them out and reprimanded them. But God made for them garments of skins and clothed them. Their sin and anxiety directed them not to be grounded on God, but nothingness (*die Nichtigkeit*).[144] Kierkegaard believes that spiritlessness leads to a lack of spirit and the inability to see anything in a spirit, despite being able to superficially grasp at everything. Nothingness did not liberate them from God's presence and the world. While Adam falls into their spiritlessness on account of others, including the serpent, spiritlessness can be transformed into being spiritual as Adam put himself before God, according to Kierkegaard.[145]

Kierkegaard argues that the self is not simply the human self, but the theological self who put the self in the sight of God. He also asserts that a

---

140. *SD* 166–67.
141. *SD* 212.
142. *SD* 212.
143. *SZ* 270; *BTM* 314; *BTS* 249.
144. Heidegger, "What Is Metaphysics?," 103.
145. *CA* 95.

self viewed only by other humans is a low self, using examples like a herdsman seen only by cows or a ruler seen only by slaves. He suggests that true selfhood is achieved when one measures oneself by God, thus attaining an infinite reality.[146] What Kierkegaard claims is that humanity has to put or stand itself before God and have a relationship with God for the sake of humanity whose selves are finite, temporal, and perishable, in contrast to God who is infinite, permanent, and imperishable. Kierkegaard's search for synthesis and relation between God and humanity is illuminated by Paul's search for the synthesis and relationship between Adam and Jesus Christ.

2. Adam and Jesus Christ

Kierkegaard picked Genesis 2 and 3 to discuss the origin of anxiety and paradoxical existence of humanity. Paul, in Romans 5, affected to formulate Kierkegaard's view of anxiety, paradox from Jesus Christ regarded as the unity of God and humanity, and death. Paul finds anti-God's words in Adam and pro-God's words in Jesus Christ. Adam brings disobedience to God, death, and hopelessness to humanity, while Jesus shows obedience to God, offers life and hope or expectation for the future (*elpis*, ἐλπὶς) to people. Adam delivers sin or transgression to humanity, but Jesus Christ gives grace (*charis*, χάρις) to humanity. Paul makes us consider which death each individual dies, "the death of Adam or the death of Christ."[147]

As Adam confronted anxiety and paradox between pro-God's words and anti-God's words, so humanity as the race of Adam faces the confrontation, paradox, and anxiety between Adam and Jesus Christ; Adam represents anti-God's words, while Jesus Christ pro-God's words. In the juxtaposed confrontation between Adam and Jesus, what Paul assert in epistles is that if we repeat Adam, who committed the disrelationship with or no-synthesis with God's words, we will end up with the death that Adam could not run away from. In contrast, if we have the relationship with Jesus Christ as "God and the man"[148] drawn as the relational being with God and humanity, and characterized as synthetic being between God and humanity, he/she does not have the consequence of death different from Adam, but is resurrected or transformed, and encounters *parousia* or the presence of the resurrected LORD or divinity.

God's words that are offered to Adam but challenged by him indicate that his freedom is limited, saying, he may freely eat of every tree of the

---

146. *SD* 210.
147. Rahner, *On the Theology of Death*, 36.
148. See Pannenberg, *Jesus—God and Man*.

garden, but is prohibited from eating the tree of the knowledge of good and evil; Adam's limited freedom entails his-self is not grounded on himself, but God's words, as Matthew 4:4 says, "People will not exist only by bread, but God's words"; Deuteronomy 8:3 says, "People don't live on bread alone, but God's words." The way of Jesus Christ as pro-God's words in contrast to Adam's anti-God's words is disclosed in "reconciliation or peacemaking," "humiliation," and "being suffering and sacrificed."

Jesus Christ as the peacemaker or reconciler performed God's words. As Matthew 5:9 says, "Blessed are the peacemakers, for they shall be called sons of God," Paul in Romans 5:1–2 states that we have peace with God through (*dia*, διά) Jesus Christ and through him we have obtained access to connection or synthesis with God whose words are not connected to humanity, since Adam or the race of humanity has disrelated God's words in its existence, and as Romans 3:23 says, "all have sinned and fall short of the glory of God." Jesus Christ as the synthesis between God and Man, or the synthesis between divinity and humanity is considered the reconciler between God and humanity. To reconcile is termed as "*katallasso* (καταλλάσσω),*"* which signifies a human being's relation to God.[149] Paul in Corinthians 5:18–19 says "*en Christo kosmon heauto* (ἐν Χριστῷ κόσμον ἑαυτῷ),"[150] which means that God's reconciliation with the world is in Christ; God's words in Jesus despite Adam's disrelationship with them are reconnected and reconciled with human existence as Adam's descendants through the participation of Jesus Christ in the world.

Jesus Christ as pro-God's words also reveals himself in being humble in spirit, which means privation from Jesus' prestige and significance. Jesus Christ emptied his divinity and became humanity, which is called incarnation. Paul in Philippians 2:5–8 says,

> Although Jesus Christ was in the form of God, he did not count equality with God a thing to be grasped, but emptied himself, taking the form of a servant, being born in the human likeness. And being found in human form, he humbled himself and became obedient unto death—even death on a cross (*santatou de staurou*, θανάτου δὲ σταυροῦ).

Paul asserts that Jesus Christ emptied himself in three forms: taking the form of a slave apart from holy divinity, thus discarding the Master of the world, being born in the likeness of human beings, and being found in human form. Finally he became obedient unto death.

---

149. *GEL* s.v. "καταλλάσσω."
150. *GEL* s.v. "καταλλάσσω."

The emptiness (*kenosis*, κένωσις) that Jesus Christ carried out through emptying of himself of the outer form of God and taking on an outer form of a man[151] brings about the issue of who Jesus Christ really is. Paul says Jesus emptied himself and participated in the world, but some people argue that Jesus "appeared on earth in a disguise and was not really man."[152] Jesus' existence in the world as appearance instead of a real person is termed "*dokeo* (δοκέω)," which means "to seem" or "to appear to existence."[153] Docetism, from a Greek root *dokeo* that means to appear, suggests Jesus' embodiment in the world was not really such, but simply an appearance. For docetic believers, Jesus was a purely divine spirit, and his humanity was only apparent; he did not suffer like us. In defense of Docetism, its adherents deny Jesus' real humanity and actual death, believing He came not in the flesh but in a ghost-like appearance. This view is seen as an early form of Gnosticism and was a significant feature in Gnostic teaching.[154]

On the other hand, there are Ebionites who reject Jesus' divinity and hold in the person of Jesus Christ only one nature, that is, humanity devoid of divinity. For Ebionites, Jesus was seen as the son of Joseph and Mary who perfectly fulfilled Jewish law, leading God to choose Him as the Messiah. They believed He improved the law and would return to establish a Messianic kingdom for the Jews.[155] Apart from whether Jesus Christ is considered the Docetic who stresses the divinity of Christ or the Ebionitic humanity of Christ, Paul understands Jesus Christ as the union of God and the human being, divinity's participation in humanity through emptiness. The concept of Jesus Christ as the union of God and humanity is difficult for people to understand so they turn to the Monophysite, which claims one *physis* (φύσις) or nature of Jesus Christ, not synthesis of divinity and humanity.[156] Docetism later joined Monophysites—which is why Pannenberg in *Jesus—God and Man* points out that the doctrine of Jesus' knowledge was consistently threatened by a docetic-Monophysite influence, which was sometimes dominant.[157]

Jesus Christ's emptiness is understood that while he is God, he does not want to exist only as God, but is embodied into or incarnated in the human being to be with and relate to the human being, according to Christ's

---

151. *IDB* s.v. "emptied."
152. *IDB* s.v. "emptied."
153. *GEL* s.v. "δοκέω."
154. Walker, *History of the Christian Church*, 51.
155. Walker, *History of the Christian Church*, 35.
156. Walker, *History of the Christian Church*, 140–47.
157. Pannenberg, *Jesus—God and Man*, 398.

obedience to the will of God that the relationship between God and humanity, broken by Adam, is reconnected, and thereby effects reconciliation.[158] Paul does not use the technical term "incarnation," but expresses synthesis of divinity and humanity and identifies the divinity of Christ with the human situation.[159] Kierkegaard uses an analogy to illustrate Jesus' existence as an emptied or incarnate being to identify divinity with human existence in his *Philosophical Fragments or A Fragment of Philosophy*.

A related to allegory describes a king who, out of love for a humble maiden, disguises himself as a beggar to win her love genuinely. He renounces his throne and adopts a new identity to bridge the gap between them, achieving union through descent rather than elevation, all to be truly equal in love.[160]

Finally, Jesus Christ performed and obeyed God's words through his death by crucifixion manifested in a suffering servant (*ebed YHWH*). Jesus Christ's death as sacrifice is displayed, for he gives up himself and gives himself as the burnt offering to God. Paul in Romans 3:24-25 states that Jesus' death as obedience to God's words, in contrast to Adam's disobedience to God's words or his own way of words enticed by the serpent's words, is considered the ransom for Adam's disrelationship with God. Paul in Romans 3:25 describes Jesus' death as an expiatory sacrifice, in 1 Corinthians 5:7 Jesus' death as a Passover sacrifice (1 Corinthians 5:7), and in Ephesians 5:2 Jesus' death as a sacrifice for sins.[161] Oscar Cullmann explains that the Old Testament concept of high priesthood involves the mediator bringing a sacrifice for the atonement of the people's sins but does not include the idea of the high priest's self-sacrifice. He indicates that the concept of the suffering servant (*ebed YHWH*) is more appropriate than that of the High Priest to convey the New Testament perspective on what Jesus viewed his work to be.[162]

3. Jesus' Death as Sacrifice

As a human being is born in the world or *Dasein* is thrown into the world, they grow and change until they die. This natural progression is likened to fruit ripening until it is ready to be harvested. Heidegger discusses how

---

158. *NIB* 11:515.
159. *NIB* 11:515.
160. Kierkegaard, *Philosophical Fragments*, 32-38.
161. *IDB* s.v. "Death of Christ."
162. Cullmann, *Christology of the New Testament*, 91.

unripe fruit progresses towards ripeness.¹⁶³ The Old Testament echoes this view, describing a mature human life as being plucked like ripe fruit (Job 5:26).¹⁶⁴ However, Jesus' death is distinct from this natural fulfillment. His death was an act of obedience to the will of God, making him as the suffering servant who bore the cross and died by crucifixion, not the fulfillment of being but to obey God's words in his existence as the suffering servant who bore the cross and died in crucifixion. This Crucifixion stands as a significant demonstration of Jesus' sacrificial act aimed at restoring humanity's communion with God.¹⁶⁵

Jesus performed God's words through following Isiah 52:12—53:12. Cullmann in *The Christology of the New Testament* describes a servant, who, despite being disfigured and rejected, embraces human suffering and sin, thereby bringing peace and healing through his wounds.¹⁶⁶ The scripture says a servant who will succeed and be highly honored despite being disfigured and unrecognizable. Many will be astonished by him, including kings who will be speechless upon seeing him. Growing up without beauty or majesty, he was despised and rejected, familiar with suffering. He took on our infirmities and sorrows, yet was considered afflicted by God. He was pierced and crushed for our transgressions, bringing us peace and healing through his wounds. Although oppressed and afflicted, he remained silent, like a lamb led to slaughter.¹⁶⁷

Jesus embodied this suffering servant, fulfilling God's prophetic words and contrasting sharply with Adam's disobedience. Paul explains in Philippians 2:8 that Jesus' self-emptying was a complete pouring out of his life unto death.¹⁶⁸ Hebrews 5:1 also refers to Jesus Christ as the priest who is embodied in humanity and appointed to make a union and relationship or peace with God through carrying out sacrifices, as the priest of the Old Testament performed the ritual for sinners to connect and relate to God through sacrificing and submitting burnt offerings. Christ is viewed as the sacrificer like the priest.¹⁶⁹ Unlike Old Testament priests who offered sacrifices, Jesus became both the sacrificer and the sacrifice.¹⁷⁰

---

163. SZ 243; BTM 287; BTS 226.
164. *IDB* s.v. "Death."
165. *IDB* s.v. "Crucifixion."
166. Cullmann, *Christology of the New Testament*, 53.
167. I readapted the scripture from my dissertation.
168. *IDB* s.v. "emptied."
169. Cullmann, *Christology of the New Testament*, 91. See also *IDB* s.v. "Death of Christ."
170. Cullmann, *Christology of the New Testament*, 91.

Kierkegaard, in *Fear and Trembling*, delves into the story of Abraham and Isaac, highlighting the profound faith and obedience required to offer a sacrifice to God. God's calling to Abraham to sacrifice and dedicate his son Isaac as the burnt offering to God suspends universal principles of *nous* or ethics. What is important from the biblical narrative is not only Abraham's struggle to have a relationship with God, but also Isaac himself, who nearly became a burnt offering. Christ as the sacrificer and sacrificed is the synthesis between Abraham and Isaac that Kierkegaard investigated. While Adam, fell into death, the synthesis of Abraham and Isaac heard a voice from God who said that Abraham should find something else as the burnt offering. Likewise, Jesus Christ as the synthesis of Abraham and Isaac, the sacrificer and the sacrificed who obeyed God's words is transformed into the eternal being called the resurrected Christ, providing humanity with a path back to God.

4. Resurrection as Transformation

Heidegger, in *Being and Time*, discusses the inescapability of death called "no-longer existence" or "impossibility of existence," leading to the mood of anxiety and emptiness, for *Dasein*'s death is *"non-relational (unbezügliche), certain . . . not to be outstripped (unüberholbare)."*[171] While *Angst* directs *Dasein* to view everything of the world as nothingness that leads to emptiness, emptiness liberates *Dasein* from the attachment to the world, and serves *Dasein* to lie in *"being-ahead-of-itself,"*[172] and to project the possibility of its new existence. *Dasein*'s emptiness as nothingness arouses freedom, displacement, openness or disclosedness (*die Erschlossenheit*), and openness provides for *Dasein* to envision the new possibility of its existence.

Emptiness (*kenosis*, κένωσις) that Paul asserts in the epistles is carried out by Christ, who was in the form of God, was emptied of his divinity, and took the form of a slave. Jesus' emptiness is to make him low and poor, to be the same as humanity apart from being considered to the high, supernatural, holy being, but to exist together with humanity, and to love people. Jesus' emptiness is understood as the shift of the paradigm from the hierarchical or the privileged to the underprivileged in status and condition. Significantly, what Jesus did then was to take the radical emptiness called death and became a sacrifice. His radical emptiness, or *kenosis*, led to his resurrection, symbolizing transformation, openness, new creation, hope, and victor over death.

171. *SZ* 258; *BTM* 303; *BTS* 239.
172. *SZ* 337; *BTM* 386; *BTS* 310.

Kierkegaard, in *The Sickness unto Death*, argues that humans live in a state of contradiction or paradox between the infinite and the finite, the temporal and the eternal, the spiritual and the physical, freedom and necessity. This contradiction leads to anxiety, sin, and death. However, he believes that our spirit, or relationship with God, can help us integrate these opposing elements into a unified being. Similarly, in *The Concept of Anxiety*, Kierkegaard discusses how anxiety and sin originated with Adam, who disobeyed God's command and brought death into the world. Kierkegaard's ideas were influenced by Paul, who also saw humanity as caught in a paradox between Adam and Jesus Christ, between the spirit and the flesh, leading to sin and death. According to Paul, overcoming this paradox, sin, and death requires faith in God.

Paul specifically contrasts Adam's fall into sin and death with Jesus Christ's obedience to God, which overcame sin and death. He suggests that just as Adam faced a choice between obeying and disobeying God, humanity faces a similar choice between following Adam or Jesus Christ. Adam represents disobedience to God, while Jesus represents obedience. Paul emphasizes in his epistles that if we follow Adam's example of disobedience, we will face the same fate of death that Adam did. In contrast, if we follow Jesus Christ, who embodies a harmonious relationship with God and humanity, we will experience a different kind of transformation and ultimately encounter eternal life.

While Adam, who prefers anti-God's words to God's words, falls into death, Jesus Christ's adherence to God's words led to his resurrection. As Paul discovered human paradox and inconsistency from both Adam and Jesus representing humanity, Paul finds human contradictoriness from its ontological existence constituted by the flesh (σαρξ) and the spirit (πνεῦμα). The flesh and spirit, which are in opposition, shape the human being called *soma* (σῶμα),[173] as *soma* is born in the world; "*Flesh and spirit* = the whole personality, in its outer and inner aspects [exist in *soma* throughout its life]."[174]

The flesh in *soma* is earthly, materialistic, corporeal, restrictive, mortal, perishable, and peripheral but animate and active. Bultmann in *Theology of the New Testament* differentiates between the flesh of the *soma* and animal flesh intended for food. He clarifies that the flesh of *soma* refers to the animate flesh of a person, active in its sensual manifestations and perceptible to the senses, which are formed and animated in the person, for the flesh of

---

173. *GEL* s.v. "σῶμα."
174. *GEL* s.v. "πνεῦμα."

the person is existent along with the spirit as the whole personality in *soma*, contrasting with the simple matter or material of the animal.[175]

The spirit (*pneuma*, πνεῦμα) in *soma* is incorporeal, celestial, boundless, unrestrictive, measureless, renewable, and regenerative to *soma*. The root meaning of *pneuma* or the spirit is "'a movement of air,' 'breeze,' or 'wind,' and so 'breath.'"[176] Since the spirit is incorporeal or non-physical, or immaterial, God's nature is understood as the spirit, and God is pure spirit. However, the spirit is found in *soma*, for humanity is created in the image of God, as Genesis 1:27 says, "So God created humanity in God's own image, in the divine image God created them, male and female God created them." Paul in Romans 8 states that in the spiritual nature God has endowed every male or female that makes it possible for the Spirit of God to dwell in the person. The nature of spirit provides a basis for the continuing conversation between a human's spirit and the divine Spirit, which comes to dwell with humanity.[177]

As the flesh and the spirit are mutually exclusive and juxtaposed to each other, and thereby are in tensions and contradictoriness in human existence, Jesus Christ, as the synthesis of man and God, the flesh and the spirit, and the corporeal and incorporeal, ontologically has to confront dichotomy, paradox, and oppositeness in his being. Since docetic believers, Ebionites, and Monophysites argue that Jesus Christ is only in one nature, either the flesh or the spirit, they do not understand that Jesus Christ is considered the being of the synthesis of divinity and humanity, and the spirit and the flesh, which are connected to Christ's suffering, death, and resurrection.

As Adam in himself had confronted dichotomy and anxiety between pro-God's words and anti-God's, he had a disrelationship with pro-God's word-self but extends a relationship with anti-God's words, departed from God, and eventually fell into death. Jesus Christ as the second Adam that Paul calls in 1 Corinthians 15:47 ontologically also confronted the dichotomy between the flesh rooted in corporeal and materialistic earth—the flesh-self, and the incorporeal, celestial spirit set in heaven—the spirit-self. In this contradictoriness, Jesus Christ sacrificed himself as the burnt offering through giving up himself engaged in the flesh of the earth but having a relationship with the spirit based on God's words or God's Spirit. First Corinthians 15:47 states that the first human or Adam was based on the flesh or earthly being, and the second Adam or Jesus Christ is rooted in heavenly spirit. Paul in 1 Corinthians 15:45–46 states that the first human,

---

175. Bultmann, *Theology of the New Testament*, 1:233.
176. *IDB* s.v. "Spirit."
177. *IDB* s.v. "Spirit."

Adam, became, a living being and the last Adam, Jesus Christ, became a life-giving spirit despite the beginning of life with Adam. Jesus Christ as the sacrificer sacrificed anti-God's words or the flesh, but is united or synthesized with God's words or God of the Spirit. Jesus Christ, who sacrificed Himself as the burnt offering to follow God's words and dedicated Himself to God, does not become self-independent being but is dependent on the will of the Creator.[178] Sacrifice or crucifixion of anti-God's words or the flesh led Jesus Christ to join God's Spirit and become the Resurrected LORD in contrast to the first Adam, who was transformed into the dead or the being of temporality.

The greatest and worthiest Judeo-Christian biblical narrative tells us of God's creation of humanity and the world. Since God created humanity, I can exist in the world, as parents made me exist in the world. Of course, God's creation is neither understood by Reason or *Nous*, nor is it scientifically proven. However, as Hebrews 11:3 says, "By faith we understand that the world was created by the word of God," in faith to which Kierkegaard refers, God created Adam and Eve as the race of humanity. But Adam's disrelationship with God's words inverted humanity and the world. I-self, he/she-self, and they-selves come to exist as the no-longer existence or the existence of temporality inherited from Adam. The narrative of creation with Adam come to be insignificant and meaningless despite the beginning of existence with Adam and Eve until the second greatest, worthiest narrative is presented by Paul, who refers to Christ' death and resurrection. While Adam's existence and death are the beginning of creation, Jesus Christ's death and resurrection is the recreation of the world. As Paul in 1 Corinthians 15:22 says, "Everyone dies in Adam, so also everyone will be given life in Christ," Christ's death and resurrection offers us faith, hope, and future. Death originated from Adam is unworthy, for non-being started with Adam's being and ended with death. However, the beginning of the human being—the new being by Jesus' death and resurrection—has to start with the non-being of Adam. Verse 46 of 1 Corinthians 15 emphasizes that the spiritual being is not first but the natural being is first and the spiritual being starts because of the natural being. Therefore, we can celebrate the creation of Adam by God and the resurrection of Jesus for humanity.

Death is viewed as confinement or restriction on life. It is commonly believed that the dead continued to exist in Sheol or Hades or in the family sepulcher.[179] John Hick in *Death and Eternal Life* compares the ancient Hebrew Sheol to the Greek Hades, describing Sheol as a vast underground

---

178. Hick, *Death and Eternal Life*, 340.
179. *IDB* s.v. "Death."

cavern where the dead persist.[180] Karl Rahner's *On the Theology of Death* asserts that Christ's death made his spiritual reality open and accessible to the entire world, suggesting this as a permanent and ontological determination. He links this to the teaching of Christ's descent into Sheol, saying, "we might refer to the teaching of our faith that concerns Christ's descent into hell, that is, Sheol, the lower world."[181] Jesus' death and Resurrection imply emancipation out of restriction and the inclusion of and openness to the Gentiles and the world. In contrast, Pannenberg posits that the Gentile mission emerged from the belief in Jesus' exaltation to Lordship in heaven, prompting the spread of this news to all nations.[182]

Resurrection as transformation does not mean to restore what the past has done or lost but recreation and reformation for the future. While restoration of the past is regarded as resuscitation or restoration, resurrection is transformation toward the future. Pannenberg argues that for Paul, resurrection signifies the beginning of new life in a new body rather than a return to life in a previously decayed fleshly body.[183] Resurrection is not resuscitation. Luke 7:11–17 tells about Jesus' rejuvenating a young man whose breath has stopped. Nevertheless, the young man died eventually, for resuscitation is distinguishable from the resurrection of the dead that Jesus disclosed. Jesus' resurrection and the Christian hope of resurrection is transformation from the perishable body into the imperishable body, from physical body to spiritual body, from the past body to the future body.

5. *Parousia* (Παρουσία) as Presence of Divinity

After Jesus Christ was crucified, transformed unto resurrection, and was absent from his disciples, they expected something meaningful and hopeful for their future: "*parousia* (παρουσία)." *Parousia* is used in the general sense of the "arrival" or "coming" as well as "presence."[184] The term *parousia* brings about two questions: (1) what *parousia* is like, and (2) when *parousia* comes about. Similarly, Heidegger raises two questions: "1. How does it stand with the dead, who no longer experience the *parousia* (1 Thessalonians 4:14–18)? 2. When will the *parousia* take place (1 Thessalonians 5:1–12)?"[185]

---

180. Hick, *Death and Eternal Life*, 59.
181. Rahner, *On the Theology of Death*, 63–64.
182. Pannenberg, *Jesus—God and Man*, 71.
183. Pannenberg, *Jesus—God and Man*, 75.
184. *IDB* s.v. "parousia."
185. Heidegger, *Phenomenology of Religious Life*, 69.

What *parousia* is like is disclosed in three ways: first, classical Greek philosophy, second, Hebrew-Jewish tradition of the Old Testament, and third, Paul's use of the term.[186] Heidegger says, "In classical Greek παρουσία [*parousia*] means arrival (presence)."[187] The classical Platonic-Aristotelian meaning of *parousia* is *ousia* (οὐσία), which means substance or essence; substance or essence is equivalent to "beingness as presentness,"[188] which makes an entity what it fundamentally is and properly appears. Beingness as presentness is to manifest what an entity properly holds instead of hiding itself. Thus, *parousia* is served as the coming out of concealment of the entity.[189] The coming out of hiddenness is demonstrated by not only the official visit of a person of higher rank or ruler, but also the epiphany of divinity.[190] *Parousia* in Greek philosophy is to be considered an ontological presence of the entity.

In Hebrew-Jewish tradition it is relating to soteriology. *Parousia* of Hebrew-Jewish background means God's deliverance illustrated in the story of Exodus about Israelites' Egyptian bondage and emancipation out of their enslavement. *Parousia* shows that God does not hold back God-self, but emerges to save captives. *Parousia* entails God's rescue and "the arrival of [the prophet like Moses] as representative of God."[191]

However, in Paul *parousia* is distinct not only from the Greek meaning of beingness as presentness, but also the arrival of the Messiah for whom Jewish people have waited, for Paul believes that the Messiah called Jesus Christ has already come to the world. What Paul unveils is *parousia* divided into two kinds: the first coming and the second coming of Jesus Christ. The first *parousia* called "incarnation" is the presence of Christ, whose deity is embodied in the flesh of the human being, while the second *parousia* is to encounter the resurrected or transformed Christ in the future. His presence as the incarnated being from God to the human being implies the significance of humanity and that every human being as the descendant of Adam is worthy to exist, as the human being is born in the world. His presence shows people the way of existence, enactment, love, and death in the world. Jesus' resurrection or transformation as the transformed being by God implies that humanity's spirit goes beyond the death of the flesh.

---

186. See *IDB* s.v. "parousia."
187. Heidegger, *Phenomenology of Religious Life*, 71.
188. Sheehan, "Introduction to Phenomenology of Religion," 56.
189. *GEL* s.v. "παρουσία."
190. *GEL* s.v. "παρουσία."
191. Heidegger, *Phenomenology of Religious Life*, 71.

Human existence is ultimately *"at the point of death"* called *"eskhatos* (ἔσχατος)."[192] In response to *eskhatos*, Paul proclaims that people have belief, hope, and projection toward the second coming or *parousia* of Christ, who died but was transformed into the living being as the first fruit of humanity. Heidegger reflects that just as God resurrected Christ, he will also bring the dead to him along with Christ.[193] While *parousia* in Paul begins with Christ's first presence as the incarnated being in the world, people can expect to encounter the resurrected Christ called the *"second* coming of the Christ."[194] Thomas J. Sheehan argues that in Paul, while *parousia* begins with Jesus' first coming to the world, after his resurrection, to encounter his presence as *parousia* for us in the future means the *"second* coming of the Christ in glory."[195] Heidegger says, for Paul, *"parousia* means 'the appearing again of the already appeared Messiah.'"[196] Thus, *parousia* in Paul is ontological, soteriological and eschatological.[197]

When *parousia* takes place is a significant question Heidegger noted. "How does *parousia* stand with the dead, who no longer experience the *parousia*?"—does it come to people after or before their death? Paul in 1 Thessalonians 4:15–17 writes that first, those who are dead in Christ will rise, and then, we who are living will be taken up with them to experience the second coming of Christ. The answer to the question whether *parousia* takes place before death or after it is to include both dead and living ones.

Paul's answer to the question of "when" *parousia* comes about is in 1 Thessalonians 5:1–2. He writes that regarding chronological and sudden time, it is acknowledged that the day of the LORD will come unexpectedly, emphasizing that the timing of the parousia is beyond objective grasp.[198] Paul does not say that the LORD will come at this or that time. Instead, he says that the day of the LORD will come like a thief in the night. Heidegger stresses the importance of personal awareness and decision-making based on one's own life in the context of the timing of events.[199] The decisive factor is how one comports themselves in life, which influences the meaning of the timing and moments.[200] How I comport myself to *parousia* in actual life is

---

192. *GEL* s.v. "ἔσχατος"; "ἔσχάτως."
193. Heidegger, *Phenomenology of Religious Life*, 81.
194. Sheehan, "Introduction to Phenomenology of Religion," 56.
195. Sheehan, "Introduction to Phenomenology of Religion," 56.
196. Heidegger, *Phenomenology of Religious Life*, 71.
197. Sheehan, "Introduction to Phenomenology of Religion," 56.
198. Heidegger, *Phenomenology of Religious Life*, 73.
199. Heidegger, *Phenomenology of Religious Life*, 72.
200. Heidegger, *Phenomenology of Religious Life*, 70.

called "factical life-experience,"²⁰¹ which matters how people in temporality or a short time live and enact individually and genuinely interrelate with others and God.

The way people comport themselves to *parousia* in actual life is disclosed in 1 Thessalonians 5:3–8: "When people say, 'There is peace and security' at that time sudden destruction will attack them. But you are not in darkness so that the day of *parousia* won't catch you by surprise like a thief. So then, let's not sleep like a drunkard, but stay awake and stay sober." To be awake is opposed to simply looking forward to the future event of *parousia*.²⁰² Those who stay awake and sober are depicted as actively engaged in continuous life rather than idling in anticipation of the parousia.²⁰³ "The question of the 'when' of the *parousia* [comes] back to [the] question of the 'how' of life—and that is, '*wachsam sein*,' to be awake."²⁰⁴ Thus, Paul in 1 Corinthians 15:51–54 argues the experiencing of *parousia* takes place in a moment of the twinkling of an eye (*ecstasis*, ἔκστασις) as the involvement of the infinite to the finite, which is considered the unity of the future, past and present.

Paul first believed that *parousia* would happen in his lifetime. But he later modified his views and at the close of his life felt that he would die before the LORD' coming.²⁰⁵ In *Jesus/God and Man*, Pannenberg says that Paul believed in the imminent arrival of the resurrected Jesus.²⁰⁶ There might be many reasons why the followers of the resurrected Christ expected the imminent return of Christ or *parousia*. Since some of them had to confront persecution and martyrdom under Roman emperors, they could not patiently wait for but impatiently expected *parousia*. Others might misunderstand in reference to time that *parousia* happens immediately, which brings about the issue of time—*chronos* (χρόνος), or a period of time, *hora* (ὥρα), or a short period of time, and *kairos* (καιρός) or a right, favorable, proper time, or the time determined by God.²⁰⁷ Others might also overlook that Jesus' resurrection is carried out by the engagement of the Spirit of God after emptying Jesus' being—sacrifice as the burnt offering. That is to say that resurrection is not undertaken by one's own determination but by the Spirit of God. Paul in 1 Corinthians 15:20–28 states that Christ has been

---

201. Sheehan, "Introduction to Phenomenology of Religion," 57.
202. Sheehan, "Introduction to Phenomenology of Religion," 57.
203. Heidegger, *Phenomenology of Religious Life*, 76.
204. Sheehan, "Introduction to Phenomenology of Religion," 57.
205. Walker, *History of the Christian Church*, 29.
206. Pannenberg, *Jesus—God and Man*, 66.
207. See GEL s.v. "χρόνος"; "ὥρα"; "καιρός."

raised from the dead as the first fruit of those who have died; while death came through Adam and all die in Adam, the resurrection of the dead has come through Jesus Christ and all will be made alive in Christ, the second Adam, who surrendered Himself to the Creator, who created the first Adam and became the resurrected Christ. *Parousia* is not determined by people's expectation but belongs to the Spirit of God, who raised the crucified Christ so that people have to patiently anticipate *parousia*.

VI

Epilogue

WHY AND HOW HAVE I written this book? The answers to these questions are elaborated by sharing my previous experiences. Conscience, life, death, sin, and salvation were issues that interested me from a young age.

1. EXPERIENCE OF DEATH

When I was five, I had a sister, who was younger than me by eleven months. My sister was healthy and chubby, but I was weak and skinny, and both of us had measles at the same time. We were confined to bed, suffering severely. One day my mother and grandmother came to the room to give us medicine. I was awakened by the sound of the door opening, but I did not open my eyes until they administered medicine to us. My mother and grandmother whispered that my healthy sister would survive, but I would die before long. They did not recognize that I heard and understood what they said. A few weeks later my sister unfortunately died, but I survived. Since she had disappeared, I asked my grandmother where she had gone. My Christian grandmother answered that my sister went up to heaven, for she was innocent and God saved her. She made me certain that I could see her someday in heaven. Thus, life and death and heaven and hell are deeply impressed on my mind, and the thought of death and hell haunts me.

I started to go to the church at a very young age with my grandmother. I just learned and believed what Sunday school teachers taught me without challenging them until high school when a Sunday Bible teacher emphasized that salvation is only granted to those who believe in Jesus Christ. He, who was a Christian theological seminary student, taught high school

EPILOGUE

students that no one can go to heaven without believing in Jesus Christ. I wondered if my sister, who had passed away at the age of 4, went to heaven or not, for she died too young to be aware of Jesus Christ. Thus, I told the Sunday school teacher it was not fair that those who did not have an awareness of, and belief in, Jesus Christ were destined to hell. Soteriological belief and faith and Jesus Christ as the means to redemption were debated in the Sunday school class for several weeks. The Bible teacher said that salvation is related to the human conscience and is available to those who had not heard the gospel and are unaware of faith in Jesus Christ. Salvation that does not absolutely depend on a belief in Jesus Christ implies that salvation is open and inclusive, and universal. This idea reduces the strength of the idea of hell in favor of a belief in universal salvation.[1] However, I was not satisfied with his conclusion and disturbed by this question: can't I be guided by conscience without considering a personal commitment to or faith in Jesus Christ? The controversial issue between openness of salvation and restricted salvation occupied my youth and made me determine to study more and to find theological-philosophical foundations through advanced studies.

As I studied Eastern and Western philosophy, Christian theology, and diverse religions such as Buddhism, Hinduism, Taoism, and Islam, I was occupied by the issues of conscience, death, open or restricted salvation, and damnation. The question of whether or not those who do not have explicit acknowledgement and faith in Jesus Christ are to be accessible to God's salvation still holds me. Karl Rahner, who inclines toward openness to or universal salvation, responds to the question with two aspects.

The first is the understanding of the universality of God's grace and the access of all people to grace. Those who belong to the universality of God's grace, apart from whether or not they confess Jesus Christ as their savior, are called "anonymous Christians." The term "anonymous (*anonymen*)" (epistemologically, *anonumos*, ἀνώνυμος, nameless) is used for those whose names or identities are not known. Someone's name implies the person's properness, identity, and individuality.[2] The anonymous Christians to whom Rahner refers are those who live in accord with the grace of God,[3] but they are neither related to a Christian community nor named as Christians. Very simply, an anonymous Christian is a person who isn't a Christian but who acts like one. In *On the Theology of Death*, Rahner describes anonymous Christians as those who embody Christian spirit, even if not in name, as long as they do not oppose Christianity at the time

---

1. Hick, *Death and Eternal Life*, 93.
2. *GEL* s.v. "ὄνομα." See also *IDB* s.v. "Name."
3. Duffy, "Experience of Grace," 54.

of their death.[4] What Rahner asserts in reference to anonymous Christians is that God's love and blessing are pervasive or "pancosmic,"[5] by which he refers to the universe; non-Christians, because of God's universal salvific will, can live in a Christian manner.[6] The anonymous Christians presuppose that grace is universal or pancosmic and extended to the outside of the historical church; God's self-gift is neither discontinuous nor exceptional.[7] Thus, Rahner in "Nature and Grace" says "Our whole spiritual life is lived in the realm of the salvific will of God, of [God's] prevenient grace, [as defined by St. Augustine], of his call as it becomes efficacious: all of which is an element within the region of our consciousness, though one which remains anonymous as long as it is not interpreted from without by the message of faith."[8] H. F. Stewart in *Thirteen Homilies of St. Augustine on St. John XIV* says, "For Augustine's doctrine of preventing grace—to him we owe the term *gratia praeveniens* [prevenient grace]."[9] Rahner's view on the prevenient grace is similar to the view of the prevenient grace of John Wesley, who founded Methodism and taught that God's grace had spread to all humans; the prevenient grace, which refers to the grace of God in a person's life which precedes and prepares to conversion allowed anyone to come to faith.[10]

God's love and blessing are pancosmic to the world through Jesus Christ's death. Of course, Jesus' death is traditionally understood in relation to Saint Anselm's notion of *satisfaction*, which means "the death of Christ regarded as a ransom paid to the lack of Adam's original righteousness by the Devil [the serpent]."[11] Rahner, as mentioned by John Hick, critiques the traditional Catholic atonement doctrine, questioning why Christ's death specifically redeemed humanity rather than his life, despite scripture emphasizing his death.[12] Hick in *Death & Eternal Life* further says, "Rahner

---

4. Rahner, *On the Theology of Death*, 112.
5. Rahner, *On the Theology of Death*, 19, 21, 52–53, 67.
6. Marmion and Hines, *Cambridge Companion to Karl Rahner*, xiii.
7. Carr, "Karl Rahner," 529.
8. Rahner, "Nature and Grace," 180, quoted from Carr, "Karl Rahner," 529.
9. Augustine, *Thirteen Homilies*, 131.
10. Melton, *Encyclopedia of Protestantism*, 374.
11. Williams, *Idea of the Fall and of Original Sin*, 397–98, 524. See also Hick, *Evil and the God of Love*, 262.
12. Hick, *Death and Eternal Life*, 230. See Rahner, *On the Theology of Death*, 60.

EPILOGUE

draws upon his theory of 'the opening out of a pancosmic relation of the spirit'[13] at death."[14]

Just as Kierkegaard conceives the human being as the synthesis of soul and body,[15] so Rahner understands the human being constituted by the body and the soul (the spirit) based on the traditional Catholic doctrine. While the body as the flesh is materialistic, perishable, and bindable, the soul, like the spirit, is boundless, unrestrictive, and measureless. The unrestrictive, boundless soul has to relate to and adjust with the perishable and bindable body for the human being to exist in the world. Rahner, according to the traditional Catholic doctrine, believes that death is the separation of soul from body.[16] He argues that the soul is at death released from the limitation bound to the body and becomes related to the world as a whole. Rahner states that the spiritual soul will not become non-cosmic in death but rather "pancosmic."[17]

Rahner further explains that the death of Jesus Christ made him the pancosmic being. Jesus Christ is the synthesis of man and God, the flesh and the spirit, and the corporeal and incorporeal. His being and love were revealed, existed, and expressed in the spatio-temporal boundary. Jesus Christ was restricted during the period of his incarnation to exerting an influence in one place at a time.[18] However, Christ, who was truly human as well as truly divine, died a human death, and at death his soul entered into the pancosmic state. Christ as spirit entered into "the intrinsic, radically unified, ultimate and deepest level of the reality of the world"[19]—this going down of the Christ-spirit into the depths of the cosmos being traditionally symbolized by his descent into hell.[20] The result of this is that the Christ-spirit entered into the pancosmic state, restricted during the period of the incarnation to exerting an influence in one place at a time, and is now able to influence the world as a whole, changing the environment in which the

---

13. Rahner, *On the Theology of Death*, 58.
14. Hick, *Death and Eternal Life*, 230.
15. *SD* 158.
16. Hick, *Death and Eternal Life*, 228.
17. Rahner, *On the Theology of Death*, 21.
18. Hick, *Death and Eternal Life*, 230.
19. Rahner, *On the Theology of Death*, 64.
20. "According to non-biblical sources, the soul (spirit) or the pneuma (πνεῦμα) are in the underworld . . . or in the air . . . where evil spirits can prevent them from ascending higher . . . τοῖς ἐν φυλακῇ πνεύμασιν πορευθεὶς ἐκήρυξεν: to the spirits in prison, having gone, Jesus Christ preached, 1 Peter 3:19 belongs if it refers to Jesus' preaching to the spirits of the dead in hell" (*GEL* s.v. "πνεῦμα").

human being has lived ever since.[21] Rahner states that the question why his death is redemption for us is still left unanswered. It is only in death that the human being enters into an open, unrestricted relationship to the cosmos as a whole.[22] Rahner believes that Christ's spiritual reality, through his death, becomes accessible to the entire world and is a permanent ontological determination.[23] He further argues that if we suppose that through death Christ established an open, real ontological relationship to the world in its unity in reference to its spatio-temporal diversification, we may understand why his death has more than one redemptive significance for us.[24] Jesus Christ's death, according to Rahner, offers all people their future salvation instead of hell, which is to be called universal salvation. Rahner's argument about Christ's death and pancosmic pervasiveness of grace means salvation already openly and universally dwells in all people.

However, Rahner's universality of God's grace is challenged by some critics, who say that his view negates the uniqueness of Jesus as a form of relativism.[25] Rahner's openness or universal salvation confronts the question of whether universal salvation is unconditionally and effortlessly offered to anyone. If unconditional and universal grace is endowed to people through Jesus Christ's death, the grace is already carried to all people. Does Rahner need to bring up Christ's death and pancosmic redemption through Christ? According to Rahner, Christ's death brings God's blessing and salvation to all people, which eases humanity's fears about the afterlife. However, if we accept his view of universal salvation, there would be no distinction between being saved and not being saved, or between grace and non-grace, except for the transition from earthly life to heavenly life without any sacrifice or effort.

In contrast, Friedrich Bonhoeffer in *The Cost of Discipleship*[26] argues that God's grace and salvation are not cheaply made available to people, but costly, and sacrificially. For that reason, God's grace is seen as restricted, for it demands sacrifice, commitments, and efforts, even if Bonhoeffer does not mention that his view is the restricted salvation. If we rely on universal salvation without personal involvement or commitment to God, the salvation might fall into the "cheap" grace to which Bonhoeffer refers: "Grace is costly because it compels a [human being] to submit to the yoke of Christ and

---

21. Hick, *Death and Eternal Life*, 230.
22. Rahner, *On the Theology of Death*, 63.
23. Rahner, *On the Theology of Death*, 63.
24. Rahner, *On the Theology of Death*, 64–65.
25. Duffy, "Experience of Grace," 54.
26. Bonhoeffer, *Cost of Discipleship*, 48.

follow him; it is grace because Jesus says: 'My yoke is easy and my burden is light.'"[27] Bonhoeffer criticizes the notion of cheap grace, arguing that it misleads people and prevents them from understanding the costly grace offered by Christ.[28]

Paul argues that Jesus Christ' death and resurrection, which became the first fruit of resurrection for those who have already died (1 Corinthians 15:20; Romans 8:29), were not with ease carried out, but effected by Jesus' commitment to God by crucifixion. Jesus' death or crucifixion is not the natural death that is the cessation of human body's organic function, but death on the cross or crucifying oneself before God. Crucifixion is Jesus' commitment to emptiness or "*kenosis* (κένωσις)," which is "the self-emptying of the God-man [Jesus Christ] in the condition of his humiliation."[29] Michael J. Gorman in his *Cruciformity: Paul's Narrative Spirituality of the Cross* encourages people to have "cruciformity," which Gorman refers to as "his own term for a concept . . . [as] conformity to the crucified Christ."[30] While the costly grace and salvation to which Bonhoeffer refers is divergently expressed, what is certain is that God's grace and salvation are not obtained cheaply, but are costly and sacrificially endowed to those who have their commitment and faith in Christ.

We need both Rahner's universal salvation and Bonhoeffer's costly salvation to have a comprehensible apprehension as far as the issue is concerned with salvation. If we only emphasize Rahner's universal salvation, the salvation seems to be cheap and people are not aware of the value of salvation, as Bonhoeffer indicates. On the other hand, if people are bent on Bonhoeffer's costly salvation, they are concerned with how much they sacrifice themselves to be saved, for the human being is finite; can anyone be saved without God's prevenient mercy? Since both universal and costly salvation are paradoxical to what Kierkegaard refers, they have to relate to each other for comprehending God's grace. Kierkegaard argues that the relation between them is not established by human reason, but faith in God, that is, self-relation to God.[31] These are two different ways in which God can bestow salvation upon humanity. In either case salvation is dependent upon God.

Paul in 1 Corinthians 15 discusses the resurrection (*he anastasis*, ἡ ἀνάστασις), a spiritual body (*soma pneumatikon*, σῶμα πνευματικόν), and

27. Bonhoeffer, *Cost of Discipleship*, 48.
28. Bonhoeffer, *Cost of Discipleship*, 59.
29. Pannenberg, *Jesus—God and Man*, 287.
30. Gorman, *Cruciformity*, 4.
31. *SD* 147.

a physical or natural body (soma psychikon, σῶμα ψυχικόν). Paul asserts that *soma* or the human being consists of two beings: the physical and spiritual bodies. The physical body is temporal and perishable, while the spiritual body is transtemporal and imperishable. When the resurrection or transformation takes place, the natural or physical body is put into the ground, but the spiritual body is raised. While the perishable, physical body might be considered unholy and disgraceful, and the imperishable, and the spiritual body be holy and graceful, Paul argues that the physical body is presupposed prior to the spiritual body; that is, the physical body comes first, not the spiritual body—the spiritual body comes afterward. While the spiritual body and the physical body are juxtaposed from each other, each cannot be understood without the other. Paul argues that we do not need to remove the physical body to search for the spiritual body, but instead to add the spiritual body to the physical body. In 1 Corinthians 15:44–49, he states that if there's a physical body, there's also a spiritual body; Adam became a living person and Jesus Christ became a spirit that gives life; it is not the spiritual which is first but the physical, and then the spiritual.

While in Christian church ministry, I was invited to officiate a funeral service in a high school gymnasium for a young woman who was supposed to graduate from the high school but was killed in a car accident two weeks before. She was immigrated from western Europe to the United States of America and grew up under a single father. I heard from high school students that life is unfair with the question why God didn't protect the teenager if God is good and love; and can they have any hope to meet her in the future? They asked me whence death come from; and what is the relationship between death and life in the human being? Are there any possibilities of existence after death?

I had to comfort the students who attended the funeral service by delivering three messages to them. The first message was I introduced the Holy Spirit called "Paracletes (*Parakletos*, Παράκλητος)," who is considered an advocate, aid, or support, hence, the Consoler, Comforter, or Intercessor.[32] The second message was she was innocent and her future after death was on God's blessed hand. The third message was I urged the participants of the funeral service to have a commitment to love, justice, and faith in God. The grieving students were confronted by some of the same questions I had had as a five-year-old.

---

32. *GEL* s.v. "παράκλητος."

2. PARADOXICAL HUMAN BEING BETWEEN EXISTENCE AND DEATH

Kierkegaard in *The Concept of Anxiety* and *The Sickness unto Death* refers to humanity as the paradoxical being between the finite and the infinite, of the temporal and the eternal. He further searches for having a relationship and synthesis beyond the paradox through the spirit. Heidegger, who was influenced by Kierkegaard, also understands humanity's or *Dasein*'s way of being in paradox between *Dasein*'s existence and death, possibility and impossibility, and he undertakes to get over the paradox through nothingness (*Nichtigkeit*) or emptiness,[33] which is *Dasein*'s way of being.

As soon as *Dasein* or the human being is thrown into the world, it, as the unfinished being, becomes, is potential, and exists,[34] and thereby grows, and projects its future possible being. Heidegger says *Dasein* is different from other things, that while *Dasein* only exists, other entities such rocks and trees *are*, but they do not exist; horses are, but they do not exist.[35] What *Dasein* "exists" instead of "is" implies that *Dasein* exists as "being-there," or "standing-out-there" in an inescapable relationship with the world;[36] "being-there" or "standing-out-there" involves "disclosure" or being "away from" the inside of *Dasein*'s consciousness.[37] *Dasein*'s way of being as "being-there" involves the un-concealment, openness, possibility, and incompleteness of its existence in the world.

However, if *Dasein* perpetually exists, opens, grows, and projects in an endless way, it would be boundless and unable to be *Dasein* in its totality, unless it exists as the termination of *Dasein* called "death (*Tod*)." Thrown into the world *Dasein* exists in potentiality and openness in the essence of an unfinished quality of being,[38] but it is unavoidable to experience its death as its no-longer existence or impossibility of its existence. Sartre in "Merleau-Ponty" says, "To survive birth, even for an instant, is an adventure, as it is an adventure not to survive. . . . It is not enough to say that we are born to die[;] we are born at the moment of death."[39] *Dasein*'s existence constituted by death always runs toward its death (*das Sein zum Tode*). *Dasein*'s

---

33. Sartre, "Existentialism," 260. See also Zimmerman, "Heidegger, Buddhism, and Deep Ecology," 244–54.
34. SZ 236; BTM 279; BTS 219–20.
35. Heidegger, "Way Back into the Ground of Metaphysics," 214.
36. Hick, *Death and Eternal Life*, 97.
37. Heidegger, "Way Back into the Ground of Metaphysics," 214.
38. SZ 236; BTM 279; BTS 219–20.
39. Sartre, "Merleau-Ponty," 304.

possibility of its existence must at the same time be the being toward death or the impossibility of its existence as non-being.[40] Hence *Dasein* is to be considered a paradoxical and tensional being between existence and death, possibility and impossibility, openness and hiddenness, and infiniteness and finiteness in its being, even if Heidegger in his writings does not use the term "paradox" or "contradiction" to characterize *Dasein*. Since *Dasein* is the being of paradox, I think that *Dasein* is different from other beings, while Heidegger argues that *Dasein*'s existence makes it different from other entities.

Heidegger searches for having a relationship between *Dasein*'s paradoxical and tensional existences like Kierkegaard, whose essential ideas are "paradox," "relationship," and "synthesis," in which humanity engages in its existence. The relationship is accomplished by synthesizing two juxtaposed, paradoxical ways of being into one way of being through *Dasein*'s resoluteness carried by nothingness (*die Nichtigkeit*) or emptiness. Nothingness that Heidegger in "What Is Metaphysics?" refers to is that *Dasein* releases it from the attachment to the world into nothing or liberates itself from the world.[41] Nothingness is "nihilation,"[42] and nihilation frees *Dasein* from the world by which it is determined, and thereby helps it openly see the world.[43] Nevertheless, *Dasein* cannot totally free itself from the world, for it exists as "being-there" "standing-out-there," which entails *Dasein*'s possibility and unfinishedness in the relationship with the world. Rather, *Dasein* restrictedly exists in its freedom and possibility of its existence under the condition of anticipating its death, finitude, and impossibility of existence, and thereby inhibiting its possibility within its finitude of existence or impossibility of existence. Hence nothingness is to be considered the possibility of impossibility of existence. What Heidegger examines is how *Dasein* exists limitedly in the world under the inescapable condition of death. Even if *Dasein* exists as the potential and projective being toward its future in the world, it cannot surpass its death and eventually collapses into the non-being of death.

While death is the unavoidable condition to affect humanity whose existence will be no longer soon or later, according to Heidegger, Kierkegaard and Paul have philosophically and theologically searched for ways to get out of the condition of death and find a vision or hope. Kierkegaard argues that humanity is rooted in contradiction or paradox, which is shaped by

---

40. Hick, *Death and Eternal Life*, 98.
41. Heidegger, "What Is Metaphysics?," 112.
42. Heidegger, "What Is Metaphysics?," 105.
43. Heidegger, "What Is Metaphysics?," 112.

two opposite factors—inwardness and outwardness,[44] death and life, the finite and the infinite, the temporal and the eternal, freedom and necessity.[45] Since the two paired factors are exclusive, tensional in the human existence, the factors make humanity fall into discrepancy and anxiety of its existence—unless two factors are related to each other and synthesized into one. The relation and synthesis of two juxtaposed factors are undertaken by a third factor distinct from *Dasein*'s own resoluteness of nothingness that Heidegger argues. Kierkegaard posits that spirit is essential for synthesis, as synthesis requires this third factor to resolve contradictions.[46]

The spirt to which he refers is contrasted to human reason, and logic, but is manifested in faith in God, for "all things are possible for God"; "to believe is precisely to lose one's understanding [human reason or rational thought] in order to win God."[47] Kierkegaard in *Fear and Trembling* explores Abraham's way of being to explain faith in God, for Abraham is said to be the father of faith.[48] Abraham heard and followed God's voice to offer his son Isaac as the burnt offering, but eventually offered a ram as offering. Abraham's action was inexplicable and awkward on the basis of universal ethics and reason,[49] but his deed makes him the father of faith. Kierkegaard explains that faith provides the eternally certain antidote to despair through the possibility, as with God, all things are possible.[50]

While Heidegger thinks of death as *Dasein*'s impossibility of existence or no-longer existence, Paul refers to death as the transformation from the temporal to the transtemporal being of humanity. In Paul's view, the individual's existence did not end with his/her death, but he/she would be raised again to appear before God.[51] Paul's views on death and transformation are illuminated in three ways: (a) Jesus Christ' resurrection experienced by his disciples and followers, and Paul's experience of the resurrected Christ, (b) the difference and relationship between Jesus' resurrection and Greek idea of the immortality of the soul, and (c) anticipation of *parousia*.

a) The four gospels illustrate who Jesus is despite some differences depending on perspectives. However, the experience of the resurrected Christ is divergent. Different experiences of the resurrected Christ are

44. *FT* 79.
45. *SD* 146.
46. *CA* 85.
47. *CA* 171.
48. *FT* 33.
49. *FT* 77.
50. *SD* 173.
51. Hick, *Death and Eternal Life*, 182.

especially disclosed in the distinction between Jesus' disciples and followers' experiences that the crucified Christ was buried in the tomb and came out of the tomb, and Paul's experience of the resurrected Christ on the way of Damascus. Paul's experience of the resurrected Christ is here similar to the story of Luke 24:13–35: "On Easter Day two disciples were traveling to a village called Emmaus. They were talking to each other about death and resurrection. While they were discussing these things, the resurrected Christ joined them on their journey. They did not recognize Him. They talked about Jesus' death and resurrection, but they did not understand His resurrection. Then the resurrected Christ interpreted for them. When they came to Emmaus, the resurrected Christ spent the night with them and then disappeared. His disciples experienced the resurrected Christ." The burial of Jesus' body in the tomb and later emptiness of the tomb where the body was physically transformed into the new form of his body are called the ontic transformation of Jesus' entity. The resurrected Christ whom Paul and Jesus' disciples encountered on the way to Damascus and Emmaus is to be called the ontological transformation of Jesus' being.

The gospel narratives refer to Jesus' bodily resurrection. Luke 24:39–40 and John 20:20 present the risen Christ as the revived body from the tomb, with the marks of crucifixion upon him, and John 21:13 depicts him as eating, and John 20:24–29 refers to inviting doubting Thomas to touch him; the risen Christ could become physically present within a locked room and could disappear without any restraints. These gospel narratives of Jesus' resurrection are held by those who accept the case for a bodily resurrection that while the raised body was buried and confined in the tomb, Jesus' dead body was ontically transformed into the living body and the glorified state of body; his resurrection implies that he is "no longer subject to all the conditions governing ordinary objects in space."[52] Jesus' disciples and followers gathered together at Pentecost after his resurrection; Peter and John proclaimed Jesus was not bound in the tomb, but emptied the tomb where he was buried, and was alive. As Jesus' dead body was transformed into the living body, Peter moved and touched by the state of Jesus' ontic transformation also miraculously healed a man lame from birth.

However, Paul did not mention the empty tomb. It is suggested that although Paul might have known about the empty tomb stories, he did not consider them relevant to countering doubts about the resurrection of the dead within the Corinthian church.[53] Acts 9 refers to Paul's experience of the resurrected Christ. As he approached Damascus, suddenly a light from

---

52. Hick, *Death and Eternal Life*, 174.
53. Hick, *Death and Eternal Life*, 175.

heaven encircled him. There is neither an embodied presence nor a visual appearance of someone. He fell to the ground and heard a voice asking him why he attacked those who followed Jesus Christ as the messiah and believed in the resurrected Christ. He was seriously sick and carried by his companions to the city, Ananias prayed for him, and Paul was healed. This narrative is to be considered Paul's subjective experience as an instance of a resurrection appearance, apart from any empty tomb stories.[54] The resurrected Christ, whom Paul encountered, ontologically also transformed Paul's way of being from the adherence to traditional and exclusive Judaism to openness and an inclusive way of Christian being, from strictness of legalism to lenient conformism, from Hebrew chauvinism to anthropological and comprehensive views of the world about God.

b) In Galatians 2:7-8 Paul expresses that his responsibility is to proclaim the gospel to the Gentiles or non-Jews. Since the Gentiles, whose ancestors are not Jews, have not the Law that God offered through Moses, they appear to be lawless, foolish, directionless, and excluded from God's blessing. However, Paul in Romans 2:14 emphasizes that Gentiles as the feature of likeness to God have their direction called "conscience" written in the hearts so that they are not aimlessly drifting, and are also to be called God's people.

As Paul proclaims that the heathen is a determinative, regulative, and responsible being because of conscience,[55] he contrastingly states that all people have sinned and are corrupted. While heathens have the ability to make their resoluteness because of conscience, they are destined to fall into unrighteousness and injustice, apart from whether they have observed the law or not, and whether they keep to what their conscience directs them or not. All that they have to do is to receive the gospel revealed in Jesus' way of being filled with love, faith, and hope to which Paul referred in 1 Corinthians 13. Paul preached the heathen to add the gospel of Jesus' incarnation in the world to their conscience. Paul addressed to the heathen's conscience of heart God's grace through Jesus' manifestation in the world.[56]

What Paul further preached to Gentiles was that humanity's sin and corruption make not only people fail to be just and righteous despite the faculty of conscience, but also causes them to fall into death. Paul argues that death is originated from Adam whose existence is created by God and who disobeyed God's words. Adam as the race of people, to which Kierkegaard refers in *The Concept of Anxiety*, caused people to fall into sin

---

54. Hick, *Death and Eternal Life*, 175.
55. Bultmann, *Theology of the New Testament*, 1:216-19.
56. Bultmann, *Theology of the New Testament*, 1:117.

and death. The way out of sin and death is not performed by humanity, but God's soteriological love to rescue people as manifested in Christ's death and resurrection.

Paul's preaching of Christ's death and resurrection to Gentiles does not mean that they did not have their own idea and conviction on death and life after death. Greek ideas regarding death as "the immortality of the soul"[57] were already popular. The immortality of soul as a philosophical form of Platonism was embedded in Greek-Roman civilization.[58] Plato in *Phaedo* argues that humanity consists of the soul and body; when a person dies, the body is destroyed, but the soul is indestructible and has its eternal existence, saying, "death separates the soul from the body";[59] "the soul must be immortal, since after death it operates and knows."[60] Jacques Maritain in *The Range of Reason* describes the human soul as a spiritual substance that gives existence and countenance to the body through its union with matter.[61] Maritain asserts that the spiritual soul is incorruptible, self-subsisting, and contains all sources of its energies within itself.[62] The immortality of the soul is challenged by questions whether people need to think of the soul, which eternally exists without being destroyed, apart from whether it is with the body or non-body after death. Do people need to discuss and examine what and why death is, what will be after death, and how to transcend death in the view of the immortality of the soul?

Henry Cadbury in "Intimations of Immortality in the Thought of Jesus" distinguishes between the ideas of the resurrection of the body and the immortality of the soul.[63] Cullmann argues that the unending of the existence of the soul does not exist by itself, but by the involvement of God. The contrast between natural immortality and the resurrection of the body depends on a particular act of God in raising or rescuing the individual from the dead.[64] In "Immortality of the Soul or Resurrection of the Dead?" Cullmann distinguishes between the immortality of the soul and the resurrection of the body, stating that resurrection involves a miraculous act of creation by God, unlike the mere continuity of the soul's existence.[65]

57. Walker, *History of the Christian Church*, 29.
58. Russell, *History of Western Philosophy*, 331.
59. Plato, *Immortality of the Soul*, 3.
60. Plato, *Immortality of the Soul*, xl.
61. Maritain, *Range of Reason*, 58.
62. Maritain, *Range of Reason*, 60.
63. Cadbury, "Intimations of Immortality in the Thought of Jesus," 132.
64. Hick, *Death and Eternal Life*, 179–80.
65. Cullmann, "Immortality of the Soul," 27.

EPILOGUE

In these distinct ideas about death, the resurrection of the body is considered a theistic idea, while the immortality of the soul is non-theistic metaphysics.[66] The immortality of the soul does not necessarily require theistic God's involvement in human death, for it eventually dies and its body naturally is demolished, but its soul is non-destructive, but existent. In contrast, the resurrection of the body does not happen by itself, but depends on God's engagement of power with human death. When Paul accessed Gentiles to introduce the resurrection of the dead to them, he did not try to exclude the immortality of soul, which was popular in Greek-Roman civilization. Rather, he wanted to discuss with them God's creation, existence, and participation in the world through Jesus' incarnation. He told them to add God's creation and partaking in the world through Jesus' personification, death, and resurrection to the immortality of the soul supported by the pagan.

Acts 17:22–34 refers to Paul's preaching to Athens: "People of Athens, I see that you are very religious in every way. As I was walking through town, I found one altar with inscription 'To an unknown God.' I now proclaim to you God, who made the world and everything in it. God created every human nation to live on the whole earth; God made the entire human race for living so we could seek after God. God is not far away from us, but near and involves the world. God set a day to judge the world by a man called Jesus Christ whom God appointed as the savior of dying people. God confirms Jesus Christ before everyone by raising him from the dead." In Romans 8:11 Paul also preached to Romans, saying, "The Spirit of the one who raised Jesus from the dead will give life to your human bodies also, through his Spirit that lives in you."

What Paul preached to Athenians and Romans was the reality of God, and the reality of God, who is not indefinite God but definitely exists and involves the world, does not make Gentiles confuse the contrast between the immortality of the soul and the resurrection of the body. Since the fundamental issue between two distinct ideas of death is theistic or non-theistic, what is important for the heathen is to have the theistic God, who created the world. In *Death and After Life* Hick states that if we presuppose the reality of God, the difference between immortality and resurrection is insignificant. Hick argues that the soul's capacity to survive bodily death is a gift of divine grace, making humans dependent on God for their existence both now and in the hereafter.[67] The difference between immortality and

---

66. Hick, *Death and Eternal Life*, 180.
67. Hick, *Death and Eternal Life*, 181.

resurrection is further examined by questioning what resurrection looks like, and when and how it happens.

c) God's involvement in the world to rescue people from death is undertaken through Jesus' death and resurrection. The resurrection that Jesus Christ carried out is the new life of a new, transformed body. Resurrection is not restoration from what was lost in the past, but recreation and reformation for the future. The restoration of the past is considered resuscitation like the person whose breath was suspended but later is revived. John 11 refers to Lazarus whose breath was stilled but later was brought back by Jesus' power or God's power.[68] However, Lazarus eventually died, for his revival was temporal, not resurrectional, which is eternal. Paul in 1 Corinthians 15 said that resurrection is transformation from the perishable to imperishable, a physical to spiritual body, the body in dishonor to the body in glory, the earthly to heavenly body. In Philippians 3:21 Paul also refers to transformation, saying, "God will transform our humble bodies so that they are like the resurrected Christ's glorious body, by the power that also make him able to subject all things to himself." Henry Cadbury in "Intimations of Immortality in the Thought of Jesus" argues that the afterlife or transformed being was taken for granted by Jesus and by his hearers generally.[69]

After Jesus Christ was transformed from the earthly, physical body to the spiritual body, he stayed with his disciples and followers for a while, and then he disappeared, that is, ascended to heaven, leaving them to hear that he as the resurrected Christ will come and encounter them and us as certainly and mysteriously (Acts 1:7–11). The risen Christ left his disciples eschatological hope and future before he departed from them. In *Theology of Hope: On the Ground and the Implications of a Christian Eschatology* Jürgen Moltmann argues that eschatology is not a supplemental idea to Christians, but, rather that all Christian beliefs are based on eschatology. He states that the *parousia* of Christ is conceived as an expected event rather than an eternal presence, signifying his "coming."[70]

Disciples' and followers' hopeful future to encounter the resurrected Christ is to be called "*parousia* (παρουσία)," the encounter with the resurrected Christ, or presence of divinity in the future beyond the unavoidable hopeless death in a moment of dramatic transformation for humanity. Moltmann states that the *parousia* of Christ is conceived as an expected event rather than an eternal presence, signifying his "coming."[71] He also dis-

---

68. SD 144.
69. Cadbury, "Intimations of Immortality in the Thought of Jesus," 139.
70. Moltmann, *Theology of Hope*, 16.
71. Moltmann, *Theology of Hope*, 31.

tinguishes the "now" of the New Testament as a moment of eschatological significance, unlike the eternal presence in Parmenides of Elea whose idea is "existence is timeless and uniform," where it represents the newness of the promised future.[72]

Paul in 1 Thessalonians 4:15–17 writes that those who are dead in Christ will rise, and then, we who are living will be taken up with them to experience the *parousia*. In 1 Thessalonians 5:1–2 Paul answers the question when the *parousia* will come about, saying, "We don't need to write to you about the chronological time (*chronos*, χρόνος) and sudden time (*kairos*, καιρός), for you know that the day of the LORD is going to come like a thief in the night. The when of the *parousia* of the LORD is based on the objective time that everyone can acknowledge, but it is not objectively graspable.[73] The question of when is to be replaced by how to live or comport ourselves in our daily lives with hope for our future, as Moltmann argues. In 1 Thessalonians 5:6 Paul says, "So then let us not sleep like a drunkard, but stay awake and stay sober." The question of the "when" of the *parousia* is replaced by how to live.[74] In short, the experiencing of *parousia* takes place in a moment of the twinkling of an eye (*ecstasis*, ἔκστασις) as the involvement of the infinite to the finite, which is considered the unity of the future, past and present that Kierkegaard argues in *The Concept of Anxiety* and *The Sickness Unto Death*.

---

72. Moltmann, *Theology of Hope*, 31.
73. Heidegger, *Phenomenology of Religious Life*, 73.
74. Sheehan, "Introduction to Phenomenology of Religion," 57.

Bibliography

Apte, V. S. *The Practical Sanskrit-English Dictionary*. Bombay: Gopa Narayen, 1924.
Archer-Hind, R. D., ed. *The Timaeus of Plato*. London: Macmillan, 1888.
Arndt, William F., and F. Wilbur Gingrich, eds. *A Greek-English Lexicon of the New Testament and "Other Early Christian Literature."* Chicago: University of Chicago; Cambridge: Cambridge University Press, 1957.
Augustine. *Confessions*. Translated by R. S. Pine-Coffin. Harmondsworth, England: Penguin, 1961.
———. *Thirteen Homilies of St. Augustine on St. John XIV*. Translated and Edited by H. F. Stewart. Cambridge: Cambridge University Press, 1902.
Ayer, J. C. *A Source Book for Ancient Church History, from the Apostolic Age to the Close of the Conciliar Period*. New York: Standard Work, 1913.
Barth, Karl. *The Epistle to the Romans*. Translated by Edwyn C. Hoskyns. London: Oxford University Press, 1968.
———. *The Theology of Schleiermacher*. Translated by Geoffrey W. Bromiley. Grand Rapids: Eerdmans, 1982.
Barthes, Roland. *Image, Music, Text*. Translated by Stephen Heath. London: Fontana, 1977.
Bernstein, Richard J. *Beyond Objectivism and Relativism: Science, Hermeneutics, and Praxis*. Philadelphia: University of Pennsylvania Press, 1985.
———. "The Constellation of Hermeneutics, Critical Theory, and Deconstruction." In *The Cambridge Companion to Gadamer*, edited by Robert J. Dostal, 267–82. Cambridge: Cambridge University Press, 2002.
———. *Praxis and Action: Contemporary Philosophies of Human Activity*. Philadelphia: University of Pennsylvania Press, 1971.
Blattner, William D. "The Concept of Death in *Being and Time*." *Man and World* 27 (1994) 49–70.
Bonhoeffer, Dietrich. *The Cost of Discipleship*. Translated by R. H. Fuller. New York: Macmillan, 1979.
Buber, Martin. *I and Thou*. Translated by Ronald Gregor Smith. New York: Macmillan, 1958.
———. *Two Types of Faith*. Translated by Norman Goldhawk. New York: Macmillan, 1951.
Bultmann, Rudolf. *Theology of the New Testament*. 2 vols. Translated by Kendrick Grobel. New York: Scribner's, 1951, 1955.
Buswell, Robert E., Jr., ed. *Encyclopedia of Buddhism*. New York: Thomson Gale, 2004.

BIBLIOGRAPHY

Buttrick, George Arthur, ed. *The Interpreter's Dictionary of the Bible: An Illustrated Encyclopedia*. Nashville: Abingdon, 1962.

Cadbury, Henry J. "Intimations of Immortality in the Thought of Jesus." In *Immortality and Resurrection*, edited by Krister Stendahl, 115–49. New York: Macmillan, 1965.

Carel, Havi. *Life and Death in Freud and Heidegger*. Amsterdam: Rodopi, 2006.

Carman, Taylor. "The Concept of Authenticity." In *A Companion to Phenomenology and Existentialism*, edited by Hubert L. Dreyfus and Mark A. Wrathall, 229–39. Oxford: Blackwell, 2006.

———. *Heidegger's Analytic: Interpretation, Discourse, and Authenticity in "Being and Time."* Cambridge: Cambridge University Press, 2003.

Carr, Anne E. "Karl Rahner." In *A Handbook of Christian Theologians*, edited by Martin E. Marty and Dean G. Peerman, 519–42. Nashville: Abingdon, 1987.

Chan, Wing-tsit, ed. *Source Book in Chinese Philosophy*. Princeton: Princeton University Press, 1963.

Chang, Garma C. C. *The Buddhist Teaching of Totality: The Philosophy of Hwa Yen Buddhism*. 1971. Reprint, New York: Routledge, 2008.

Cleary, Thomas. *Entry into the Inconceivable: An Introduction to Hua-yen Buddhism*. Honolulu: University of Hawaii Press, 1983.

Conze, Edward. *Buddhist Thought in India*. London: Allen & Unwin, 1977.

Cook, Francis H. "Fa-tsang's *Treatise on the Five Doctrine*: An Annotated Translation." PhD diss., University of Wisconsin, 1970.

———. "The Jewel Net of Indra." In *Nature in Asian Traditions of Thought*, edited by J. Baird Callicott and Roger T. Ames, 213–29. Albany: State University of New York Press, 1989.

Cullmann, Oscar. *The Christology of the New Testament*. Translated by Shirley C. Guthrie and Charles A. M. Hall. Revised ed. Philadelphia: Westminster, 1963.

———. "Immortality of the Soul or Resurrection of the Dead?: The Witness of the New Testament." In *Immortality and Resurrection*, edited by Krister Stendahl, 9–53. New York: Macmillan, 1965.

de Bary, William Theodore. *The Buddhist Tradition in India, China, and Japan*. New York: Random, 1972.

de Nys, Martin J. *Hegel and Theology*. New York: T&T Clark, 2009.

Derrida, Jacques. "Force of Law: The 'Mystical Foundation of Authority.'" In *Deconstruction and the Possibility of Justice*, edited by Drucilla Cornell et al., 3–67. Translated by Mary Quaintance. New York: Routledge, 1992.

———. "Interpreting Signatures (Nietzsche/Heidegger): Two Questions." In *Dialogue and Deconstruction*, edited by Diane P. Michelfelder and Richard E. Palmer, 58–71. Albany: State University of New York Press, 1989.

———. *Of Grammatology*. Translated by Gayatri Chakravorty Spivak. Baltimore: Johns Hopkins University Press, 1997.

———. *Speech and Phenomena and Other Essays on Husserl's Theory of Signs*. Translated by David B. Allison and Newton Garver. Evanston, IL: Northwestern University Press, 1973.

Dreyfus, Hubert L. *Being-in-the-World: A Commentary on Heidegger's "Being and Time."* Cambridge, MA: MIT Press, 1991.

———. "Interpreting Heidegger on *Das Man*." *Inquiry: An Interdisciplinary Journal of Philosophy* 38.4 (1995) 423–30.

BIBLIOGRAPHY

Duffy, Stephen J. "Experience of Grace." In *The Cambridge Companion to Karl Rahner*, edited by Declan Marmion and Mary E. Hines, 43–62. Cambridge: Cambridge University Press, 2007.

Edwards, Paul. "Heidegger and Death as a 'Possibility.'" *Mind* 84 (1975) 546–66.

Eitel, Ernest J., ed. *A Sanskrit-Chinese Buddhism*. London: Trübner, 1888.

Fa-tsang. "Cultivation of Contemplation of the Inner Meaning of the Huayen: The Ending of Delusion and Return to the Source." In *Entry Into the Inconceivable: An Introduction to Huayen Buddhism*, edited by Thomas Cleary, 147–69. Honolulu: University of Hawaii Press, 1983.

———. "Hundred Gates to the Sea of Ideas of the Flowery Splendor Scripture." In *A Source Book in Chinese Philosophy*, edited by Wing-Tsit Chan, 414–24.

———. "Treatise on the Divisions of Doctrine in the Unitary Vehicle of Huayen" (*Huayen ich'eng chiaoi fench'ichang*). In *Taisho Shinhsu Daizokyo*, edited by J. Junjiro Takakusu and Kaigyoku Watanabe, 45:406–14. Tokyo: Daizo Shuppan, 1924–1934.

———. "A Treatise on the Golden Lion (*Huayen Chin Shihtzu Chang*)." In *A Source Book in Chinese Philosophy*, edited by Wing-Tsit Chan, 409–13. Princeton: Princeton University Press, 1963.

Fung, Yu-lan. *A History of Chinese Philosophy*. Princeton: Princeton University Press, 1983.

Gadamer, Hans-Georg. *Philosophical Hermeneutics*. Translated by David E. Linge. Berkeley: University of California Press, 1976.

———. *Truth and Method*. Edited and translated by Garrett Barden and John Cumming. New York: Seabury, 1975.

Garff, Joakim. *Kierkegaard: A Biography*. Translated by Bruce H. Kirmmse. Princeton: Princeton University Press, 2005.

Geter, Kenneth David. "Missed Appropriations: Uncovering Heidegger's Debt to Kierkegaard in *Being and Time*." PhD. diss., Iliff School of Theology, University of Denver, 2016.

Gimello, Robert M. "Chih-yen (602–663) and the Foundations of Hua-yen Buddhism." PhD diss., Columbia University, 1976.

Gorman, Michael J. *Cruciformity: Paul's Narrative Spirituality of the Cross*. Grand Rapids: Eerdmans, 2001.

Gregory, Peter N. *Tsung-mi and the Sinification of Buddhism*. Princeton: Princeton University Press, 1991.

Hakeda, Yoshito S. *The Awakening of Faith*. New York: Columbia University Press, 1967.

Hartshorne, Charles. "Sankara, Nagarjuna, and Fa Tsang, with Some Western Analogues." In *Interpreting Across Boundaries*, edited by Gerald James Larson and Eliot Deutsch, 98–115. Princeton: Princeton University Press, 1988.

Hegel, Georg W. F. *The Philosophy of History*. Translated by J. Sibree. New York: P. F. Collier & Son, 1857.

Heidegger, Martin. *The Basic Problems of Phenomenology*. Translated by Albert Hofstadter. Revised ed. Bloomington: Indiana University Press, 1982.

———. *Der Begriff der Zeit/The Concept of Time*. Translated by William McNeill. Oxford: Blackwell, 1992.

———. *Being And Time*. Translated by John Macquarrie and Edward Robinson. New York: Harper & Row, 1962.

———. *Being And Time*. Translated by Joan Stambaugh. Albany: State University of New York Press, 1996.

———. *History of the Concept of Time*. Translated by Theodore Kisiel. Bloomington: Indiana University Press, 1985.

———. *An Introduction to Metaphysics*. Translated by Ralph Manheim. New Haven: Yale University Press, 1959.

———. *Kant and the Problem of Metaphysics*. Translated by Richard Taft. Bloomington: Indiana University Press, 1991.

———. "Letter on Humanism." In *Martin Heidegger: Basic Writings from Being and Time (1927) to the Task of Thinking (1964)*, edited by David Farrell Krell, 189–242. New York: Harper & Row, 1977.

———. *Logic: The Questions of Truth*. Translated by Thomas Sheehan. Bloomington: Indiana University Press, 2010.

———. *Metaphysical Foundations of Logic*. Translated by Michael Heim. Bloomington: Indiana University Press, 1984.

———. *On the Way to Language*. Translated by Peter D. Hertz. New York: Harper & Row, 1982.

———. *Ontology—The Hermeneutics of Facticity*. Translated by John van Buren. Bloomington: Indiana University Press, 1999.

———. *Pathmarks*. Edited by William MacNeill. Cambridge: Cambridge University Press, 1998.

———. *The Phenomenology of Religious Life*. Translated by Matthias Fritsch and Jennifer Anna Gosetti-Ferencei. Bloomington: Indiana University Press, 2010.

———. *Poetry, Language, Thought*. Translated by Albert Hofstadter. New York: Harper & Row, 1971.

———. *Sein und Zeit*. Tübingen: Max Niemeyer, 1967.

———. "The Way Back into the Ground of Metaphysics." In *Existentialism from Dostoevsky to Sartre*, edited by Walter Kaufmann, 206–21. New York: Meridian, 1968.

———. "What Is Metaphysics?" In *Basic Writings*, edited by David Farrell Krell, 91–112. New York: Harper & Row, 1977.

Hick, John. *Death and Eternal Life*. Louisville, KY: Westminster John Knox, 1994.

———. *Evil and the God of Love*. New York: Harper & Row, 1977.

Hoy, David Couzens. *The Critical Circle: Literature, History, and Philosophical Hermeneutics*. Berkeley: University of California Press, 1982.

———. "Heidegger and the Hermeneutic Turn." In *The Cambridge Companion to Heidegger*, edited by Charles B. Guignon, 170–94. Cambridge: Cambridge University Press, 1993.

Humbert, David J. "Freedom and Time in Kierkegaard's *The Concept of Anxiety*." PhD diss., McMaster University, 1983.

Husserl, Edmund. *The Crisis of European Sciences and Transcendental Phenomenology: An Introduction to Phenomenological Philosophy*. Translated by David Carr. Evanston, IL: Northwestern University Press, 1970.

Hwang, Bong-Choul. "Process and Harmony: A Comparison between Whitehead and Fa-tsang Metaphysics on the Notion of Reality." PhD diss., Iliff School of Theology, University of Denver, 1994.

Inwood, Michael. *A Hegel Dictionary*. Oxford: Blackwell, 1999.

———. *Heidegger: A Very Short Introduction*. Oxford: Oxford University Press, 1997.

———. *A Heidegger Dictionary*. Oxford: Blackwell, 1999.
James, William. *The Varieties of Religious Experience: A Study in Human Nature*. New York: Macmillan, 1961.
Keck, Leander E. *The New Interpreter's Bible*. Vol. 1. Nashville: Abingdon, 1994.
Kepnes, Steven. *The Text as Thou: Martin Buber's Dialogical Hermeneutics and Narrative Theology*. Bloomington: Indiana University Press, 1992.
Kiekegaard, Søren. *Christian Discourses*. Translated by Walter Lowrie. London: Oxford University Press, 1952.
———. *The Concept of Anxiety*. Edited and translated by Reidar Thomte with Albert B. Anderson. Princeton: Princeton University Press, 1980.
———. *Either/Or: A Fragment of Life*. Edited and translated by David F. Swenson et al. New York: Modern Library, 1944.
———. "Fear and Trembling: A Dialectical Lyric by Johannes De Silentio (1983)." In *Fear and Trembling and The Sickness unto Death*, 21-139. Translated by Walted Lowrie. Princeton: Princeton University Press, 1968.
———. *Philosophical Fragments or A Fragment of Philosophy*. Translated by David F. Swenson. Princeton: Princeton University Press, 1962.
———. *The Present Age: A Literary Review*. Translated by Alexander Dru. New York: Modern Library, 1944.
———. "The Sickness Unto Death: A Christian Psychological Exposition for Edification and Awakening by Anti-Climacus." In *Fear and Trembling and The Sickness unto Death*, 141-262. Translated by Walter Lowrie. Princeton: Princeton University Press, 1968.
———. "The Tame Geese: A Revivalistic Meditation." In *The Journals (1850-1854)*, edited by Robert Bretall, 433. New York: Modern Library, 1944.
Kimmerle, Heinz. "Foreword to the German Edition." In *Hermeneutics: The Handwritten Manuscripts*, by Friedrich Schleiermacher, 19-40. Edited by Heinz Kimmerle. Translated by James Duke and Jack Forstman. Atlanta: Scholars, 1997.
———. "Hermeneutical Theory or Ontological Hermeneutics." In *History and Hermeneutic*, 107-21. Translated by Friedrich Seifert. New York: Harper & Row, 1967.
Krell, David Farrell. *Ecstasy, Catastrophe: Heidegger from Being and Time to the Black Notebooks*. Albany: State University of New York Press, 2015.
Lai, Whalen. "Chinese Buddhist Causation Theories: An Analysis of the Sinitic Mahayana Understanding of *Pratityasamutpada*." *Philosophy East and West* 27.3 (1977) 241-64.
———. "The Meaning of 'Mind-Only' (*Wei-hsin*): An Analysis of a Sinitic Mahayana Phenomenon." *Philosophy East and West* 27.1 (1977) 65-83.
Lehmann, Paul. "The Anti-Pelagian Writings." In *A Companion to the Study of St. Augustine*, edited by Roy W. Battenhouse, 203-34. Grand Rapids: Baker, 1979.
Liu, Ming-Wood. "The Doctrine of the Buddha-Nature in the Mahayana *Mahaparinirvana Sutra*." *Journal of the International Association of Buddhist Studies* 5 (1982) 63-94.
———. "The Problem of the *Icchantika* in the Mahayana *Mahaparinirvana Sutra*." *Journal of the International Association of Buddhist Studies* 7 (1984) 57-81.
———. "The Teaching of Fa-tsang—An Examination of Buddhist Metaphysics." PhD diss., University of California, 1979.

Löwith, Karl. *From Hegel to Nietzsche: The Revolution in Nineteenth-Century Thought.* Translated by David E. Green. New York: Columbia University Press, 1964.

Macann, Christopher. *Four Phenomenological Philosophers: Husserl, Heidegger, Sartre, Merleau-Ponty.* London; New York: Routledge, 1993.

Magurshak, Dan. "The Concept of Anxiety: The Keystone of the Kierkegaard-Heidegger Relationship." In *International Kierkegaard Commentary: The Concept of Anxiety*, edited by Robert L. Perkins, 167–95. Macon, GA: Mercer University Press, 1985.

Maritain, Jacques. *The Range of Reason.* New York: Scribner's, 1953.

Marmion, Declan, and Mary E. Hines, eds. *The Cambridge Companion to Karl Rahner.* Cambridge: Cambridge University Press, 2007.

Marshall, Alfred, trans. *The RSV Interlinear Greek–English New Testament.* Michigan: Zondervan, 1958.

Meeks, Wayne A., ed. *The Harper Collins Study Bible: New Revised Standard Version.* London: Harper Collins, 1989.

Melton, J. Gordon. *Encyclopedia of Protestantism.* New York: Facts on File, 2005.

Moltmann, Jürgen. *Theology of Hope: On the Ground and the Implications of a Christian Eschatology.* Translated by James W. Leitch. New York: Harper & Row, 1965.

Mulhall, Stephen. *Heidegger and Being and Time.* 2nd ed. London: Routledge, 2005.

Neville, Robert C. *The Tao and the Daimon: Segments of a Religious Inquiry.* Albany: State University of New York Press, 1982.

Niebuhr, Richard R. "Friedrich Schleiermacher." In *A Handbook of Christian Theologians*, edited by Martin E. Marty and Dean G. Peerman, 17–35. Nashville: Abingdon, 1987.

Odin, Steve. *Process Metaphysics and HuaYen Buddhism.* Albany: State University of New York, 1982.

Oh, Kang Nam. "A Study of Chinese Hua-Yen Buddhism with Special Reference to the *Dharmadhatu (Fa-Chieh)* Doctrine." PhD diss., McMaster University, 1976.

Palmer, Richard E. *Hermeneutics: Interpretation Theory in Schleiermacher, Dilthey, Heidegger, and Gadamer.* Evanston, IL: Northwestern University Press, 1969.

Pannenberg, Wolfhart. *Jesus—God and Man.* Translated by Lewis L. Wilkins and Duane A. Priebe. Philadelphia: Westminster, 1977.

Perrin, Norman, and Dennis C. Duling. *The New Testament: An Introduction.* 2nd ed. New York: Harcourt Brace, 1982.

Pierce, C. A. *Conscience in the New Testament.* London: SCM, 1955.

Plato. *The Immortality of the Soul.* Translated by Charles S. Standford. New York: Hurst, 1833.

Rahner, Karl. "Nature and Grace." In *Sacramentum Mundi: An Encyclopedia of Theology*, edited by Karl Rahner, 2:165–88. Baltimore: Helicon, 1966.

———. *On the Theology of Death.* New York: Herder and Herder, 1967.

Reynolds, Frank E., and Charles Hallisey. "Buddha." In *The Encyclopedia of Religion*, edited by Mircea Eliade et al., 2:319–32. New York: Macmillan, 1987.

Richardson, William J., SJ. *Heidegger: Through Phenomenology to Thought.* New York: Fordham University Press, 2003.

Ricoeur, Paul. *Interpretation Theory: Discourse and the Surplus of Meaning.* Fort Worth: Texas Christian University Press, 1976.

Rorty, Richard. *Philosophy and the Mirror of Nature.* Princeton: Princeton University Press, 1979.

BIBLIOGRAPHY

Russell, Bertrand. *A History of Western Philosophy*. New York: Simon and Schuster, 1945.
Sartre, Jean-Paul. *Being and Nothingness*. Translated by Hazel E. Barnes. New York: Washington Square, 1971.
———. "Existentialism." In *Existentialism from Dostoevsky to Sartre*, edited by Walter Kaufmann, 222–311. New York: World, 1968.
———. "Merleau-Ponty." In *Situations*, 227–326. Translated by Benita Eisler. New York: George Braziller, 1965.
Sarup, Madan. *An Introductory Guide to Post-Structuralism and Postmodernism*. 2nd ed. Athens: University of Georgia Press, 1993.
Schleiermacher, Friedrich. *The Christian Faith*. 2nd ed. Edited by H. R. Mackintosh and J. S. Stewart. Philadelphia: Fortress, 1976.
———. *Hermeneutics: The Handwritten Manuscripts*. Edited by Heinz Kimmerle. Translated by James Duke and Jack Forstman. Atlanta: Scholars, 1997.
———. *Hermeneutik: Nach den Handschriften new herausgegeben und eingeleitet von Heinz Kimmerle*. Heidelberg: C. Winter, 1959.
———. *On Religion: Speeches to Its Cultured Despisers*. Translated by John Oman. New York: Harper & Row, 1968.
Schumacher, Stephan, and Gert Woerner, eds. *The Encyclopedia of Eastern Philosophy and Religion*. Boston: Shambhala, 1989.
Sheehan, Thomas J. "Introduction to Phenomenology of Religion." In *A Companion to Martin Heidegger's Being and Time*, edited by Joseph J. Kockelmans, 40–62. Washington, DC: University Press of America, 1986.
Soothill, William Edward, and Lewis Hodous. *A Dictionary of Chinese Buddhist Terms*. Taipei: Ch'eng-wen, 1968.
Stcherbatsky, Th. *The Central Conception of Buddhism and the Meaning of the Word "Dharma."* Calcutta: Susil Gupta, 1956.
Steiner, George. *Martin Heidegger*. Chicago: University of Chicago, 1989.
Stendahl, Krister. "The Apostle Paul and the Introspective Conscience of the West." *Harvard Theological Review* 53 (1963) 199–215.
Streng, Frederick J. *Emptiness: A Study in Religious Meaning*. Nashville: Abingdon, 1967.
Takakusu, Junjiro, and Kaigyoku Watanabe, eds. *Taisho Shinshu Daizokyo*. Tokyo: Daizo Shuppan, 1924–1932.
Taylor, Charles. "Comparison, History, Myth." In *Myth and Philosophy*, edited by Frank Reynolds and David Tracy, 37–55. Albany: State University of New York Press, 1990.
Taylor, Mark C. *Deconstructing Theology*. New York: Crossroad, 1982.
Tennant, F. R. *The Sources of the Doctrines of the Fall and Original Sin*. Cambridge: Cambridge University Press, 1903.
Thiselton, Anthony C. *The Two Horizons: New Testament Hermeneutics and Philosophical Description with Special Reference to Heidegger, Bultman, Gadamer, and Wittgenstein*. Grand Rapids: Eerdmans, 1980.
Tracy, David. *The Analogical Imagination: Christian Theology and the Culture of Pluralism*. New York: Crossroad, 1981.
———. "On the Origins of Philosophy of Religion: The Need for a New Narrative of Its Founding." In *Myth and Philosophy*, edited by Frank Reynolds and David Tracy, 1–36. Albany: State University of New York Press, 1990.
Walker, Williston. *A History of the Christian Church*. 3rd ed. New York: Scribner's, 1970.

Warnke, Georgia. *Gadamer: Hermeneutics, Tradition, and Reason*. Stanford: Stanford University Press, 1987.

Watson, Burton, trans. *Chuang Tzu: Basic Writings*. New York: Columbia University Press, 1964.

Whitehead, Alfred North. *Process and Reality: An Essay on Cosmology*. Edited by David Griffin and Donald Sherburne. New York: Free Press, 1978.

Williams, Norman Powell. *The Idea of the Fall and of Original Sin*. New York: Longmans, 1927.

Williams, Paul. *Mahayana Buddhism: The Doctrinal Foundations*. New York: Routledge, 1989.

Williams, Robert R. *Schleiermacher the Theologian: The Construction of the Doctrine of God*. Philadelphia: Fortress, 1978.

Windelband, Wilhelm. *An Introduction to Philosophy*. Translated by Joseph McCabe. London: Adelphi Terrace, 1921.

Wright, Dale Stuart. "Emptiness and Paradox in the Thought of F-tsang." PhD diss., University of Iowa, 1980.

Zimmerli, Walther. "The Word of God in the Book of Ezekiel." In *History and Hermeneutic*, 1–13. Translated by James F. Ross. New York: Harper & Row, 1967.

Zimmerman, Michael E. "Heidegger, Buddhism, and Deep Ecology." In *The Cambridge Companion to Heidegger*, edited by Charles B. Guignon, 240–69. Cambridge: Cambridge University Press, 1993.